Development of the Constitutions in China and the Visegrad States

Development of the Constitutions in China and the Visegrad States

Lu Da

Development of the Constitutions in China and the Visegrad States

A Comparative Perspective

Lu Da
School of Law
Wuhan University
Wuhan, Hubei, China

ISBN 978-981-16-5635-4   ISBN 978-981-16-5636-1 (eBook)
https://doi.org/10.1007/978-981-16-5636-1

© The Editor(s) (if applicable) and The Author(s), under exclusive license to Springer Nature Singapore Pte Ltd. 2021
This work is subject to copyright. All rights are solely and exclusively licensed by the Publisher, whether the whole or part of the material is concerned, specifically the rights of translation, reprinting, reuse of illustrations, recitation, broadcasting, reproduction on microfilms or in any other physical way, and transmission or information storage and retrieval, electronic adaptation, computer software, or by similar or dissimilar methodology now known or hereafter developed.
The use of general descriptive names, registered names, trademarks, service marks, etc. in this publication does not imply, even in the absence of a specific statement, that such names are exempt from the relevant protective laws and regulations and therefore free for general use.
The publisher, the authors and the editors are safe to assume that the advice and information in this book are believed to be true and accurate at the date of publication. Neither the publisher nor the authors or the editors give a warranty, expressed or implied, with respect to the material contained herein or for any errors or omissions that may have been made. The publisher remains neutral with regard to jurisdictional claims in published maps and institutional affiliations.

This Springer imprint is published by the registered company Springer Nature Singapore Pte Ltd.
The registered company address is: 152 Beach Road, #21-01/04 Gateway East, Singapore 189721, Singapore

Foreword by Prof. Qianhong Qin

As Dr. Da's postdoctoral cooperative supervisor, I am very glad to write something about Dr. Da's new book and the comparative constitutional law in China.

This book is about the constitutional development in China and the V4 countries. The comparative works mainly focus on the differences and similarities of the text of the constitutions in China and the Visegrad states. It started from the dissolution of Austria-Hungary. After the dissolution, Czechia, Slovakia and Poles created their own counties. Later, after the Revolutions of 1989, the V4 countries witnessed the democratization by making or amending the constitutions and (re)introducing the constitutionality review system. The rule of law and constitutionalism is realized in respective countries, while, in China, the socialist constitution has been amended. The discussion of benign unconstitutionality and the practice of judicialization of constitution had attracted a lot of attention at home and abroad.

To study constitutions of the Eastern Europe has a long history in China. In the drafting of Constitution of PRC (1954), Mao Zedong, the founding father of the PRC sent a message by telegraph to other leaders of the CPC and asked them to read the Polish and Czechia constitutions.

To teach constitution of the Eastern Europe also has a long history at the School of Law, Wuhan University. The prominent Prof. He Huahui offered the course of comparative constitutional law since 1980s. His book on comparative constitutional law is one of the most popular ones to the law school students. In this book, he introduced the constitutions of the Eastern Europe in the socialist system part (this book was published in 1988).

I taught the course of comparative constitutional law over 20 years at the School of Law, Wuhan University. In recent years, we payed a great attention on the constitutional development of Western Europe (e.g. Germany, France and, the UK) and the USA. The development of constitutions of the Eastern Europe has been overlooked. As far as I know, there are only a few Chinese books on the topic of the constitutions of the Eastern Europe. It is glad to see more and more young researchers are interested in this important topic.

Since March 2019, Dr. Da conducted his postdoctoral research on the comparative constitutional law with a special attention on China and the V4 countries under my supervision. This is the very first book from his research. He told me he is preparing his second book on the topic of constitutionality review in China and V4 countries. I am looking forward to reading his new book soon!

June 2021

Prof. Qianhong Qin
Vice President of China Association of Constitutional Law
of the China Law Society
Wuhan, China

Foreword by Assoc. Prof. Norbert Varga

Hungary, along with its neighbors, Poland, Czech Republic and Slovakia experienced the socialist system for nearly forty years. In the socialist regime, the countries not only adopted the planned socialist economy, but followed the Soviet constitution. The constitutional development of the Visegrad states was thoroughly examined by legal scholars within/beyond this region.

He conducted his Ph.D. research on this topic under my supervision from 2015 to 2018 at the University of Szeged, Hungary. In his work, the Chinese legal history of the constitutional law had been compared to the Visegrad one. In his book, he used comparative and historical methods, not to mention textualism and functionalism, to analyze the constitutional development of China and the Visegrad states. He argued that China and the Visegrad states chose different roads of development based on four reasons: socioeconomic conditions, the culture, the relationship with the Soviet Union, and the relationship with the EU.

I noted in Dr. Da's book that he added a new chapter to compare the constitutions of China and the Visegrad states after the transformation period. He pays special attention to the review of constitutionality of China and the Visegrad states by introducing an abortion case in Poland (by the way, the Hungarian Constitutional Court also adjudicated an abortion case in 1991) and the custody-and-education policy in China, he compared how to access the review of constitutionality of China and the Visegrad states. He tries to describe a phenomenon that the organs for the review of constitutionality of China and the Visegrad states are more self-restraint compared to previous activism.

However, as he mentioned in his book, this research mainly focuses on the comparative analysis of the text of the Constitutions of China and the Visegred states. I do believe European readers will be glad to see how the Constitution and Law Committee of the NPC and the Legislative Affairs Commission of the Standing Committee of the NPC decide the cases.

At last, I am glad to know that he is conducting his research on the comparative studies of the constitutional developments of China and the Visegrad states after he completed his Ph.D. in Szeged, Hungary. I am looking forward to reading more of his research works.

June 2021

Associate Prof. Dr. Norbert Varga
Vice Dean of the Faculty of Law and Political Science
University of Szeged
Szeged, Hungary

Preface

Constitutional law, or fundamental law in some countries, usually regulates a state's ultimate rules and general principles. In socialist states, following the Soviet model, fundamental rights of citizens and the competences of each constitutional institution were regulated by the constitution and typically adopted by the highest organ of state power.

This monograph addresses a topic that is rarely touched upon by Chinese scholars or scholars from the Visegrad states: a comparative study of constitutional development in China and the Visegrad states. I first visited the Visegrad states in 2013. I spent one year in Bratislava, the capital city of Slovakia, and learned the Slovak language there. In 2015, I revisited the Visegrad states. This time, I spent three and half years in Szeged, the southern Hungarian city that is famous for its sunshine, and obtained my Ph.D. in law at the University of Szeged in 2018.

In this monograph, I compare the constitution-making, text of the constitutions and constitutional movements in China and the Visegrad states from the late nineteenth century to the present. I must acknowledge that the comparative works are rough and basic, since they were mainly based on Chinese and English materials. Surely, a considerable number of books and papers written in Slovak, Czech, Polish and Hungarian are sitting on bookshelves waiting to be read. However, the materials that I have reviewed provide a sufficient basis to conduct a comparative study and to make some comparative conclusions.

This monograph covers legal history studies, looking back to the communist period and examining the establishment of communist regimes in China and the Visegrad states, one the one hand; and comparative studies, comparing the constitutional development in China and the Visegrad states from the late nineteenth century to the present, on the other. It is readily apparent that China and the Visegrad countries have had common histories of socialist experiences and systems since the late 1940s. However, the history of the communist party in each state, which is presented in this monograph, is much longer than the histories of these socialist states. Therefore, after the introduction, I give a detailed introduction to the communist party in each state, paying special attention to China and Hungary. During that time, the communist parties in both countries tested the possibility of establishing a Soviet republic. Provisional constitutional documents were introduced to the public in both countries, although neither document ever entered into force.

I give a detailed introduction to the first written communist constitution in each state and examine the structure and important provisions of these documents. I also explain the constitution-making process. In the final section, I employ a comparative method to analyze the differences and similarities in the countries' constitutions.

During the reform period, a socialist system was established in each state. I examine the important constitutional amendments. Because this is a legal study, I do not wish to describe the details of the 1956 Hungarian revolution, 1956 Poznan protest, Prague Spring or Cultural Revolution in the reform period. Instead, I put my energy into examining the changes in concrete provisions in different versions of each state's constitution. Additionally, this section presents comparative work on the highest organs of state power in China and the Visegrad states.

This monograph considers the next stage a transformational period. After the Revolutions of 1989, the Visegrad states abandoned the socialist system, and this was immediately reflected in their constitutions. The socialist system was removed from these documents, and Western-style constitutions were quickly established. The Revolutions of 1989 also affected China, leading to the Tiananmen incident. However, the Communist Party of China (CPC) insisted on the socialist system in the constitution, and some important economic reforms were made. These reforms were ensured in the constitution through an amendment. The constitution should not only exist on paper but should be followed by everyone and every institution in the state. Therefore, a constitutionality review system has been established in many countries. In this section, I also provide a comparative analysis of these constitutionality review systems.

The chapter on constitutionality review after the transformation period in this monograph is new. It analyzes the constitutional development in China and the Visegrad states after the transformation period. These initiatives occurred during a new stage in China and the Visegrad states. China declared that it would improve its constitutionality review system. Hungary and Poland were accused of violating their constitutions, which caused so-called constitutional crises in both countries. Most of this monograph is based on my Ph.D. dissertation, and when I was in Hungary, friends advised me, "It will be much better if you can give some extra attention to the current constitutional development in China and the Visegrad states" and "Why don't you compare the constitutional cases in your work?" I usually argued that I did not plan to do so because this research is a legal history work and that my plan for the research project was based on the text of the constitutions of China and the Visegrad states and on analyzing their similarities and differences. However, after nearly two years of research on constitutionality review back in China, it was time to start a new chapter of this research project comparing the constitutionality review in China and the Visegrad states.

China and the Visegrad states share many common memories: the emergence of communist parties, the establishment of socialist states, socialist constitution-making and turmoil in the late 1980s. After the Revolutions of 1989, the Visegrad states turned to the West and reestablished democratic societies in the process of constitution-remaking and establishing a constitutionality review system. In China, the CPC continued in its ruling position, and the Constitution of 1982 just witnessed its fifth amendment in 2018. Constitutionality review was also emphasized in the 2017 CPC annual report.

Naturally, amid such changes, numerous differences emerge in this comparative study. For example, Chinese constitutionality review is conducted by the National People's Congress (NPC) and its Standing Committee. In the Visegrad states, countries followed the Austrian or German constitutional court model. Similarities also existed in the constitutionality review in China and the Visegrad states. Protection of citizens' basic rights is the general purpose of constitutionality review, and political facts are highly involved in it, with some commentators from China and the Visegrad states even insisting that the process should take only constitutional law into account. Additionally, in this chapter, I note a general principle of constitutionality review systems, that is, constitutional consensus. The constitutional order, or more specifically, the effectiveness of constitutionality review, requires two things: a consensus on constitutional values from the people and a legal system that follows the constitution.

This monograph uses three research methods to compare constitutional development in China and the Visegrad states. First, I employ the historical method by reviewing the history of constitutional development chronologically in each state. I also address how historical conditions influenced constitution-making. Second, contextualism is used in this research. I compare the contexts of the constitutions in each state. Third, as most comparative scholars do, I employ functionalism. The development of the socialist constitutions in each state differed, especially between China and the Visegrad states, which are considered as a group. The most significant example is the Revolutions of 1989. They affected every socialist state, including China and the Visegrad states. Soon, the Visegrad states abandoned their socialist constitutions, and China continued its socialist constitution and made some significant amendments.

In conclusion, after the Revolutions of 1989, China and the Visegrad states chose different roads along which to develop. In the last part of this monograph, I provide four reasons for the different choices in China and the Visegrad states. The first is socioeconomic conditions, the second is different cultures, and the last two are related to the relationship with the Soviet Union and the EU. I hold that in the contemporary constitutional development in China and the Visegrad states, constitutionalism was employed as an instrument, and so-called rule by constitutionalism was (re)established on both sides. It is difficult to judge the pros and cons of the roads taken by China and the Visegrad states and declare which was the best. However, there are still some conclusions. First, a prosperous country cannot exist without a constitution. Second, a constitution must be respected and fully enforced, and a constitutionality review system should be established. Finally, there are some common grounds in the constitutions that are shared by all the countries. However, it is difficult to say that there is a model of constitution that every country can follow; each state's constitution should reflect its own conditions.

Wuhan, China
May 2021

Lu Da

Acknowledgements

I still remember it is an early summer night, I was sitting in a dormitory of Southwest University of Political Science and Law (SWUPL) and I found the university Website posted an information of China Scholarship Council (CSC) scholarship for regional studies. I applied this scholarship and was accepted. With this scholarship, I spent one year in Bratislava, Slovakia. This is the first time I have been lived and studied in the Visegrad States.

Luckily enough, after I finished my LLM at SWUPL with the paper on Slovakia Presidential election, I was accepted by University of Szeged, Hungary, for my Ph.D. studies. The program is sponsored by CSC (China) and stipendium hungaricum (Hungary), and I had a great time in Szeged with my learned and kind-hearted colleagues and friends from Hungary and beyond.

The monograph is based on my Ph.D. dissertation and with a new chapter focuses on contemporary constitutional development in China and the V4 countries. In Chinese, there is a word to describe the fateful coincidence and relationships, 缘分 (Yuanfen). My *yuanfen* with the V4 countries started in an early summer night of 2013, and I wish it will last forever!

For these reasons, I would like to express my special appreciation and thanks to my Ph.D. Supervisor, Dr. Norbert Varga. I would like to thank you for encouraging my research and for allowing me to do the research which I really want to study. Your valuable advice on both my future career and my personal life has inspired me so much.

I would like to thank my dear colleagues from Hungary. Professor Dr. Maria Homoki-Nagy, Prof. Krisztina Karsai, Dr. habil. Peter Mezei, Dr. habil. Tamas Antal, Dr. Zsuzsanna Fejes, Dr. Mate Petervari, and Santiago Vallejo Galárraga and his family and thank Prof. Dr. Attila Bado, Prof. Dr. Ivan Halasz, and Dr. Gyorgy Kepes for your kind advice. Dr. Zsuzsanna Peres and Dr. Gergely Salat helped me a lot on the monograph, thank you so much for your brilliant opinions.

My insightful colleagues from Poland, Dr. Wladyslaw Peksa, Dr. Maciej Mikula and Prof. Dr. Ralph Schattkowsky, and Dr. hab. Piotr Grzebyk thank you so much for your opinions on the monograph and for encouraging me on my research.

Dear knowledgeable colleague Prof. Dr. Tomas Gabris from Slovakia, thank you for your help on the monograph of the Czechoslovakia part.

In China, Prof. Qin Jie and my master program supervisor Prof. Zhang Yonghe also helped me a lot for my Ph.D. application. Prof. Qianhong Qin, as my postdoctoral supervisor, helped me a lot to improve the research on the Chinese constitutional development and for the generous research fund on this program. Thanks to my colleagues from room 420, School of Law, Wuhan University, for providing a friendly research environment, and their insightful opinions always inspired me.

I am very grateful to Ms. Lydia Wang and Mr. Arulmurugan Venkatasalam, and Mr. Vishnu Muthuswamy for their professionally publication support.

Last but not least, a special thanks for my family; my parents always encouraged me chasing my dream, even that means we cannot meet often. They also taught me the importance of responsibility.

This work is sponsored by the Stipendium Hungaricum Scholarship Program and China Scholarship Council, and without their generous support, this project cannot be completed.

Wuhan, China   Lu Da
May 2021

Contents

1 **Introduction** 1
   1.1 Brief Introduction to Comparative Constitutional Law 1
        1.1.1 History of Comparative Constitutional Law 1
        1.1.2 Concept of Comparative Constitutional Law 2
        1.1.3 Value of Comparing Constitutional Law 3
   1.2 Methodology 5
   1.3 Terminology 6
        1.3.1 Brief Introduction to Visegrad and the Visegrad Group 6
        1.3.2 Central Europe or Eastern Europe? 6
        1.3.3 Definition of the Visegrad States in This Research 7
        1.3.4 China and Its Constitutions 7
        1.3.5 Same Terminology in the Constitutional Text,
               Different Practical Effects 7
   1.4 Structure of This Research Work 8
   References 10

2 **Birth of the Communist Party and Its Early Activities in China
and the Visegrad States** 11
   2.1 Birth of the Communist Party of China and Its Early Activities 12
        2.1.1 Birth of the Communist Party of China 12
        2.1.2 First United Front 13
        2.1.3 End of First United Front and "White Terror"? 15
        2.1.4 Reason for the Breakup of the First United Front 16
        2.1.5 Communist-Controlled China and the Chinese Soviet
               Republic 19
   2.2 Birth and Early Activities of the Communist Parties
       in the Visegrad States 24
        2.2.1 Spread of Communist Ideology in the Visegrad States 24
        2.2.2 Birth of the Hungarian Communist Party and Its Early
               Activities 25

		2.2.3	Birth of the Communist Parties and Their Early Activities in Czechoslovakia and Poland	34
	2.3	Conclusion		38
	References			39
3	**The First Written Communist Constitutions in China and the Visegrad States**			43
	3.1	First Communist Constitution in China		44
		3.1.1	Adoption of the Constitution of the People's Republic of China	44
		3.1.2	Analysis of the Text and Structure of the Constitution of the People's Republic of China	49
	3.2	First Written Communist Constitutions in the Visegrad States		56
		3.2.1	Hungarian People's Republic	56
		3.2.2	Czechoslovak Republic	60
		3.2.3	Polish People's Republic	64
	3.3	Comparative Analysis of the Structure and Text of the First Written Communist Constitutions of China and the Visegrad States		69
		3.3.1	Comparative Analysis of the Structures of the First Written Communist Constitutions of China and the Visegrad States	69
		3.3.2	Comparative Analysis of Text of the First Written Communist Constitutions of China and the Visegrad States	71
	3.4	Conclusion		75
	References			76
4	**Development of the Constitutions of China and the Visegrad States in the Reform Period**			79
	4.1	Development of the Constitution of the People's Republic of China in the Reform Period		80
		4.1.1	1975 Constitution of the People's Republic of China	81
		4.1.2	1978 Constitution of the People's Republic of China	83
		4.1.3	1982 Constitution of the People's Republic of China	85
		4.1.4	Conclusion	88
	4.2	Development of the Constitutions of the Visegrad States in the Reform Period		89
		4.2.1	Development of Constitutional Amendments in the Hungarian People's Republic in the Reform Period	90
		4.2.2	Development of the Constitutional Documents of Czechoslovakia in the Reform Period	92
		4.2.3	Development of Constitutional Amendments in the Polish People's Republic in the Reform Period	96
		4.2.4	Conclusion	98

	4.3	Comparative Analysis of the Development of the Constitutions of China and the Visegrad States in the Reform Period	98
		4.3.1 Similarities	99
		4.3.2 Differences	101
	4.4	Comparative Analysis of the Supreme Organs of State Power in China and the Visegrad States	103
		4.4.1 Development of the National People's Congress of the People's Republic of China	104
		4.4.2 Development of the National Assembly of the Hungarian People's Republic	105
		4.4.3 Development of the National Assembly of the Czechoslovak Republic	106
		4.4.4 Development of the Sejm of the Polish People's Republic	107
		4.4.5 Similarities in the Development of the Supreme Organs of State Power in China and the Visegrad States	107
		4.4.6 Differences in the Development of the Supreme Organs of State Power in China and the Visegrad States	109
	4.5	Conclusion	109
	References		110
5	**Development of Constitutions in China and the Visegrad States in the Transformation Period**		**113**
	5.1	Development of the Constitution of China in the Transformation Period	114
		5.1.1 First Amendment to the Current Constitution of China	114
		5.1.2 Second Amendment to the Current Constitution of China	115
		5.1.3 Third Amendment to the Current Constitution of China	116
	5.2	Development of the Constitutions of the Visegrad States in the Transformation Period	118
		5.2.1 Development of the Constitution of Hungary in the Transformation Period	118
		5.2.2 Development of the Constitution of Czechoslovakia in the Transformation Period	120
		5.2.3 Development of the Constitution of Poland in the Transformation Period	123
	5.3	Comparative Analysis of the Development of Constitutions in China and Visegrad States in the Transformation Period	126
		5.3.1 Similarities	127
		5.3.2 Differences	128
	5.4	Comparative Analysis of the Constitutionality Review Systems in China and the Visegrad States	131
		5.4.1 Constitutionality Review System in the People's Republic of China	132

		5.4.2	Constitutionality Review System in Hungary	133
		5.4.3	Constitutionality Review System in Czechoslovakia	134
		5.4.4	Constitutionality Review System in Poland	135
		5.4.5	Similarities	136
		5.4.6	Differences	137
	5.5	Conclusion		138
	References			138
6	**Development of the Constitutions in China and the Visegrad States After the Transformation Period**			141
	6.1	Development of the Constitution of China After the Transformation Period		142
		6.1.1	Fourth Amendment to the Current Constitution of China	142
		6.1.2	Fifth Amendment to the Current Constitution of China	144
		6.1.3	Conclusion	145
	6.2	Development of the Constitutions in the Visegrad States After the Transformation Period		146
		6.2.1	Development of the Constitution of Hungary After the Transformation Period	146
		6.2.2	Development of the Constitution of the Czech Republic After the Transformation Period	148
		6.2.3	Development of the Constitution of the Slovak Republic After the Transformation Period	151
		6.2.4	Development of the Constitution of the Republic of Poland After the Transformation Period	155
		6.2.5	Comparative Analysis of the Development of Constitutions in China and the Visegrad States After the Transformation Period	159
	6.3	Comparative Analysis of the Constitutionality Review Systems in China and the Visegrad States After the Transformation Period		161
		6.3.1	Introduction: Abortion Ban and Custody-and-Education Abolition	162
		6.3.2	Constitutionality Review in China After the Transformation Period	165
		6.3.3	Constitutionality Review in Hungary After the Transformation Period	166
		6.3.4	Constitutionality Review in the Czech Republic After the Transformation Period	169
		6.3.5	Constitutionality Review in Slovakia After the Transformation Period	171
		6.3.6	Constitutionality Review in Poland After the Transformation Period	173

		6.3.7	From Activism to Self-restraint in Constitutionality Review: A Comparative Perspective	175
	6.4	Conclusion		178
	References			179
7	**Conclusion**			185
	7.1	Brief Review		185
	7.2	Reasons for the Different Roads		188
		7.2.1	Socioeconomic Conditions	188
		7.2.2	Culture	189
		7.2.3	International Relationships with the Soviet Union	190
		7.2.4	Relationships with(in) the European Union (EU)	191
	7.3	Rule by Constitutionalism in China and the Visegrad States After the Transformation Period		192
	7.4	Conclusion		195
	References			196

Chapter 1
Introduction

Abstract The introduction chapter addressed the history and concept of comparative constitutional law and why should we compare the constitutional development in China and the Visegrad States. Three methodologies have been employed in this research work, historic method, textualism, and functionalism. In order to make the text more understandable, terminologies have been dealt with. The last part is the structure of the monograph.

1.1 Brief Introduction to Comparative Constitutional Law

Clearly, this is a research work on comparative law, specifically comparative constitutional law. This section presents a brief literature review of comparative constitutional law. The author introduces its history and concept and discusses why we should compare constitutional law in different states.

1.1.1 History of Comparative Constitutional Law

Michel Rosenfeld and Andras Sajo's edited book describes comparative constitutional law as a subfield of comparative law and even as making up only a small portion of the field of comparative law. Comparative law, in an academic sense, appeared in 1900. However, the discipline of comparative constitutional law was established much later as comparative law was initially much more focused on private law. It is believed that comparative constitutional law arose as an academic discipline in Europe after the Second World War. In the United States, the Supreme Court also played an important role in the establishment of comparative constitutional law. Later, this discipline was gradually integrated into the legal education system in the US and Europe (Rosenfeld & Sajo, 2012).

Ran Hirschl's introduction states that several books on comparative constitutional law were published in the late nineteenth century in the United States. However, at that time, the narrative of this topic was given only in the political domain (Jellinek,

© The Author(s), under exclusive license to Springer Nature Singapore Pte Ltd. 2021
L. Da, *Development of the Constitutions in China and the Visegrad States*,
https://doi.org/10.1007/978-981-16-5636-1_1

1905).[1] Hirschl agrees with Rosenfeld and Sajo that the field came into existence after the Second World War, especially the establishment of communist regimes, which brought different type of constitutions into the world. Comparative constitutional inquiry arose and was later revived in the mid-1980s (Hirschl, 2014).

Dixon and Ginsburg's edited handbook clearly introduces the development of comparative constitutional law. Comparative constitutional studies can be traced back to Aristotle's Politics. However, as a discipline in the education system, especially in the United States, it suddenly became a heated topic in the early 1950s, and later developments in social science and new constitutional design in several states greatly enriched the study of comparative constitutional law (Dixon & Ginsburg, 2011).

Frankenberg argues that the study of comparative constitutional law may be traced back to Aristotle's comparative work Politics. Nevertheless, comparative constitutional law as an academic discipline was still not established, and it remained a subfield of comparative law. However, later developments on this topic were increasingly notable (Frankenberg, 2012).

In conclusion, the study of comparative constitutional law has a long history; it can be traced back to ancient Greece if not earlier. Aristotle's comparative works, especially Politics, presented different constitutional systems in different political systems. However, most scholars agree that comparative law as an academic discipline appeared in the beginning of the twentieth century[2] (Halasz, 2015) and that it mainly focused on private law. In the 1940s and 1950s, comparative constitutional law as a discipline was recognized in Europe and the United States; in the 1950s, numerous comparative constitutional law courses were offered in law schools in the US (Dixon & Ginsburg, 2011). This subject has developed and become increasingly popular up to the present day.

1.1.2 Concept of Comparative Constitutional Law

Relatively, comparative constitutional law remains a very new subject even in the legal field.[3] Its meaning and scope are still being debated.

It is difficult to find a simple definition of comparative constitutional law. However, as the name of the subject implies, it is a subfield of comparative law and specifically related to constitutional law. Meuwese and Versteeg's article refers to comparative constitutional law as the "comparative study of constitutional law", and the new trend in the field is "quantitative constitutional comparison", which employs a statistical method to analyze numerous constitutional documents (Meuwese & Versteeg, 2012).

---

[1] In general, most scholars agree that the discipline of comparative constitutional law was established later than 1900, since the widely recognized masterpiece on state law was first published in 1900 by Georg Jellinek. However, only the second (1905) edition is available online.

[2] A Hungarian legal scholar, Prof. Elemér Balogh, even contributed his knowledge to comparative law.

[3] As mentioned above, most scholars agree that comparative constitutional law as an academic discipline appeared in the late 1940s and 1950s.

Harding and Leyland's article emphasizes that "comparative constitutional law is the branch of comparative law that studies constitutions as legal phenomena." The authors also reference comparative politics since there is no clear boundary between the two subjects. In their opinion, the main scope of comparative constitutional law includes constitution-making, constitutional reform and constitutional adjudication (Harding & Leyland, 2007). Frankenberg argues that comparative constitutional law still does not form a discipline, instead "oscillating" among several, such as political science, philosophy and comparative law. He also agrees that comparative constitutional law is a subfield of comparative law rather than an independent discipline (Frankenberg, 2012). In their introduction to their handbook on comparative constitutional law, Dixon and Ginsburg use several terms to describe the subject, including "interdisciplinary interest" and "institutionalized". Comparative constitutional study is a maturing field, as Dixon and Ginsburg note. Therefore, it is difficult to give a clear and comprehensive definition.

However, most scholars agree that comparative constitutional law is a subfield of comparative law, and Zweigert and Kotz's book provides a simple enough definition. In a more internationalistic sense, "comparative law is the comparison of the different legal systems of the world" (Zweigert & Kotz, 1998). Therefore, it may be possible to consider comparative constitutional law the comparison of constitutions in different legal systems in the world.

1.1.3 Value of Comparing Constitutional Law

It is worth inquiring why we should compare constitutional law and what is the value of comparing the constitutions of different countries. This is a question that constitutional comparatists cannot avoid.

In their book, Dorsen, Rosenfeld, Sajo and Baer present reasons why we should compare constitutional law. First, our curiosity pushes us to do so, and recently, with the development of communication, it has become much easier to access constitutional materials in different countries. Second, the world has become "smaller", and constitutions in different states are much more interdependent and may cross national boundaries, which means that they have more similarities. At the same time, each state has its own social conditions and historical background, and although constitutions may cross boundaries, each one will still have some unique characteristics. Third, an increasing number of constitutional materials are available since almost every country has its own constitution (Dorsen et al., 2010). Basu also provides a new perspective on this question: Referring to the domestic sphere, comparing former constitutions is very important for constitution-making (Basu, 2014).

The author addresses this question relating to his research work, which compares the development of constitutions in China and the Visegrad states during the communist period on the textual level, because it is much more complicated to compare the text in the constitutions and also in real life.

Why should we compare constitutional development in these countries? To answer this question, the author performed a quick search for any studies on this topic, and the result is somewhat shocking. There is no single research work that focuses only on comparing constitutional development in China and the Visegrad states. Monographs on the Constitution of the People's Republic of China by foreigners are rare, and the most notable recent work is Zhang's "The Constitution of China: A Contextual Analysis". Therefore, this work also offers a comprehensive picture of Chinese constitutional development at the textual level. Nevertheless, constitutional practice in China may operate differently. Readers of this work must be aware that from ancient times until now, the practical role of law has in most cases been considered as a leadership tool (Salat, 2006).[4] However, this does not mean that this atypical Western legal system is inferior to the Western system. It has functioned well in China.

Why is there little comparative constitutional law scholarship in this area? The following facts must be considered. First, As Dixon and Ginsburg mention in their edited handbook, "90% of comparative work in the English language covers the same ten countries" (Dixon & Ginsburg, 2011). It is true that most research in the comparative field focuses on "important countries". Second, countries in the Visegrad region have their own languages. For Chinese, Hungarian, Czech, Slovak and Polish are not familiar at all. Like the languages of scholars who live in the Visegrad states, Chinese is a very exotic language. Exacerbating this dilemma is that these languages are difficult to learn: In the language difficulty rankings by the Foreign Service Institute, Chinese belongs to Category Five out of five, and languages in the Visegrad states are ranked in Category Four.[5] The distance between China and the Visegrad states may intensify this unfamiliarity. For this reason, the author must rely on the Chinese and English literature; most literature used here is in English and Chinese, and some Hungarian, former Czechoslovakian and Polish literature is also used in cases where there are only Hungarian, Czech, Slovakian or Polish versions of constitutional provisions.

The above context generates the first answer to the question of why the author is conducting this comparison. There is little scholarship on this topic, and the author hopes this work may contribute to comparative research on both sides.

With the strengthening of cooperation between China and the Visegrad states, China has proposed the Road and Belt Initiative. It is worth comparing the development of constitutions on the two sides.

Another reason for this work is that both sides experienced similar systems. After the Second World War, China and the Visegrad states entered communist periods and established socialist systems in their constitutions. However, each country had its own

---

[4] For example, a masterpiece of Qin's criminal law from Hungary is Gergely Salat's Ph.D. Dissertation, The System of Criminal Law of the Ancient Chinese State of Qin. Through his work, Hungarian readers may realize how law was treated in China, and his work made it clear that some theories from the antient China still existed.

[5] The Language Difficulty Ranking is a ranking of languages based on a native English speaker's perspective. Retrieved June 16, 2021, from http://www.effectivelanguagelearning.com/language-guide/language-difficulty.

conditions. Therefore, similarities and differences are examined in their periods of constitutional development.

1.2 Methodology

It remains difficult to find a standard methodology for comparative legal research. Because it is an academic discipline, some general concerns must be fully discussed (Zweigert & Kotz, 1998).[6] Comparative constitutional law is still "maturing" (Dixon & Ginsburg, 2011). Therefore, there is no well-recognized methodology for it. Hoecke's article provides several methods for comparative legal research, namely, the functional, structural, analytical, law-in-context, historical, and common-core methods (Hoecke, 2015). More specific methodologies for comparative constitutional law are introduced by Jackson and Venter. Jackson's article presents the methods of classificatory work, historical work, universalist research, functionalism and contextualism (Jackson, 2012). Venter provides his view on the methodology of comparative constitutional law, naming the following five methods: functionalism and neofunctionalism, transplantation, dialogical interpretation, contextualism and observance of difference (Venter, 2010).

This research uses three main methods. First, as the title may imply, the author employs the historical method. During the communist period, China and the Visegrad states witnessed the development of socialist constitutions in each state. The author reviews the histories of constitutional development in each state in chronological order, as well as how historical conditions influenced the constitution-making. Second, contextualism or the law-in-context method is used. The author compares the contexts of the constitution in each state. For instance, the first communist constitutions in each state were strongly influenced by the 1936 Soviet Union Constitution, as is clear from an examination of their contexts. Third, like most comparative scholars, the author employs functionalism in this research. The development of socialist constitutions in each state differed, especially between China and the Visegrad states, which are considered as a group. The most significant example is the Revolutions of 1989. They affected every socialist state, including China and the Visegrad states. However, later, the Visegrad states abandoned their socialist constitutions, while the Chinese socialist constitution remained in force, although some crucial amendments were adopted (Michaels, 2006).

---

[6] Researchers agree that the modern concept of comparative legal research can be traced back to 1900 in Paris, where some leading scholars have identified an International Congress for Comparative Law.

1.3 Terminology

In this part, the author explicitly addresses the meaning of the term Visegrad states in this research work, and the same terms used in the constitutions of different countries may function differently.

1.3.1 Brief Introduction to Visegrad and the Visegrad Group

Visegrad is a historical town in northern Hungary. Today, this name is widely known due to the Visegrad Group, which currently consists of the four countries of Hungary, the Czech Republic, the Slovak Republic, and the Republic of Poland. This organization formed in February 1991; three state leaders met in Visegrad, inspired by a historical meeting of three kings in this area in 1335. In 1993, Czechoslovakia split into two states, the Czech Republic and the Slovak Republic, and both successor countries kept their membership in the group.

1.3.2 Central Europe or Eastern Europe?

This research has two main sections; the first focuses on the People's Republic of China, and the second on Hungary, Czechoslovakia before 1993 and the Republic of Poland. Giving these three countries an accurate general name is not simple. From geography to political geography, several terms have been used to describe this region. For example, in the official introduction to the Visegrad Group, this area is referred to as Central Europe.[7] However, considering the location of these countries from a political geography perspective during the communist period, many studies instead describe them as Eastern Europe (Stokes, 1998).[8] In addition, countries in this region are often categorized as belonging to the political geographical conception of East Central Europe or Central and Eastern Europe. Numerous scholars present comparative studies, and not only the Visegrad countries but also several former socialist states belong to this group (two very common examples are given here) (Gabris, 2018; Zagorski, 2015).

---

[7] About the Visegrad Group. Retrieved June 16, 2021, from http://www.visegradgroup.eu/about.

[8] During the Cold War period, this area was considered the Eastern Bloc. For instance, in Ramet's edited book, the term Eastern Europe refers to thirteen countries, including some in this area.

1.3.3 Definition of the Visegrad States in This Research

As mentioned in the last section, whether one uses the term Central Europe, Eastern Europe or East Central Europe, it is difficult to determine whether these terms refer to Hungary, the Czech Republic, the Slovak Republic, and the Republic of Poland. The author defines the term Visegrad states to more accurately describe the countries in this region. More specifically, in this work, the Visegrad states means Hungary, Czechoslovakia and Poland during the communist period, and after the dissolution of Czechoslovakia, it means Hungary, Poland, the Czech Republic and Slovakia.

1.3.4 China and Its Constitutions

Most of the time in this monograph, China refers to the People's Republic of China (PRC). In Chap. 2, China may refer to the Qing Dynasty or the Republic of China. After the civil war in China, the Communist Party of China (CPC) abolished the Six Codes (including the Constitution of the Republic of China) and established the PRC. The counterpart of the CPC, the Kuomintang, moved to island of Taiwan, and continued its governance on the island of Taiwan and the peripheral islands.

This monograph mainly deals with the Constitution of the PRC and conducts a comparative analysis of the Visegrad states' constitutions. However, the Constitution of the Republic of China (1946) undeniably has a special status in China's constitutional history.

1.3.5 Same Terminology in the Constitutional Text, Different Practical Effects

Of course, some terminology used in the Visegrad constitutions and the Chinese constitution during the communist period may have been used by the governments in different ways in reality. Taking "election" as an example, in the 1954 Constitution of the PRC, detailed regulations on elections of different levels of deputies to the People's Congress were presented in the Electoral Law of the PRC for the National People's Congress and Local People's Congresses in 1953 (thereafter 1953 Electoral Law).

Compared with deputy elections in the Visegrad states during the communist period, the first impression of such elections in China is generally that the entire process was conducted in an unprofessional way. Approval by acclamation even became the main procedure in some elections.

Then, the secret ballot was restored with a thoughtless approach. In practice, the city- and higher-level deputy elections operated in an indirect way. The deputy was elected by the lower-level People's Congress, and during the election, each deputy received a ballot. If the deputy did not support a candidate, then he or she was to mark an "x", and if he or she wished to abstain, he or she would mark a "√". For an affirmative vote, the deputy did not need to make any mark on the ballot (Wang, 2014). This thoughtless procedure ultimately destroyed the value of the secret ballot. It was obvious to the public whether deputies were abstaining or voting no, since they needed to use a pen to mark the ballot in those cases and did not need to so for an affirmative vote.

Other constitutional terminology, such as "legislative" and "judicial" institutions, functioned differently. As noted at the beginning of this monograph, the PRC neglected the rule of law for a long period, and the first Criminal Law of the PRC was not adopted until 1979, thirty years after the PRC's establishment. The first General Principles of Civil Law were not even adopted until 1987.

1.4 Structure of This Research Work

This entire research work consists of six chapters. This chapter presents a brief introduction and literature review. The final chapter concludes the work and presents some comments. The remaining sections contain the main discussion of the topic, namely, the comparison of the development of the constitutions of China and the Visegrad states.

This chapter presents the introduction and contains four parts. The first part contains the literature review on comparative constitutional law, the history of this subdiscipline, and the definition of comparative constitutional law. The second part presents the methodology of this research work. The third part explains terminology used in this article, and the final part describes the structure of this article.

Chapter 2 discusses the early exchanges of communist parties and the Soviet constitution between China and the Visegrad states. There are four parts in this chapter. The first part examines the birth of the Chinese Communist Party and its early activities. The Soviet Republic was established in China in the 1930s, and an outline of the Soviet constitution was also provided. However, this regime soon lost its ruling power. The second part examines Bela Kun's Communist Party and the 133-day Soviet Republic in Hungary in 1919. The third part explores the early activities of the communist parties in Czechoslovakia and Poland. The fourth part presents a comparison.

Chapter 3 examines the first communist constitutions in China and the Visegrad states. After the Second World War, communist systems were established in the Visegrad region and in China. The PRC adopted its first communist constitution in 1954, and this section conducts a very detailed examination of the text and structure of that document, as well as the constitution-making process. In this chapter, the author also examines the 1949 Hungarian constitution, 1948 Czechoslovakian constitution and 1952 Polish constitution one by one. The third part compares the first communist constitutions in each state, focusing on differences and similarities in the text and structure. The fourth part concludes this chapter.

1.4 Structure of This Research Work

Chapter 4 focuses on the development of the constitutions in the PRC and the Visegrad states during the reform period. In this article, the reform period refers to the mid-1950s to the 1980s. In China, three different versions of the constitution were adopted by the National People's Congress (NPC). Among these, the first two were strongly influenced by the Cultural Revolution; the current constitution was adopted in 1982 and restored many provisions of the 1954 constitution. The second part discusses constitutional development in the Visegrad states. In the Hungarian case, the author pays special attention to the 1972 constitutional amendment. In the Czechoslovakian case, two constitutional documents are examined. The 1960 constitution declared Czechoslovakia a socialist state, and the 1968 constitution declared it a federal state. In the Polish case, several important constitutional amendments were introduced. The third part compares the development of constitutions in China and the Visegrad states during the reform period. The final part of this chapter examines the supreme organ of state power in each state, employing a comparative analysis approach.

Chapter 5 explores the development of constitutions in China and the Visegrad states during the transformation period. After the Revolutions of 1989, the socialist system was abandoned in the Visegrad states. In this part, the author focuses on this vital point, and although the communist constitutions in each state were not abandoned immediately, crucial amendments were adopted by the legislative bodies in all of them. In China, the Revolutions of 1989 also affected the rule of the Chinese Communist Party, several constitutional amendments were adopted by the NPC, and economic reform was reflected in the context of the current constitution. The third part compares the constitutional development in each state during the transformation period. Finally, the author investigates the constitutionality review system in each state.

Chapter 6 focuses on constitutional development after the transformation period. The relationship between China and the Visegrad states entered a new era. The Belt and Road Initiative (BRI) connected China with the Visegrad states. All the states have participated in the BRI. Warsaw and Budapest hosted the 17 + 1 Summit in 2013 and 2017. China announced that it had built a socialist legal system and that it would be governed by the constitution. In 2017, the process of constitutionality review in China was updated, considered to usher in a new chapter in constitutional development in China. In the Visegrad states, constitutionality review has been conducted for over 30 years. Recently, Poland and Hungary have faced accusations of constitution violations, which has caused constitutional crises. The main topic of this chapter is the constitutionality review process in each state.

Chapter 7 concludes this research work. The first part briefly reviews the development of the constitutions in each state during the communist period and after the Revolutions of 1989. Next, the author presents several reasons why China and the Visegrad states chose different roads to develop their countries after the Revolutions of 1989. The author argues that in their contemporary constitutional development, China and the Visegrad states have employed constitutionalism as an instrument, and so-called rule by constitutionalism has been (re)established in both regions.

References

Basu, D. D. (2014). *Comparative constitutional law* (3rd ed.). Lexis Nexis.
Dixon, R., & Ginsburg, T. (2011). Introduction. In R. Dixon & T. Ginsburg (Eds.), *Comparative constitutional law* (1st ed., pp. 1–14). Edward Elgar Publishing Ltd.
Dorsen, N., Rosenfeld, M., Sajo, A., & Baer, S. (2010). *Comparative constitutionalism: Cases and materials* (2nd ed.). West Academic Publishing.
Frankenberg, G. (2012). Comparative constitutional law. In M. Bussani & U. Mattei (Eds.), *The Cambridge companion to comparative law* (1st ed., pp. 171–190). Cambridge University Press.
Gabris, T. (2018). *Prolegomena to legal history of East-Central Europe*. Wolters Kluwer.
Halasz, I. (2015). The institutional framework and methods of the implementation of soviet legal ideas in the Czechoslovakia and Hungary during Stalinism. *Journal on European History of Law, 6*(2), 29–37.
Harding, A., & Leyland, P. (2007). Comparative law in constitutional contexts. In E. Esin Orucu & D. Nelken (Eds.), *Comparative law: A handbook* (1st ed., Chap. 14). Hart Publishing.
Hirschl, R. (2014). *Comparative matters: The renaissance of comparative constitutional law*. Oxford University Press.
Hoecke, V. M. (2015). *Methodology of comparative legal research*. Law and Method. Retrieved June 16, 2021, from https://biblio.ugent.be/publication/7145504
Jackson, C. V. (2012). Comparative constitutional law: Methodologies. In M. Michel Rosenfeld & A. Sajo (Eds.), *The oxford handbook of comparative constitution law* (1st ed., Part I, Chap. 2). Oxford University Press.
Jellinek, G. (1905). *Allgemeine Staatslehre*. Only the second edition is available online. Retrieved June 16, 2021, from https://archive.org/details/allgemeinestaat00jellgoog
Meuwese, A., & Versteeg, M. (2012). Quantitative methods for comparative constitutional law. In M. Adams & J. Bomhoff (Eds.), *Practice and theory in comparative law* (1st ed., pp. 230–257). Cambridge University Press.
Michaels, R. (2006). The functional method of comparative law. In M. Mathias Reimann & R. Zimmermann (Eds.), *The oxford handbook of comparative law* (1st ed., Part II). Oxford University Press.
Rosenfeld, M., & Sajo, A. (2012). Introduction. In M. Rosenfeld & A. Sajo (Eds.), *The oxford handbook of comparative constitution law* (1st ed., pp. 1–19). Oxford University Press.
Salat, G. (2006). *Az ókori kínai Qin állam büntetőjogának rendszere [The System of Criminal Law of the Ancient Chinese State of Qin]* (Doctoral dissertation). Retrieved June 16, 2021, from http://doktori.btk.elte.hu/lingv/salat/salat_disszertacio.pdf. An English version of summary of his dissertation is available online. Retrieved June 16, 2021, from http://doktori.btk.elte.hu/lingv/salat/salattezis_eng.pdf
Stokes, G. (1998). Eastern Europe's defining fault lines. In S. P. Ramet (Ed.), *Eastern Europe: Politics, culture, and society since 1939* (1st ed., pp. 15–34). Indiana University Press.
Venter, F. (2010). *Global features of constitutional law* (1st ed.) Wolf Legal Publishers.
Wang, Y. (2014, March 7). "两会"表决"进化史": 从投豆子到按键子 [The "Evolution" of "The Two Meeting": From Bean Voting to Electronic Voting]. *Jiefang Daily*. Retrieved June 16, 2021, from http://www.chinanews.com/cul/2014/03-07/5922944.shtml
Zagorski, A. (Ed.). (2015). *Russia and East Central Europe after the cold war: A fundamentally transformed relationship*. Human Rights Publishers.
Zweigert, K., & Kotz, H. (1998). *Introduction to comparative law* (Tony Weir tr, 3rd ed.). Oxford University Press.

Chapter 2
Birth of the Communist Party and Its Early Activities in China and the Visegrad States

Abstract In this chapter, the author dealt with how the communism influenced China and the Visegrad States. The first part addressed the birth of the CPC and its early exercises, in the following part, how communist parties in the Visegrad countries established and how they operated has been studied. In this part, the early exercises of constitutional-making were analyzed in the respective countries.

China and the Visegrad countries clearly share histories of socialist experiences and social systems after the late 1940s.[1] However, some regions in these states had longer socialist experiences and communist party activities than others. In China, the socialist experience can be traced back to Russia's October Revolution. Since the failure of the Paris Peace Conference, Chinese scholars and generations of young people have sought a new solution to the misery wrought by colonization; as Mao Zedong stated, "With the cannon of October Revolution, the Revolution brings us Marxism–Leninism." Marxism-Leninism was considered a new way to solve China's problems. Chen Duxiu and Li Dazhao, the pioneers of socialism in China, organized the country's earliest communist group (Fairbank, 1993). The Hungarian Soviet Republic was considered the world's second Soviet Republic, although it lasted only 133 days (Hajdu, 1979). In Poland, the activities of the Communist Party can be traced back as far as the nineteenth century (Regula, 1934). Czechoslovakia's Communist Party was established in 1921, and Lenin even asked his secretary to bring him more information about the Congress of the Czechoslovak Social-Democratic Party (Lenin, 1921).

Part of this chapter was published in the Journal on European History of Law.

[1] China has been a socialist state since 1949, when the country was suffering from eight years of war against Japan and four years of civil war. In the Visegrad countries, the situation was quite similar: after the Second World War and with the "help" of the Soviet Union, the Visegrad countries began their socialist experiences in the very late 1940s or early 1950s. Also, it should be pointed out that when we talk about the socialist experiences and systems in what are today the Czech Republic and Slovakia, we always mean what was formerly Czechoslovakia, a unified country at that time. Additionally, the Visegrad countries refer to Hungary, Czechoslovakia, and Poland until 1 January 1993, at which time Czechoslovakia was divided into two countries, the Czech Republic and Slovakia.

© The Author(s), under exclusive license to Springer Nature Singapore Pte Ltd. 2021
L. Da, *Development of the Constitutions in China and the Visegrad States*,
https://doi.org/10.1007/978-981-16-5636-1_2

In this chapter, the author discusses the births of the communist parties and their early activities in these countries; however, it is impossible to present the full picture of all of these countries' communist parties' activities in this period in one chapter. Therefore, the most relevant aspects are presented, specifically, those that relate to the countries' constitutional practices. Regarding China, the author examines the birth of the CPC, the White Terror period and the Constitution of the Chinese Soviet Republic.[2] Regarding the activities of the Hungarian Communist Party, the author focuses on the Constitution of the Hungarian Soviet Republic[3] and the White Terror. Regarding Poland and Czechoslovakia, the author gives a detailed introduction to the formation of their communist parties and their early activities.

Finally, the author notes the difficulty of choosing research materials and presenting historical narratives in this monograph because from different perspectives, completely opposite stories may have been presented to the public. As Wu Dayou writes in a preface, "The biggest problem in modern Chinese history books is the biased opinions from the official narrative of the Kuomintang and the Communist Party" (Wu, 2009). A similar situation occurs in narratives on the Hungarian Soviet Republic and the White Terror in Hungary, with materials published in Hungary's socialist period usually displaying sympathy for the Hungarian Soviet Republic and a negative view of the White Terror, while newly published materials take the complete opposite position. Therefore, the author uses materials from both sides and seeks to present the full picture to the readers.

2.1 Birth of the Communist Party of China and Its Early Activities

As of the time of writing (2021), the CPC is celebrating its 100th birthday. Below, the author explores how the Chinese people accepted the ideology of communism and how it emerged and began to play a role in China 100 years ago.

2.1.1 Birth of the Communist Party of China

After the first Opium War opened the door of China (Fairbank, 1978; Liu, 1998)[4] the Chinese suffered from colonization and made numerous attempts to eject their

---

[2] The Constitution of Chinese Soviet Republic (1931). Chinese version only. Retrieved June 17, 2021, from https://www.marxists.org/chinese/reference-books/ccp-1921-1949/07/066.htm.

[3] Constitution of Hungarian Soviet Republic, Hungarian version only. Retrieved June 17, 2021, from https://hu.wikisource.org/wiki/A_Magyarorsz%C3%A1gi_Szocialista_Sz%C3%B6vets%C3%A9ges_Tan%C3%A1csk%C3%B6zt%C3%A1rsas%C3%A1g_alkotm%C3%A1nya.

[4] The reasons behind the First Opium War are still debated. However, the result of this war was clear: it opened the door for great powers to come to China and begin the division of their spheres of influence.

colonizers (Purcell, 1959).[5] However, the new leadership and the new Republic did not give the Chinese dignity and equality. China, as a victor in the First World War, joined the Paris Peace Conference, did not reach its goal and became an independent country again.[6] After the failure of the Paris Peace Conference, the May Fourth Movement broke out in Beijing, and Chinese scholars and young people began to seek a new road to independence for China (Fairbank, 1993).

One of the new methods that was provided to the public was socialism (Li, 2005; Zhang, 2009).[7] Some Chinese scholars noticed the events in Russia after 1917 and their outcomes and brought Marxism-Leninism to China. With the help of the Communist International, Chen Duxiu and Li Dazhao and their followers formed the first Marxist-Leninist group in China (Liu, 2006). The New Youth Magazine also contained numerous articles on Marxism-Leninism, and libraries and bookshops were full of translated and original books on the subject (Liu, 2006).

In the summer of 1921, the CPC was established in Shanghai and South Lake in Jiaxing with the help of the Communist International (Fairbank, 1983).[8] There were 12 delegates who represented 57 members of the CPC, and Delegate Mao Zedong represented the Hunan Communist cell. However, the pioneers of the CPC, Chen Duxiu and Li Dazhao, did not attend the meeting (Fairbank, 1983).

2.1.2 First United Front

On 26 January 1923, the Sun–Joffe Manifesto was published in Shanghai. It was considered the beginning of the First United Front between the Kuomintang and the CPC (Ding, 1990; Zhang, 1985).[9] After that, the First United Front, which, from

---

[5] Generally, the following activists are considered as the fighting Chinese: Taiping Heavenly Kingdom, the Boxer Rebellion, the reform movement of 1898 and the Xinhai Revolution.

[6] China requested the return of its sovereignty over Shandong; however, this request was refused by the conference.

[7] From the 1920s to the 1930s, many political parties and groups were established in China; they promoted their own theories across the country and sought the support of the masses; i.e., in the Chinese Youth Party, the National Association of Vocational Education of China and even within the Kuomintang, different factions were promoting their own theories. Moreover, different theories arose for helping the country shed the vestiges of colonization; for these political proposals and doctrines.

[8] The original plan was that the inaugural meeting would be held in a girls' school in Shanghai with the young representatives in their twenties. According to the schedule, the meeting started in a school in the French Concession; however, when the participants noticed that the meeting was being monitored by the secret police, the members changed the meeting place to a boat in South Lake.

[9] The formation of First United Front did not go well at the beginning; the idea to form the First United Front was a decision made by the Communist International and did not originally come from China. In order to put this idea into practice, the Communist International sent one of its members, Maring, to China to begin carrying out this idea; however, at the beginning, both the Kuomintang and the Communist Party of China rejected this idea. Moreover, there is additional debate about

Sun's perspective, united Russia and tolerated the Communist Party (联俄容共), played a very important role in the revolutionary events of the 1920s.

Before the Manifesto, with the guidance of the Communist International, the CPC decided to cooperate with the Kuomintang during the West Lake Meeting in August 1922 (Zhang, 2009).[10] As a result, Party members were to join the Kuomintang individually and spread communism (Ding, 1990; Fairbank, 1983).[11] In response, the Kuomintang, during its First National Congress in January 1924, determined to make an alliance between the Soviet Union and the CPC, decided to accept CPC members in the Kuomintang as individuals. Moreover, the Kuomintang's Central Committee offered some special high-ranking positions to CPC members (Yang, 2008). With the help of the new Communist International emissary Borodin, the entire program of the first Congress was very similar to that of meetings of the Soviet Union's Communist Party, and, in addition, a party constitution was created that was strongly influenced by that of the Russian Communist Party (Fairbank, 1983; Yang, 2008).

During the First United Front, the CPC and the Kuomintang made great progress in the Chinese revolution. At the end of the First United Front, the Kuomintang almost accomplished its goal of unifying the whole country. With the help of the Soviet Union and the Communist International emissary, the Front formed the National Revolutionary Army, and in 1926, began its new journey, the Northern Expedition.

From his decades of revolutionary experiences and multiple betrayals by warlords, Sun Yat-sen realized the importance of the army (Hsu, 2012). In May 1924, the Republic of China Military Academy opened, with nearly 500 new students from all over China (Fairbank, 1983). Chiang Kai-shek, one of the leaders of the Kuomintang, was appointed President by Sun Yat-Sen, and the principal military instructors had all graduated from military school. Notably, a particular member of the CPC made his own contribution to the school. Zhou Enlai, after studying in Europe, joined the school as a vice director of the Political Department (Yang & Luo, 1984). This military academy was considered the most important military school in China. Numerous generals of the Republic of China attended it, and many Communist military leaders graduated from it.

In the mass movement, the CPC worked extensively with the working class and farmers (Fairbank, 1983).[12] It is said that the Labor Union had approximately

---

when the First United Front began; according to Zhang Lei's article, the First National Congress of the Kuomintang, which was held in 1924, marked the beginning of the First United Front.

[10] Communist International spent a tremendous amount of time attempting to persuade the Communist Party of China to accept the idea and cooperate with the Kuomintang. In the West Lake meeting, only the Party leadership were allowed to join the Kuomintang. Late in the 3rd Plenary Meeting of the Party, held in June 1923, was it decided that all Party members would join the Kuomintang.

[11] According to the Communist International's directive to the Communist Party of China in May 1923, the latter should cooperate with the Kuomintang and start a national revolution in China.

[12] For example, in an enlarged plenum of the Party's Central Committee, a solution for achieving the goal was found: "It is absolutely true that the future destiny of the Chinese revolutionary movement depends entirely upon whether or not the Chinese Communist Party will be able to organize and lead the masses".

2.1 Birth of the Communist Party of China and Its Early Activities 15

1,241,000 members in 1926. Additionally, the CPC was very focused on young people, and the Communist Youth Corps grew by more than five times in less than two years (Fairbank, 1983).[13] In the countryside, the Communist Party greatly developed the Farmers' Association. Guangdong alone had 626,457 members in 1926 (Fairbank, 1983). On 30 May 1925, the May Thirties Incident occurred. Protesters flooded into the international settlements in Shanghai, resulting in over 10 Chinese people dead and some protesters injured. The incident soon led to nationwide anti-foreign demonstrations, also inspiring Chinese patriotism (Fairbank, 1983).[14]

2.1.3 End of First United Front and "White Terror"?

However, the ending of the First United Front is not a happy story. The discourse of the "White Terror" is presented in the complete opposite way from the official narrative of the PRC and research from the Republic of China or Western researchers. In this part, the author seeks to convey the full picture of the White Terror from different perspectives. Research works and media from the PRC have a very negative narrative of the White Terror or the April 12 Incident and show sympathy for Party members.[15] In 1927, Chiang Kai-shek launched his anti-communist policy with violence (Yang, 2008).[16] On 12 April, the Commander in Chief of the Shanghai Garrison Command, along with local gang (Fairbank, 1983)[17] members, disarmed the Workers' Inspection Corps in one day. The next day, when the General Labor Union organized a protest against the Kuomintang's violence, the Commander in Chief, Bai Chongxi, ordered his army to shoot the protesters (Fairbank, 1983; Yang, 2008). The cooperation between the Kuomintang and the CPC was officially over; the Kuomintang, led by Chiang Kai-shek, began its "counterrevolution policy" (Zhang, 2009)[18] in

---

[13] In early 1925, the renamed Communist Youth Corps only had 2500 members; in November of 1926, there were around 12,500 members in total.

[14] It was caused by a suppress on 15 May, on that day, the Japanese guards shot Chinese workers and one worker (a communist) died.

[15] Not only the school history books in the People's Republic of China but also the official media, i.e. the state-owned news agencies and academic articles from PRC, were sympathetic toward the Communist Party.

[16] On 12 March 1925, Sun Yat-sen died with his goal of unifying China unfinished. Chiang Kai-shek and Wang Jingwei became the leader of the Kuomintang. Before the Shanghai massacre of 1927, Chiang Kai-shek had already started his limited Communist Party policy; on 20 March 1926, the Zhongshan incident happened, and in May the same year, during the second plenary session of the Second National Congress of the Kuomintang, a regulation limiting the Communist Party of China was adopted. It seems that Chiang tried to solve the problem between the Kuomintang and the Chinese Communist Party peacefully.

[17] The local gang was the Green Gang, a secret society and criminal organization with a long history. The leader of the Green Gang, Du Yuesheng, was Chiang's close friend, and he was also believed to be one of the participants of the April 12th incident.

[18] The term of "counter-revolution policy" is usually used in the literature from the People's Republic of China, or mainland China. However, from the perspective of the Republic of China (Taiwan),

China, while the CPC, realizing the importance of the army, tried to establish its own revolutionary army in the countryside. This marks the end of the First United Front and the beginning of the White Terror as well.

On 15 April, two days after the 12th April "Counterrevolution Incident", Chiang Kai-shek ordered a purge of the Party. The order mentioned the Communist Party, whose members were to be investigated on suspicion of treason. Moreover, Chiang ordered the army force to arrest the leaders of the Communist Party and even published a wanted order (Yang, 2008).[19]

In Guangzhou, the Communist Party and its members also suffered a brutal massacre, and even the Republic of China Military Academy, the military school that had been run by Chiang Kai-shek, had to disarm. The government believed that there was a strong influence from the Communist Party, and approximately 200 cadets were arrested because they were considered members of the Party (Fairbank, 1983). On 27 April, this tragedy finally ended. According to the report, approximately 2000 suspected communists were arrested, and approximately 20 people died in the massacre, most of whom were young students, including two female students (Fairbank, 1983).

The purge also occurred in other parts of China, weakening the influence and power of the CPC. In response, in Wuhan and Changsha, radical CPC members killed so-called enemies (Fairbank, 1983).

2.1.4 Reason for the Breakup of the First United Front

This shift from full cooperation to brutal repression and from an independent local government to ruling the whole country showed the importance of the First United Front. However, with the triumph of the Northern Expedition, the friendship between the Kuomintang and the CPC faded.

Nevertheless, examining the full background of the First United Front, the conflicts of interest among the Kuomintang, the CPC and the Communist International (or Soviet Union) existed from the very beginning of their cooperation.

In the early 1920s, when Communist International emissary Maring helped Chen Duxiu and Li Dazhao organize the CPC, the Communist International already realized that the Party was too weak to organize a nationwide revolution in China. After the Party's establishment, Maring, its "guide", traveled with his interpreter Zhang Tailei to Guilin, a city famous for its magnificent scenery, and visited Sun Yat-sen to discuss the cooperation between the Kuomintang and the CPC (Yang, 2001). However, at that moment, Sun Yat-sen did not show great interest in cooperating with

---

this was only part of the process for removing the obstacles to uniting the whole country. Even Wang Jingwei, a former leader of the Kuomintang decided to divide the Communist Party after he saw the threat of the Communist Party. Nevertheless, the policy that Chiang took was more brutal.

[19] During the Northern Expedition, thanks to the experience of the president of the Republic of China Military Academy, Chiang Kai-shek became the highest leader of army in Kuomintang.

2.1 Birth of the Communist Party of China and Its Early Activities

the Party; he believed that the Kuomintang would be a success with his ideology. He even asked Zhang Tailei, Maring's interpreter, "Why do the young people want to find the medicine [meaning a solution to problems in China] from Marx; you can find the basic ideas of Marxism in the ancient Chinese books, can't you?" (Yang, 2001).

However, the reality forced Sun to reconsider the offer from the Communist International. At that time, Sun was facing financial difficulties, military challenges, and the chaos of the Party. He had trouble raising money from his supporters, and the tax revenue was also less than that of the previous year; at the same time, Chen Jiongming betrayed the Kuomintang and seemed to be cooperating with Sun's enemy Wu Peifu. Because Chen had betrayed the Party, Party members lost their connection with the Kuomintang (Yang, 2008).

In the summer of 1923, when Borodin, the new emissary, came to Guangzhou and talked little about the long term with Sun Yat-sen, the Kuomintang started to accept the help of the Soviet Union. In particular, when the Soviet Union promised financial and military support (Zhou, 2011),[20] the relationship between the Kuomintang and the Soviet Union or the Communist International became increasingly close.

On the CPC's side, the proposal to cooperate with the Kuomintang seemed to be a directive from the more powerful Communist International (Zhou, 2011),[21] and the only option for this still young and vulnerable Party was to obey (Ding, 1990).[22]

The First United Front was established as a result of the coordination between the Communist International and the Soviet Union. However, the wish for cooperation between the two was their own; rather, it was much more a decision made by the Communist International and the Soviet Union. As the conflicts of interest between the Kuomintang and the CPC intensified, it was very difficult to maintain this cooperation.

At the beginning, this cooperation was full of conflicts; the Kuomintang insisted on its Three Principles of the People and did not consider the CPC an equal partner. For the Kuomintang, allowing members of the CPC to join the Kuomintang as individuals and offering more leadership positions to Party members were only attempts to obtain support from the Soviet Union; once the Kuomintang became sufficiently strong, it planned to end this cooperation and "purify" itself.

---

[20] The support from Soviet Union helped the Kuomintang's development a great deal; in 1923, after the Sun-Joffe Manifesto, the Soviet Union gave the Kuomintang 2 million Mexican silver coins, and since then, each year, the Kuomintang receives millions of yen in financial support from the Soviet Union. In terms of military support, the Soviet Union provides a large number of weapons to the Kuomintang, and it helped the Kuomintang establish the Republic of China Military Academy in Guangzhou. Additionally, the new Party constitution is quite similar to that of the Party Constitution of the Soviet Union.

[21] The Communist Party of China was a branch of Communist International.

[22] At the beginning, the Communist Party of China tried to reject the proposal to cooperate with the Kuomintang; however, after the interference of Communist International, the Communist Party had to accept the proposal.

The CPC was also unwilling to accept the "task" of cooperating with the Kuomintang at first because it did not consider the Kuomintang's policies real communism. The policies of the CPC should be more radical, according to an article by Chen Duxiu, its leader: "The Party members of the Kuomintang are mainly opportunists and bureaucrats, only Sun Yat-sen is a real revolutionist…we are just joining the Kuomintang temporarily … to fix the Party's mistake of approaching Zhang Zuoling[23] and Japan … and the task of the Communist Party is…to split up the Kuomintang" (Yang, 1999). It was very clear that with this attitude, the partnership with the Kuomintang was doomed to an unhappy ending from the beginning of the First United Front (Yang, 1999).[24]

Beginning in 1927, the second year of the Northern Expedition, the Kuomintang was much stronger than at the beginning of the cooperation, and the CPC had developed greatly not only in Party membership but also through its experience of tremendous struggle. In March 1927, the National Revolutionary Army came to Shanghai and Nanjing and tried to control these two large and very important cities. The expedition went well and received strong support from the masses (Fairbank, 1983). In Shanghai, the Communist Party organized a few "uprisings" with Workers' Inspections Corps and workers. These gunmen caused major chaos in the city; at the same time, thousands of workers went on strike and demonstrated (Fairbank, 1983). Similar events occurred in Nanjing, with even more chaos.[25] In Chiang's opinion, the Communist Party's attempts to control these very important cities, which created such turmoil, would harm the Northern Expedition, so he decided to end this disorder and punish the Communist Party.[26]

Overall, the main reason for the schism of the Kuomintang and the CPC was the fundamental conflict of interest between the two parties, and their cooperation only occurred because parents asked their children to live together.[27] However, as time passed, differences multiplied, and the brotherhood ultimately ended with unhappiness.

---

[23] The most powerful warlord in Northeast China.

[24] However, this idea of the part of Chen Duxiu did not receive any criticism from Communist International.

[25] In Nanjing, the chaos resulted in many deaths and injuries. According to some Japanese reports, this chaos was caused by Communist Party members.

[26] It should be noted that this kind of reasoning came only from the Kuomintang's side; for the Communist Party, because Chiang became the spokesman of the elite bourgeoisie, he was no longer considered revolutionary.

[27] The metaphor used here is a traditional metaphor from ancient China. Before the wedding ceremony, the new couple would not have met each other, and they had to follow along with their parents' decision.

2.1.5 *Communist-Controlled China and the Chinese Soviet Republic*

Although the Kuomintang-ruled Republic of China was considered the legitimate government prior to 1949, some parts of China were controlled by the Communist Party. Therefore, the Communist Party could pursue its political goals in these areas, such as establishing a Soviet Republic in China and even adopting a constitution.

2.1.5.1 State Within a State: Communist-Controlled China

After the brutal massacre in 1927, the CPC realized the importance of the army and started to establish its own controlled territory (Shu, 2016).[28] From mid-1927 to the end of 1937, the beginning of the Second United Front, the CPC gained extensive experience in revolution and organized peasant movements (Fairbank, 1986). The Party not only controlled its own territory but also matured as a party.

From the failure of the First United Front to the establishment of the Chinese Soviet Republic, the CPC resisted the Kuomintang's "betrayal" in different ways. Qu Qiubai and other Communist leaders organized a few uprisings in different cities, but they ended in failure (Fairbank, 1986).[29] These failures caused the Communist Party to seek another means of survival. In Hunan, future People's Republic leader Mao Zedong had very rich experiences dealing with farmers in rural areas. After the failure of the Autumn Harvest Uprising, Mao Zedong went to the Jinggang Mountains with his army and tried to establish a rural Soviet republic there (Sun, 2003).[30] Rural Soviet policy was considered to have been proven useful at that time, and an increasing number of rural soviets or so-called Communist-controlled Chinese areas were established. Most of the territory of communist-controlled China was in Southern China, and the most important territory of the CPC was the Jiangxi-Fujian Soviet (Sun, 2003).[31]

---

[28] On 7 August 1927, there was a meeting held in Wuhan, Hubei Province to respond to the Kuomintang's counter revolution. There, Mao Zedong mentioned that "political power grows out of the barrel of a gun", which indicated that the Communist Party needed to focus on its own military construction.

[29] The Communist Party organized a few uprisings in Nanchang, Guangzhou and Wuhan. On 1 August of 1927, there was a uprising happened in Nanchang; although it failed, it is considered the beginning of the Communist Party of China having its own army. Therefore, the first of August was celebrated as Army Day since the Peoples' Republic of China was established.

[30] Mao Zedong had a lot of experience with peasants. He grew up in a small village in Shao Shan, Hunan Province. Unlike his fellows in the First United Front, he spent his most time in rural areas and spread communism in such areas. The reason he chose the Jinggang Mountains, according to Sun Jiang's article, was that the area was far away from the political centers of Hunan and Jiangxi, and most farming lands there were controlled by landlords. Therefore, it would be easy to initiate land reforms in this area.

[31] At that time, there were around 15 communist-controlled Soviet areas in China, and most of them were located rural areas.

However, at the beginning, because of the Soviet influence, the CPC still paid more attention to cities and its urban leadership, and communists in the cities were seemingly viewed as superior to the those in the rural soviets (Sun, 2003). The success of the communist revolution depended on the proletariat and not peasants, just as in its big brother, the Soviet Union.

The Kuomintang would allow its enemy any chance of breathing space. In 1928, the Nanjing Nationalist government started to create a new criminal code, including a special criminal law on the Communist Party issue. Tan Yankai supervised the drafting of this special law. The so-called Provisional Counter-Revolution Penalty Regulation was enacted on 9 March 1928.[32] This regulation called for an extremely harsh punishment. For example, it stipulated that anyone who attempted to subvert the nationalist government or the Kuomintang would be sentenced to death. Three Principles of the People were also considered fundamental in China; anyone who wanted to violate this principle and participate in an uprising would be sentenced to death. There was even an article stating that activists in an organization or gathering with a counterrevolutionary goal would be sentenced to imprisonment and the organization or gathering disbanded (Yang, 2008). There were also a few decisions made by the nationalist government, including collective punishment (Yang, 2008).[33]

Because of the Kuomintang's harsh punishments and predominant military power, the influence of the Communist Party in the cities was at a low ebb, and Communist Party members had more chances to spread their theories in rural areas. In the Jinggang Mountains, Mao Zedong and his army struggled to survive; Mao tried to establish his own base in this area, and he needed support from the farmers. As noted above, in the Jinggang Mountains, most farmland was owned by landlords, and farmers had miserable lives there. When Mao came to this area, he started the land reform policy. It was very popular among the poor farmers, an increasing number of poor people joined Mao's army, and finally, Mao and his army had their "home" (Fairbank, 1986).[34] To legitimize the land reform, land laws were passed in different rural areas (Fairbank, 1986; Guo, 1987).[35] This helped the Communist Party establish its own controlled area. Communism became popular among farmers, and increasingly, poor farmers sent their sons to join the communist army.

---

[32] It is very interesting to note that both sides claimed that other side was the "counter revolution". Since the Republic of China nominally united the whole country after the Northern Expedition, there was no doubt that the Kuomintang would conduct an encirclement campaign.

[33] The decision against the Communist Party regulated the punishment for the so-called ineffective Kuomintang Party members and branches.

[34] At the beginning of the Jinggang Mountains campaign with the Soviets, Mao told his army, "We are doing the revolution … it should have a home, otherwise it will be very difficult … When the enemy does not come, we can train our soldiers, and mobilize the masses; when the enemy comes, we can fight with them and rely on this home".

[35] Depending on the different social class in rural areas, the Communist Party instituted different policies. Generally, for poor peasants, the Communist Party provided a certain amount of land; for average peasants (not rich but also not poor), the CPC protected their interests; and for rich peasants, at the beginning, the CPC also protected their rights, but with the development of land reforms, rich peasants' interests were violated: for landlords, since they wish the opposite of land reform, their rights were completely violated in most of time.

2.1 Birth of the Communist Party of China and Its Early Activities 21

In early 1929, Mao Zedong, Zhu De and approximately 3600 soldiers left the Jinggang Mountains; they went to southern Jiangxi and tried to establish a new rural soviet in Gan Nan. After the difficult fight with the Kuomintang army, Mao Zedong and his army had a new home in the southern part of Jiangxi Province. In the same year, Mao and his compatriots decided to create a new rural soviet in the western part of Fujian province, since the region was wealthy and had a good base for a mass movement. After nearly a year of fighting with the Kuomintang, the Jiangxi-Fujian Soviet was finally established, and it soon became the largest component territory of the Chinese Soviet Republic.

2.1.5.2 Chinese Soviet Republic and Its Constitution

In the very beginning of the 1930s, the Communist Party controlled substantial territories in rural areas (Chen, 1982)[36] and had 15 rural soviets. More than 100,000 Chinese joined the Red Army; however, there was no central government ruling communist-controlled China (Chen, 1982). Due to the strong influence of its masses of people and its territory, the Jiangxi-Fujian Soviet has been considered central to rural soviets in China.

To ensure the legality of these rural soviets and develop guidelines for future revolution, in 1931, the CPC decided to establish the Chinese Soviet Republic and enact the Constitution of the Chinese Soviet Republic (Chen, 1982).[37] From 7 to 20 November 1931, the First National Congress of the Chinese Soviet Republic was held in Rui Jin, a small town in Jiangxi. Six hundred ten deputies attended the meeting and passed the Constitution, Land Law and Labor Law.[38] Mao Zedong was elected as the leader of the new government (Chen, 1982).

The Constitution of the Chinese Soviet Republic was considered the first communist constitution in China. However, it was strongly influence by the 1918 Constitution of the Soviet Union (Liu, 2011; Sun & Tian, 2007). Although the constitution was amended after the Second National Congress of the Chinese Soviet Republic, the main idea was not changed (Chen, 1982).[39]

The constitution consisted of a preamble and 17 articles, and it stipulated the form of the state, basic political system, tasks of the government and rights and duties of the

---

[36] The Soviet presence was felt in more than 10 provinces and in around 300 counties.

[37] In 1930, the Central Committee of the Communist Party of China made the decision to establish a central government in rural Soviet areas; however, because of the interference of the Kuomintang and the inconvenience of transportation in rural areas, the date for establishing the Soviet public area changed several times.

[38] These were the most important laws at that time. Land laws affected the legality of the land reform in rural Soviet areas, and labor laws were designed to protect workers' rights.

[39] Several places changed, and the most important change was "the consolidated alliance with middle peasants" in the first Article. The full version of the Constitution of the Chinese Soviet Republic, Chinese version only. Retrieved June 18, 2021, from https://www.marxists.org/chinese/reference-books/ccp-1921-1949/07/066.htm.

people.[40] Next, the author discusses the Constitution of the Chinese Soviet Republic in terms of these four components.

Form of the State

The form of the state is a basic question in every country. Because of the strong influence of the Soviet Union and the characteristics of the communist state, the Constitution of the Chinese Soviet Republic stated its form of state in Article 2:"What the Chinese Soviet Republic set up is a state which is based on the democratic dictatorship of the workers and peasants. All power of the Soviet regime shall belong to the workers, peasants, Red Army soldiers and the entire toiling population."[41]

It declared the Chinese Soviet Republic a democratic dictatorship, with workers and farmers the leaders of this new country. Notably, Article 1 of the 1918 Constitution of the Soviet Union stated, "Russia is declared to be a republic of the Soviets of Workers', Soldiers', and Peasants' Deputies. All the central and local power belongs to these soviets" (Liu, 2011).[42] Both constitutions ensured the leadership of workers, peasants and soldiers.

Basic Political System

Essentially, the basic political system in the Chinese Soviet Union was a copy of that described in the Soviet Union's constitution (Liu, 2011).[43]

Article 3 stipulated that "the highest organ in the Chinese Soviet Republic is the National Congress of Chinese Soviets, and when the National Congress is not in session, the highest organ shall be the Provisional Central Executive Committee of National Soviets. The Central Executive Committee shall appoint a Council of People's Commissars, which shall conduct all governmental affairs, and promulgate orders and resolutions."[44] This article regulated how the new state would function politically, and from the National Congress of Chinese Soviets to the NPC of the

---

[40] However, it should be noted that not everyone who lived in the Soviet Republic had the same rights and duties. For example, landlords, and sometimes rich peasants, were considered the enemy of the Soviet Republic; therefore they did not have the same rights and duties stated in the constitution.

[41] The full version of the Constitution of the Chinese Soviet Republic, Chinese version only. Retrieved June 18, 2021, from https://www.marxists.org/chinese/reference-books/ccp-1921-1949/07/066.htm.

[42] Constitution of the Soviet Union in 1918, English version. Retrieved June 18, 2021, from https://www.marxists.org/history/ussr/government/constitution/1918/index.htm.

[43] The Constitution of the Soviet Union in 1918 had a similar regulation, and another similar regulation was included in the Constitution of the Soviet Union in 1924.

[44] The full version of the Constitution of the Chinese Soviet Republic, Chinese version only. Retrieved June 18, 2021, from https://www.marxists.org/chinese/reference-books/ccp-1921-1949/07/066.htm.

2.1 Birth of the Communist Party of China and Its Early Activities

PRC, it also showed the historical influences on the Constitution of the Chinese Soviet Republic (Xu, 2005).

Tasks of Government

Since the Chinese Soviet Republic was only a regional regime, the constitution not only included ensured the power of the government and people's rights and duties but also declared the tasks of the government. These were guidelines for this new state.

Article 1 of the Constitution of the Chinese Soviet Republic enumerated the tasks of the government:

> The task of the Constitution of the Chinese Soviet Republic is to guarantee the democratic dictatorship of the proletariat and peasantry in the Soviet districts and to secure the triumph of the dictatorship throughout the whole of China. It shall be the aim of this dictatorship to destroy all feudal remnants, eliminate the influence of the imperialist powers in China, to unite China, to systematically limit the development of capitalism, to carry out economic reconstruction of the state, to promote the class-consciousness and solidarity of the proletariat, and to rally to its banner the broad masses of poor peasants and the consolidated alliance with middle peasants in order to effect the transition to the dictatorship of the proletariat.[45]

This article suggests the reality in China in the 1930s; the country was not fully unified, imperialist power still had great influence, and the country was not independent in its foreign policy and economy. The majority of the population and farmers still lived in very poor conditions. The democratic dictatorship indicated the form of the state in this new regime. These tasks were realistic, and the CPC followed this road, realizing the triumph of communism in China as a whole.

Rights and Duties of the People

The Constitution of the Chinese Soviet Republic also stipulated the rights and duties of the people. However, according to Article 2, the following groups were not included in the concept of "people" even though they lived in the Chinese Soviet Republic, and they were deprived of political rights: "Militarists, bureaucrats, landlords, the gentry, capitalist and monks—all exploiting and counterrevolutionary elements—shall be deprived of the right to elect deputies to participate in the government and to enjoy political freedom".[46] It is clear that the new regime was still not sufficiently mature, and this deprivation of political rights violated fundamental rights.

---

[45] The full version of the Constitution of the Chinese Soviet Republic, Chinese version only. Retrieved June 18, 2021, from https://www.marxists.org/chinese/reference-books/ccp-1921-1949/07/066.htm.

[46] The full version of the Constitution of the Chinese Soviet Republic, Chinese version only. Retrieved June 18, 2021, from https://www.marxists.org/chinese/reference-books/ccp-1921-1949/07/066.htm.

Not only Article 2 but also Articles 4, 5, 6, 9, 10, 11, 12, 13 and 14 declared people's rights and duties. According to these regulations, people lived in the Chinese Soviet Republic without distinction of sex, religion, or nationality and would enjoy freedom of speech, publishing, assembly and association. People older than 16 years would enjoy suffrage, everyone would enjoy free education and freedom of marriage and religion, and people had the right and duty to work and perform military service (Chen, 1982).

Notably, Article 14 stated, "The Soviet government of China recognizes the right of self-determination of the national minorities in China". This did not fit China's situation because of the strong influence of the Soviet Union's constitution. Most of the regulations on people's rights and duties were copied from the Constitution of the Soviet Union, including Article 14 (Liu, 2011).

From the birth of the CPC in 1921 to the establishment of the Chinese Soviet Republic in 1931, the Communist Party spent 10 years exploring its own path, and the rich experiences of the rural soviets helped the party grow from weak to strong, from a regional regime to ruling all of China. The Communist Party faced several fatal attacks from the Kuomintang and during the Sino-China war. Ultimately, it managed to survive and even enlarged the Red Army and the Communist-controlled territory in China. Thanks to the sacrifice of the proletariat and peasants and the poor administrative organization of the Kuomintang, the CPC established the PRC in 1949.

2.2 Birth and Early Activities of the Communist Parties in the Visegrad States

Compared to China, the Visegrad states were much more familiar with communism. This part discusses these countries' communist parties and their early activities. Special attention is paid to the constitutional development in each state.

2.2.1 *Spread of Communist Ideology in the Visegrad States*

Before we examine the formation of the communist parties in each state in the Visegrad region, it is worth explaining how the communist ideology spread in the Visegrad states, or more specifically in the Habsburg Empire (Gergely, 2000)[47] and later the Austro-Hungarian monarchy, after the Compromise of 1867.

---

[47] From 1790 to 1867, because of the *Pragmatica Sanctio*, Hungary was linked with the Habsburg Empire, and the emperor was also regarded as the nominal king of the Kingdom of Hungary after he took an oath to abide by Hungarian law. The independence of Hungary was only lost after the surrender at Vilagos in August 1849.

An increased worker population in the monarchy resulted from the land reforms during the Habsburg Empire. In Hungary, for example, in the 1830s and 1840s, the rulers passed a series of laws to "rectify certain imperfections and unnecessary omissions" (Gray, 2009). However, these land reforms were not as successful as expected, and life in the countryside was difficult. Meanwhile, with the development of industrialization in the Habsburg Empire, including Hungary, an increasing number of jobs were offered by factories in the cities and mineral industries, such as in Bohemia and Silesia (Palmer, 1903). With the large number of workers in the industrial sector, trade unions and other political groups grew significantly. The Hungarian Social Democratic Party was formed in 1890, and its early Declaration of Principles cited the ideology of Marxism. The Russian Revolution and Lenin's theories reached Hungary in late 1918 (Poloskei, 2000).

2.2.2 Birth of the Hungarian Communist Party and Its Early Activities

The Communist Party of Hungary was established after the First World War, and although this occurred over only four months, the Party soon had the chance to use its methodology (Tokes, 1967).[48]

In this part, the author discusses three main topics: the formation or birth of the Communist Party of Hungary, the establishment of the Hungarian Soviet Republic and its constitution—and particularly, how the Soviet Union's constitution influenced it—and finally, the failure of the Hungarian Soviet Union (Da, 2017).

2.2.2.1 Socialism in Hungary Before the First World War

The history of socialism in Hungary is much longer than that of the Communist Party of Hungary. In the 1860s, when Karl Marx sought to spread his socialism or so-called Marxism in Europe, as a part of the Austro-Hungarian monarchy, Hungary contained numerous thinkers and books on socialism. Its first political group, the General Workers' Association, mainly consisting of the Budapest proletariat, formed on 23 February 1868 (Mevius, 2005; Tokes, 1967). In 1867, Austria and Hungary enacted the Compromise along with other ethnic nationalities in both countries, and the so-called Austro-Hungarian monarchy was established. The establishment of the monarchy helped greatly develop the economy in the Hungarian region. Industrialization occurred in Hungary, and an increasing number of factories were built after the Compromise, especially in large cities, such as Budapest. Many poor farmers left their hometowns and came to large cities to make a living as well. According to

---

[48] The Communist Party of Hungary, established in November of 1918, was led by Bela Kun and his former imprisoned friends, who accepted Marxism-Leninism while held in the Russian prisoner of war camps.UHu.

Hungarian statistics, only 28,000 workers worked in factories at this time. However, over the next 40 years, the number of factory workers increased 10 times (Gyula, 2001).

Receiving the ideas of social-democratic theorists from Germany, such as Eduard Bernstein and Ferdinand Lassalle, the socialist group leading the working class mainly in Budapest made five failed attempts to form a socialist party in Hungary from 1869 to 1890. In their early activities, these socialist activists sought to achieve goals such as general suffrage for every Hungarian and electing working-class representatives to the parliament. However, the inescapable reality dashed these socialists' dreams (Tokes, 1967).

At the end of the nineteenth century, there was a new burst of socialist activity. With industrialization in Hungary, an educated middle class was growing in the large cities, and they increasingly sought legal recognition from the monarchy to ensure their rights (Tokes, 1967).

Just as there was a socialist journal in China, called New Youth,[49] there was also a journal in Hungary that spread socialism among young students and scholars. With the help of rich friends, social democrats and Hungarians who were born in the old Hungarian Kingdom (currently Romania), Oszkar Jaszi launched a monthly journal, Huszadik Szazad (Twentieth Century), in Hungary on 1 January 1900. After a few years, it became one of the most important academic publications in Hungary due to its prestigious subscribers (Tokes, 1967). Later, Jaszi came up with the idea of establishing an "eastern Switzerland" in the Hungarian Kingdom. However, this idea did not win support from other ethnic nationalities in the old Hungarian Kingdom (Hoensch, 1988).

During the war, which required many weapons and other forms of support for the monarchy, many more workers were needed; however, the workers' conditions declined dramatically. According to the War Requirement Acts, almost all industrial enterprises were controlled by the government in the spring of 1915 (Hoensch, 1988). With the prolongation of the war, the living standards of the working class in cities worsened, and the daily shortages became increasingly severe. Numerous people, especially the working classes, became dissatisfied with the government, and counter-government activists and antiwar programs were organized by the socialist group (Hoensch, 1988).

2.2.2.2 Birth of the Communist Party of Hungary

On 16 November 1918, the Karolyi government released a Declaration, and Hungary became a Republic. This marked the collapse of the Austro-Hungarian monarchy (Hoensch, 1988).

---

[49] New Youth, or La Jeunesse, was the most important journal in the early twentieth century; it spread socialist ideas among scholars and young students, and the chief editor, Chen Duxiu, was one of the leaders of the Communist Party of China during its early period.

2.2 Birth and Early Activities of the Communist Parties …

Bela Kun was the early leader of the Communist Party of Hungary. He and his comrades, such as Jozsef Kelen, and his brother Otto Korvin established the Party in 1918. The next year, the Party had the chance to build a Soviet Republic and enact some socialist policies, although this Soviet Republic only lasted 133 days.

Kun was born in a small village in Transylvania (now part of Romania) in 1886. In his early years, he worked as a journalist in Romania and joined the socialist party, the Hungarian Social Democratic Party, when he was 16 years old (Bugaiski, 2002; Tokes, 1967).[50] During WWI, Kun was captured by the Russian army and sent to a war prison camp in Tomsk. There, Kun was forced to work but also tried to form a communist group with his comrades (Tokes, 1967).[51]

While in prison, Kun and his comrades accepted the new trend of the Russian Revolution. They became Bolshevik Party members in 1917 and even had the privilege of living outside of the prison camp (Tokes, 1967).

Before Kun and his Bolshevik comrades returned to Hungary and established the Communist Party of Hungary in 1918, in March, Kun organized the Hungarian Group of the Communist Party of Russia in Moscow (Matyas & Otto, 1982).

Almost at the same time, socialist war prisoners joined the Bolsheviks in other parts of the camp in Russia (Tokes, 1967). An increasing number of former Hungarian soldiers accepted the new trend in socialism of Bolshevism or Leninism, took inspiration from the Russian Revolution and even took part in the Revolution (Tokes, 1967).

Because approximately 25% of the graduates of Russia's "Prisoner of War graduates of the October Revolution" program at that time were Hungarian, the reputable Kun was named the first president of the Federation of Foreign Groups (Tokes, 1967).

After the Brest-Litovsk agreement, Russia, the new socialist country, finally had time to take a breath and even considered spreading the revolution to other countries. Hungary was one of the most likely countries to have a socialist revolution at that time. Richard Lowenthal notes that because Hungary's economy and political structure were less developed, even though Germany had lost the First World War, Hungary was still the most likely place to experience a socialist revolution (Lowenthal, 1971).

In this context, Kun and his Bolshevist comrades were sent back to Hungary by the Communist Party of Russia and began to work toward a socialist revolution there (Tokes, 1967). When they returned to Budapest in 1918, the most important task was to orchestrate the activities of the Hungarian Communist Party.

After its failure in the First World War, the Austro-Hungarian monarchy weakened dramatically, and former nationalities in the country increasingly began establishing their own states. Because of its failure in the war, Hungary lost much of its territory, and it was no longer a great power in Europe, let alone the world. The pessimistic Hungarians had to live with depression and anxiety (Low, 1963). On 1 November, the king had to appoint Mihaly Karolyi to form the new cabinet. Soon, the monarchy had

---

[50] The Hungarian Social Democratic Party was the established in 1889 and was the main socialist party at that time.

[51] In this study group, these socialist war prisoners not only translated some German-origin Marxist books but also took Russian language classes.

to split, and Hungary established its Republic after the publishing of the Declaration on 16 November 1918 (Tokes, 1967). However, the Karolyi cabinet could not control the entire situation in Hungary, and the new Republic remained chaotic.

In November 1918, the Communist Party of Hungary was established under such conditions in Budapest. Kun was one of the leaders of the Party. The new Party then began to enact its own revolutionary program, guided by the experienced Bolshevik Kun (Tokes, 1967).

2.2.2.3 First Hungarian Soviet Republic

The Hungarian Soviet Republic lasted only 133 days, a short period in the country's history. However, this was a very important chapter not only in Hungarian history but also in the history of communist development. It is widely considered the second Soviet Republic in the world.[52]

The Austro-Hungarian monarchy's loss in the First World War deeply damaged the sovereignty of this great power, and the old political order obviously failed to control its territory and the nationalities that lived there.

Hungary established its own Republic in 1918. Mihaly Karolyi became the first Prime Minister of the Hungarian Republic. During his governance, Hungary's leading factions could be categorized into three groups: Karolyi's political group, Jaszi's Radical Bourgeois Party and the socialist Hungarian Social Democratic Party (Tokes, 1967). The group supporting Karolyi in the government was stronger than the Social Democratic Party. However, the left-wing Social Democrats and the Communist Party (not in the government) apparently had much more experience connecting with common people, especially in rural areas.

In November 1918, only a few days later, Karolyi was appointed prime minister by King Karl IV. Hungary decided to terminate its Compromise relationship with Austria and eliminated its Austro-Hungarian king. Under such conditions, the Aster Revolution broke out in Hungary in October 1918. After the revolution, King Karl IV had to make a statement dissolving the monarchy, and the First Hungarian Republic came into being. Karolyi, a widely respected politician, was elected the first president of the Republic. Dénes Berinkeywas appointed the Prime Minister in the Youth Republic.[53]

Nevertheless, the First Hungarian Republic existed for only four and a half months. After Berinkey's two months of service for this new Republic, the Social Democratic Party gained power in the government (Hajdu, 1979). In early March 1919, the left wing of the socialist party seized power. However, while it would not make any changes to Hungary's international relationships, the Vix memorandum soon brought dramatic change in Hungary (Hajdu, 1979).

---

[52] The Hungarian Soviet Republic. Retrieved June 18, 2021, from https://theorangefiles.hu/the-hungarian-soviet-republic/.

[53] The First Hungarian Republic. Retrieved June 18, 2021, from https://theorangefiles.hu/the-first-hungarian-republic/.

Birth of the Hungarian Soviet Republic

After the First World War, Hungary was part of the Central Powers that lost the war. China, as one of the Allied Powers, won the war. However, both countries lost in the Paris Peace Conference, and this led to dramatic changes in China and Hungary.

As a result of the Paris Peace Conference, Hungary was to give significant territory to the Allied Powers. On 20 March 1919, Lieutenant Fernand Vix sent his famous Vix memorandum to President Karolyi requesting that the First Hungarian Republic give away its territory of West Transylvania and part of the Great Hungarian Plain (Hajdu, 1979). When the memorandum was published, Hungarian national pride was seriously wounded, and most Hungarians hoped that their government would do something to change the situation, with some even wanting a change in government.

The leadership of the First Hungarian Republic government felt the pressure from the people, and they asked the main political groups in Hungary whether any party would take responsibility for addressing the Vix memorandum. The right wing of the government refused to take responsibility, and after a long discussion, the leadership of the Social Democratic Party announced their decision: They were willing to form a new government and take responsibility for the whole country. Meanwhile, they formulated a new plan to cooperate with the Communist Party (Hajdu, 1979).

However, the Communist Party of Hungary was suppressed by the First Hungarian Republic. As noted above, when Bela Kun and his comrades founded the Party, it began working toward its political aim of spreading communism and socialist revolution in the country. However, during a march on 20 February 1919, angry working-class protesters had a major conflict with the police, which soon became a riot. Four policemen died in the riot, and the government decided to show its strength against the public and the organizers of the march. The Communist Party of Hungary was obviously on the list, and police came to the Party's headquarters and searched its documents. The Party's propaganda leaflets and official newspaper, Vörös Ujság (the Red Newspaper), were evidence of their violent counter government position. The police arrested 68 Party members, and their trial included the Party leader Bela Kun (Tokes, 1967).

Although the Social Democratic Party had some unpleasant experiences with the Communist Party (Tokes, 1967),[54] it realized that the masses did not favor the bourgeois leading the present government, and its leaders had the idea of forming a proletariat dictatorship government. Cooperation was soon realized between the Social Democratic Party and the Communist Party of Hungary. After discussion between the leadership of the two parties over one night, the most important decision was made by both: The country would follow Russia's form of government (Hajdu, 1979),[55] and a new Soviet Republic was born in Hungary.

---

[54] For example, the riot on the 20th of February happened in front of the office of Nepszava, the official newspaper of the Social Democratic Party; out of the fear of the violence, socialists called the police and asked for protection. Then, the rioting broke out.

[55] As an example, there was no minister in the new government, the commissar was in charge, and the new government also had a new name: "the Revolutionary Governing Council".

Therefore, on 21 March 1919, the government had to hand over its power, and the Social Democratic Party shared power with the Communist Party (Hajdu, 1979; Molnar, 1978).[56] Additionally, the First Hungarian Republic changed its form of state to a Soviet Republic (Hajdu, 1979). For the Communist Party, this was an almost unbelievable event; just one month ago, the Party had suffered suppression by the government, with Kun and other Party leaders imprisoned. Nevertheless, the political victims became the rulers of the state, and the former prisoner became the leader of the Soviet-type government (Tokes, 1967).

This bloodless dramatic change in Hungry offered the ruling position to the Communist Party of Hungary, and the Party had a chance to enact communist policies in a very short period.

Legal Regime of the Hungarian Soviet Republic and Its Constitution

Although the Hungarian Soviet Republic was considered the world's second Soviet Republic, there was not much Soviet legal tradition or system that could be used for reference. Peter Apor's article cites Laszlo Reti, the director of the Institute for Party History (It was abolished in the 1990s.): "The Hungarian Soviet Republic 'created our people's democracy, which also has the function of the dictatorship of the proletariat" (Apor, 2011). Soviet Russia, as the only successful Soviet Republic in the world, therefore became the only model to follow. The leaders of the Hungarian Soviet Republic made the same observation. Laszlo states, "The Soviet Republic, which was the Third Hungarian Republic, held the Russian Soviet State up as its model" (Apor, 2011). When the new government was established, it sent a report to Lenin, the leader of Soviet Russia and the Communist Party of Russia. In the report, the Hungarian rulers showed their respect for Russia and expressed their willingness to follow the Russian Soviet model (Apor, 2011; Low, 1963).

The Hungarian Soviet Republic existed for only 133 days, and there was not much peaceful time for the new Soviet Republic to practice governance in the legal field. Like the Chinese Soviet Republic, the Hungarian Soviet Republic did not pass many new laws in this period. Most of the time, the new Soviet Republic was busy fighting its enemies, not only from abroad but also within the country (Hajdu, 1979).

Under such conditions, the legal regime in the Hungarian Soviet Republic was strongly influenced by Soviet Russia. Most administrative policies were passed as decrees. Lenin's State and Revolution were considered the directives or ruling principles in Hungary, not only on the economy but also law (Hajdu, 1979). The short ruling period along with the obstacles and hostility from neighboring countries and Szeged[57] left few chances to establish Soviet legal practices in Hungary (Hajdu,

---

[56] Two parties signed a "unity" document in March 1919, and a new party came out—the Hungarian Socialist Party.

[57] Szeged, a city in southern Hungary was at that moment the center of the anti-Hungarian Soviet Republic.

1979).[58] Therefore, most of the laws and regulations passed by the government were related to improving the living standards and working conditions among the urban working class and poor farmers in rural areas.

During the ruling period of the Hungarian Soviet Republic, the Revolutionary Governing Council passed basic rules related to agrarian policy and nationalization of private estates (Hajdu, 1979). In rural areas, as later in the Chinese Soviet Republic, widespread land reform took place. Before Hungary became a Soviet Republic, the Land Reform Law was passed in February 1919 (Hollos, 2001); during the land reform period, landlords lost their lands, and poor farmers received their own lands (Hajdu, 1979). Land reform in Hungary commenced much earlier, when Maria Theresa conducted land reform to ease conflicts, and at the end of the 1840s, land reform became one of the liberal reforms (Gary, 2009). However, insufficient land reform led to poor agricultural growth and finally caused unrest in rural areas (Kopsidis, 2008). In the cities, the working class also had the chance to improve their working conditions. The eight-hour workday was introduced by decree (Kopsidis, 2008). Workers also enjoyed higher pay; on 17 April 1919, the government passed a regulation raising workers' wages (Kopsidis, 2008).

After the First Congress of the Hungarian Socialist Party in June, the First Congress of Hungarian Soviets was held on 16 June. There, the representatives not only discussed the economic situation, foreign policy and the military situation but also created and passed the Constitution of the Hungarian Soviet Republic (Kopsidis, 2008); it was the first Soviet constitution in Hungary and was greatly influenced by Soviet Russia.

Before the adoption of this constitution, a so-called provisional constitution was introduced to resolve the confusion about the local soviets' operation. Before, no specific provision had existed to regulate the operation of the local soviets and define the powers of the local soviets and their representatives. Under such conditions, the Revolutionary Governing Council adopted Decree XXVI as the provisional constitution (Mathe, 2000).

The preparatory work for the constitution of "the Federal Hungarian Socialist Soviet Republic" (Constitution of the Hungarian Soviet Republic) was conducted by a five-member committee after the Communist Party began ruling the state. It was mainly based on the 1918 Constitution of Soviet Russia. The draft constitution was adopted on 23 June 1919 (Mathe, 2000).

The Constitution of the Hungarian Soviet Republic consisted of seven chapters and 89 articles. It had the following chapters: (1) Principles of the Constitution of the Hungarian Soviet Republic; (2) The rights and duties of workers in the Hungarian Soviet Republic; (3) The organization of the central soviet; (4) The organization of

---

[58] The newly independent neighboring countries used to be one part of the Austro-Hungarian empire or were gained from Hungary after the Paris Peace Conference. Additionally, there was not enough time to issue new regulations to cover everything.

local soviets; (5) Suffrage; (6) The budgetary law; and (7) The rights of nationalities in the Hungarian Soviet Republic.[59]

The constitution stipulated the most important principles in the first chapter, stating that the country's proletariat dictatorship made a new socialist order and ensured the ruling position of workers, soldiers and peasants. It also declared the country's foreign policy.[60]

Additionally, the constitution ensured suffrage for the masses, and while most people had the right to vote, there were several groups deprived of suffrage.[61] Under the proletariat dictatorship, the constitution also had some special protections for workers, for instance stipulating that "the State will maintain those unable to work, and such as those who want to work but for whom no work can be provided" (Hajdu, 1979).

The constitution also regulated the supreme organ of state power, the National Convention of the Federal Councils, and the Federal Central Executive Committees were designated as the executive in the central government. In addition, the Council of People's Economy was the dedicated central economic organ. The constitution did not include a section on the judiciary. However, several laws regarding judicial issues were passed by the ruling government in the period of the Hungarian Soviet Republic (Mathe, 2000).

The new constitution was modeled after the 1918 Soviet Union Constitution, and it broke the tradition of Hungarian constitutions; however, since the Soviet Republic's "life" was too short, its constitution was never enforced (Dezso et al., 2010).

2.2.2.4 Counter-Revolution and White Terror

Like its Chinese counterpart, the Hungarian Soviet Republic did not gain enough support at home or abroad. Soon, it lost its independence, and the Party members in Hungary were pursued by enemies. In the following section, the author discusses how the Hungarian Soviet Republic was failed by counterrevolutionary groups.

Worries Behind the Triumph—Hostile Neighboring Countries

While the proletariat celebrated its victory, the new Hungarian Soviet Republic faced two groups of enemies: the hostile armies of its surrounding countries, and within the country, the remaining democratic powers gathered in southern Hungary (Kaas & Lazarovics, 1931; Simon, 2000).[62]

---

[59] Constitution of Hungarian Soviet Republic. Hungarian version only. Retrieved June 18, 2021, from https://hu.wikisource.org/wiki/A_Magyarorsz%C3%A1gi_Szocialista_Sz%C3%B6vets%C3%A9ges_Tan%C3%A1csk%C3%B6zt%C3%A1rsas%C3%A1g_alkotm%C3%A1nya.

[60] Article 1–3, Chapter 1, Constitution of Hungarian Soviet Republic.

[61] Article 68, Constitution of Hungarian Soviet Republic.

[62] After the Paris Peace Conference, Hungary was forced to give away a large amount of its territory to neighboring countries; the new Soviet Republic was trying to take back its territory from its

An attack by the Romanian army started on 16 April 1919, and protecting the new Soviet Republic became Hungary's top priority. Vilmos Bohm, the Commander-in-Chief of the Hungarian Red Army, had approximately 55,000 mostly untrained young men under his command (Sugar et al., 1990). With the support of the Allied Powers, the attack progressed. On the Hungarian side, it increased the proletariat's enthusiasm for the new Soviet Republic; soon, at the end of April, the Red Army included 70,000 soldiers who gathered and fought for the Republic (Hajdu, 1979). However, the superior Romanian army destroyed the communist activities in Hungary, and within a few days after the attack, Hungary lost Nagyvarad (Oradea), Arad and Debrecen. On 26 April 1919, the Czechoslovak army started to attack northern Hungary, and the Soviet Republic was endangered (Sugar et al., 1990). Nevertheless, the working class voluntarily joined the Red Army, and the Ukrainian Soviet army attacked Romania, somehow changing the situation of the conflict. In the second half of May, Salgotarjan was saved, Miskolc was controlled by the Red Army, the threat from the north was eliminated, and the Hungarian Red Army occupied part of the territory of Czechoslovakia. The danger from the neighboring states appeared to be gone (Sugar et al., 1990). However, the Allied Powers noticed the military activities in Slovakia, and the Hungarian Red Army had already occupied Bratislava and seriously threatened the safety of Vienna. Clemenceau sent a note to the Hungarian Soviet government and asked the Red Army to stop their military activities in Slovakia (Hajdu, 1979). The Soviet government considered Clemenceau's note and tried to reach an agreement with these great powers (Hajdu, 1979).

After a short peace in July, the Red Army decided to break the "silence" and tried to cross the Tisza. This military movement failed. Finally, on 30 July, the Romanian army broke the defense and headed to Budapest. On 1 August, the government had its last meeting, and the leadership decided to resign and hand over their power to a trade union (provisional) government (Tokes, 1967).

Counter-Revolution and "White Terror"

While the Romanian and Czechoslovakian warriors attacked the Soviet Republic, counterrevolutionaries in Hungary also tried to bring it down. The counterrevolutionaries were based in the southern Hungarian city of Szeged, at that time occupied by the French. On 6 July, the very late period of the Hungarian Soviet Republic, the future ruler Miklos Horthy became a member of the counterrevolutionary army. Soon, he was appointed its Commander-in-Chief (Szinai & Szucs, 1965). When the Romanian army conquered the Hungarian Soviet Republic and entered Budapest, the counter-revolutionary army received support from the Allied Powers (mainly France, Great Britain and Russia). On 1 August 1919, the Hungarian Soviet Republic collapsed. The Romanian army occupied most of the territory of Hungary, even the capital.

---

neighboring states. This caused panic among these countries. Moreover, during the formation of the Hungarian Soviet Republic, the counter-revolution continued to exist, and this group of people suffered brutally at the hands of the Soviet Republic.

The occupation lasted three and a half months, until the Romanian army received an order from the Allied Powers requesting that it fight Soviet Russia. Therefore, on 14 November, the Romanian army left Budapest and other parts of Hungary and headed west. On 16 November 1919, the counterrevolutionary army entered Budapest and soon controlled the whole country (Szinai & Szucs, 1965).

With the rule of a counterrevolutionary government, or the so-called Kingdom of Hungary, Horthy became the country's de facto ruler. To suppress the Hungarian revolutionary spirit, the new government enacted a series of brutal policies to control the country. Under such policies, labor activists, Jews and communists became the victims of White Terror (Bodo, 2010), the Communist Party of Hungary remained illegal, and most Communist Party members had to move to other countries, with most going to Soviet Russia, including Kun. The communist activities became a secret movement.[63]

2.2.3 Birth of the Communist Parties and Their Early Activities in Czechoslovakia and Poland

Although Czechoslovakia and Poland gained their independence after the First World War,[64] their communist movements began earlier. In Czechoslovakia, although the whole country was ruled by the Austro-Hungarian monarchy, radical Czech-Slav socialist parties already existed as part of the socialist parties in the monarchy (Suda, 1980).[65] In Poland, the communist party, the Polish Socialist Party, was founded in Paris in 1892 (Blobaum, 1984).[66] In this part, the author explores the birth of the communist parties in Czechoslovakia and Poland and their important activities.

2.2.3.1 Birth of the Communist Party of Czechoslovakia

Similar to the formation of Poland's communist party, the establishment of the Communist Party of Czechoslovakia was a result of the split of the Social Democratic Party. The more radical members of the socialist party wanted to build a Soviet Republic and then form a Communist Party (Zinner, 1963).

---

[63] Regarding the "White Terror", academia currently holds a relatively positive view of the Horthy Regime and its suppression of communists.

[64] After the First World War, Czechoslovakia, established in lands from the Austro-Hungarian empire, and Poland were (re)established after a long-term partition. However, during the Second World War, both countries lost their sovereignty and had to again be reestablished after 1945.

[65] As an example, the Social Democratic Czechoslovakian party in Austria was the main socialist party in Austria, and it was also considered the foundation for the later Czechoslovakian social democratic workers' party.

[66] See also the PPS (Polska Partia Socjalistyczna). Retrieved June 18, 2021, from https://www.jewishvirtuallibrary.org/pps-polska-partia-socjalistyczna.

2.2 Birth and Early Activities of the Communist Parties ... 35

The Social Democratic Party of Czechoslovakia was considered the predecessor of its Communist Party, and the history of this socialist party can be traced back to the Czech group the Austrian Social Democrats in 1878 (Zinner, 1963).

Before regaining its independence, Czechoslovakia was under the control of the Austro-Hungarian monarchy; however, the Czech part had a much closer relationship with Austria, and the main part of the Slovakian territory had an old name, "Upper Hungary", for a long time. The Czech part enjoyed industrialization, with nearly 40% of the population working in industry. Additionally, the legalization of the socialist party in Austria and the Czech areas it controlled sped up the development of the socialist movement (Suda, 1980). In contrast, only 19% of the population of Slovakia worked in industry (Zinner, 1963). Therefore, the socialist movement was more advanced in the Czech part. Additionally, the Communist Party of Soviet Russia helped greatly before the establishment of Czechoslovakia, and there were numerous Czech and Slovakian communist activists who lived in Soviet Russia. In 1918, before the Paris Peace Conference, the independence of Czechoslovakia was supported by the Allied countries in the First World War (Suda, 1980).[67]

However, Czechoslovakia's independence did not bring a new Communist Party of Czechoslovakia, since the Social Democrats were more focused on the issue of independence, not the dictatorship of the proletariat. In 1920, the Czechoslovak Social Democratic Party won the country's first election; meanwhile, in the same year, the Second Congress of the Communist International was held in Moscow, and it decided that all the communist parties in the world should focus on the dictatorship of the proletariat and "adopt the name 'Communist' and to revise its program" (Skilling, 1955). This caused conflicts between the left and right wings of Czechoslovakia's Social Democrats. After a year of delay, the country's Communist Party was finally founded in Prague, and Sturc, Smeral and Kreibich were considered its leaders.

Therefore, after three years of Czechoslovakian independence, the Communist Party of Czechoslovakia was founded in 1921 (Skilling, 1955).

2.2.3.2 Early Activities of the Communist Party of Czechoslovakia

From the year the Party was established to 1945, which marked the end of the Second World War, the Communist Party of Czechoslovakia never ruled the country by itself; however, before the Party was formed, an experimental communist exercise occurred in the Slovakian region, the Slovak Soviet Republic.

The Slovak Soviet Republic was strongly supported by Bela Kun and his Hungarian Soviet Republic. Since the failure of the Paris Peace Conference and the loss of territory, many Hungarians felt disappointed, which also caused the collapse of Károlyi's government. The communist Kun was selected as the country's new

---

[67] There was a Czechoslovakia National Council in Moscow, and it was considered as the legitimate source of leadership in the fight for Czechoslovakian independents; there was also a Czechoslovakian Legion in Russia during the First World War that fought for the Allies. Therefore, after the war, the Allies recognized the independence of Czechoslovakia.

leader. In March 1919, the Hungarian Soviet Republic was founded (Pastor, 2003). However, the new Soviet Republic was not popular with its neighbors. Additionally, most Hungarians considered the territory of Slovakia to be part of Hungary, since it had previously been called Upper Hungary. In May 1919, Hungarian troops went to western Slovakia, and on 16 June 1919, the Slovak Soviet Republic was established in Presov, a city in northeast Slovakia. This was "pursuant to Clause 88 of Hungarian Soviet Constitution" (Suda, 1980).

However, the Slovak Soviet Republic existed for only three weeks and was considered a puppet regime. Czechs and Slovaks played a very important role in the Republic. Janousek, the leader of the Republic's government, was a Czech communist, promoted a communist revolution in Czechoslovakia and peacefully established a Soviet Republic (Toma, 1958). Moreover, the failure of the Slovak Soviet Republic was considered a symbol of the communist movement in Czechoslovakia. It encouraged the solidarity of Czechs and Slovaks during the communist movement after 1945 (Suda, 1980).

2.2.3.3 Birth of the Communist Party in Poland

Before 1918, the Poles gained independence from Russia, Austria and Prussia, and most of the territory of Poland was part of the Russian Empire.[68] However, with the spread of socialism in the mid-nineteenth century and later of Marxism (Marx, 1848) in the late nineteenth century and the development of the economy and industry (Regula, 1934), some radical socialist parties formed in Poland.

Among these socialist parties, two were considered parents of the Communist Party of Poland: the Social Democracy of the Kingdom of Poland and Lithuania (SDKPIL) and the left wing of the Polish Socialist Party (the PPS-Leftist), (Regula, 1934).

During the late nineteenth century, all of Europe experienced revolutions, not only of independent countries but also of a new ideology. Socialism and later Marxism spread throughout Europe.

In the "Russian" part of Poland, the Poles had a similar experience, and the working class or so-called proletariat organized their own political parties, fighting for their rights and the freedom of the country. In 1892, the Polish Socialist Party was founded; one year later, another important party was founded, the Social Democracy of the Kingdom of Poland. In the very early twentieth century, with the participation of socialists from Lithuania, the Party was renamed the Party of Social Democracy of the Kingdom of Poland and Lithuania (Busky, 2002).[69] Both parties led the early communist movement in Poland.

---

[68] After the collapse of the Polish–Lithuanian Commonwealth, Poland was soon divided by Russia, Germany and the Austro-Hungarian monarchy; however, the majority of the territory in today's Poland was occupied by the Russian Empire.

[69] Additionally, from an historical perspective, Poland and Lithuania had a very long history as a one country; i.e., the Polish–Lithuanian Commonwealth was a great power in the sixteenth and seventeenth centuries.

2.2 Birth and Early Activities of the Communist Parties ...

Rosa Luxemburg and Feliks Dzierzynski were considered the leaders of the Party of Social Democracy of the Kingdom of Poland and Lithuania. Luxemburg was well known for her socialist theory and her story of fighting in Germany. However, Dzierzynski was considered the soul of the Party (Blobaum, 1984). Led by Dzierzynski and Luxemburg, the Party engaged in fighting with Poland's ruler at that time, Russia (Blobaum, 1984). Meanwhile, the Polish Socialist Party divided in two, due to different programs and ideologies. The leftist part (also known as the youth faction) was planning to lead a socialist revolution and make Poland a socialist country.

Finally, in 1906, the Polish Socialist Party divided, and one part cooperated closely with the Party of Social Democracy of the Kingdom of Poland and Lithuania (Serafin, 2015). After the First World War, Poland reestablished its own country, and Russia put the first Communist Party in charge of the whole country; it finally merged with the leftist Polish Socialist Party and became the Communist Workers' Party of Poland in 1918. One year later, the Communist Party joined the Communist International.[70] Because of the changed situation in Poland and under the guidance of the Soviet Communist Party, the Communist Workers' Party of Poland changed its name to the Communist Party of Poland in 1925 (Busky, 2002).

2.2.3.4 Early Activities of the Communist Party of Poland (KPP)

During the early history of Poland's Communist Party, the Russian Communists had a very strong influence not only on the Party's members but also on its program. The Report on the Third KPP Congress stated, "However, let us remember that we must implant the Bolshevik ungrafted tree upon the trunk of contemporary Polish communism" (Regula, 1934).

In the early period of the Communist Party of Poland, the most impressive military operation occurred during the Russia-Poland War. After the First World War, Poland was reestablished. However, there was a border dispute between Poland and Soviet Russia, and this conflict later resulted in the Russia-Poland War. In 1919, the Soviet Red Army invaded Poland and soon occupied the northeastern part. On 28 July 1920, the Red Army occupied Bialystok, and two days later, Bialystok, as a Jewish city, witnessed the establishment of the Provisional Polish Revolutionary Committee (Davina, 2008; Suny, 1998). It was supported by Soviet Russia (10 million roubles were collected by the Orgburo[71]); however, the Provisional Committee was not supported by most Poles and was considered an outside invader (Davina, 2008). Therefore, the committee existed for only 23 days, and it was not possible to adopt a constitution (Davina, 2008). However, the committee prepared a Manifesto of this

---

[70] A Brief History of the Communist Workers' Party of Poland (December 19, 2015). Retrieved June 20, 2021, from https://libcom.org/history/brief-history-communist-workers%E2%80%99-party-poland.

[71] Orgburo, the Central Committee of the Communist Party of the Soviet Union, existed from 1919 to 1952.

socialist revolution. Issues of economics, agriculture and the rule of the working class were presented (Davina, 2008). With the failure of the Red Army and the Soviet-Polish peace treaty signed in Riga in 1921 (Busky, 2002), it was not possible to enact communist policies in Poland.

After the experimental Soviet Revolution in Poland, because the Communist Party of Poland shared a common ideology with the Soviet Union and wanted to establish a Soviet Republic in Poland, it was not welcomed by the Second Polish Republic. In 1925, Marshal Pilsudski engaged in a military coup in Poland, supported at that time by the Communist Party of Poland. However, with the triumph of the coup, the Soviet Union considered Pilsudski's regime fascist and opposed it. The conflict between the Soviet Union and Poland put the Communist Party of Poland in a very awkward position. As a result, the government treated it as an illegal party (Busky, 2002).

A special phenomenon of the Communist Party of Poland was the significant contribution by Jewish people to the Polish communist movement (Schatz, 1991). The Provisional Polish Revolutionary Committee in Bialystok also garnered great support among Jewish residents (Davina, 2008).

2.3 Conclusion

These communist parties did not appear out of thin air. The birth of the communist parties in China and the Visegrad states was the result of the successful revolution in Russia in 1917. After the triumph of this October Revolution, communist parties were finally established in each state. The Communist Party of Hungary was the earliest. The Hungarian Group of the Communist Party of Russia was organized in March 1918. In the same year, Bela Kun, the former prisoner of war, learned communist ideology and gained fame on campus, and his Hungarian comrades were sent back to Hungary in November. The Communist Party of Hungary was also established in the same month (Molnar, 1978; Tokes, 1967).[72] Communist activities in Poland can be traced back to December 1918, which was the birth of the Communist Workers' Party of Poland. The party changed its name to the Communist Party of Poland in 1925 (Weydenthal, 1986). The remaining two countries established their communist parties at the beginning of the 1920s. Czechoslovakia founded its Communist Party in 1921 (Wheaton, 1986), and Chinese communists established their communist organization in July of the same year (Uhalley, 1988). All of these communist parties were members of the Third International, which was based in and received guidance from Moscow. In the early activities of these communist parties, Hungary and China both had the chance to imitate the Soviet system in their own states entirely or

---

[72] There are two possibilities for the birth date and place of the Communist Party of Hungary. One is that the party was established on 4 November 1918 in Moscow, and the second is the party was established on 24 November 1918 in Hungary A session for transforming the Hungarian Group of the Communist Party of Russia was first held in Hotel Dresden in Moscow and a complete session was held in Budapestu.

partially. Therefore, in this section, the author paid special attention to the Hungarian Soviet Republic and its provisional constitution and the Soviet Republic of China and its constitutional outline. Neither constitutional document ever entered into force.

From the early activities of the communist parties in each state, Soviet Russia clearly had the leading position in the international communist community. Although most of the early practices of the communist parties in each state failed during the interwar period, the experiences of the communists and the lessons that they learned ultimately enabled their dream to come true, namely, the establishment of communist regimes in the Visegrad region and China.

References

Apor, P. (2011). Praefiguratio: Exemplary history and temporal order in the thirtieth anniversary of the first Hungarian Soviet Republic of 1919. *Politics, Religion and Ideology, 12*(2), 123–143.
Blobaum, R. (1984). *Feliks Dzierzynski and the SDKPiL: A study of the origins of polish communism* (1st ed.). East European Monographs.
Bodo, B. (2010). Hungarian aristocracy and white terror. *Journal of Contemporary History, 45*(4), 703–724.
Bugajski, J. (2002). *Political parties of Eastern Europe: A guide to politics in the post-communist Era* (1st ed.). Sharpe Inc.
Busky, D. F. (2002). *Communism in history and theory: The European experience* (1st ed.). Praeger.
Chen, Y. (1982). 中国人民当家作主的第一部根本大法——试析《中华苏维埃共和国宪法大纲》 [The first fundamental law of Chinese people in charge-analysis constitution of Chinese soviet republic]. *Journal of Xin Jiang Normal University (Social Science Edition), 2*, 10–15.
Da, L. (2017). The birth of communist party and soviet constitution between China and Hungary. *Journal on European History of Law, 8*(2), 87–99.
Database of Previous Time of the National Congresses of the CPC. 中共产党第一次全国代表大会简介 *[The Brief Introduction of the First National Congress of the Communist Party of China]*. Chinese version only. Retrieved June 17, 2021, from http://cpc.people.com.cn/GB/64162/64168/64553/4427940.html
Davina, C. K. (2008). *Soviet-polish relations, 1919–1921*. (Doctoral dissertation, University of Glasgow). Retrieved June 20, 2021, from http://theses.gla.ac.uk/663/1/2009crollphd.pdf
Dezso, M., et al. (2010). *Constitutional law in Hungary* (1st ed.). Kluwer Law International.
Ding, X. (1990). 中共第一次国共合作的策略演变 [The changes of the policy of the communist party of China during the first united front]. *Modern Chinese History Studies, 5*, 174–198.
Fairbank, J. K. (Ed.). (1978). *The Cambridge history of China, Vol. 10, Late Ch'ing, 1800–1911, Part 1* (1st ed.). Cambridge University Press.
Fairbank, J. K. (Ed.). (1983). *The Cambridge history of China, Vol. 12, Republican China, 1912–1949, Part 1*, (1st ed.). Cambridge University Press.
Fairbank, J. K. (Ed.). (1986). *The Cambridge history of China, Vol. 13, Republican China, 1912–1949, Part 2* (1st ed.). Cambridge University Press.
Fairbank, J. K. (Ed.) (1993). *The Cambridge history of China, Vol. 12* (Yang Pinquan, Zhang Yan et al. Trs. 1st ed.). China Social Science Press.
Gergely, A. (2000). Rise of the modern hungarian sate 1790–1867. In A. Gergely & G. Mathe (Eds. Trans. by D. Szekely), *The Hungarian state: Thousand years in Europe* (1st ed., pp. 168–214). Korona Publishing House.
Gray, R. W. B. (2009). *Land reform and the Hungarian peasantry c. 1700–1848*. (Doctoral dissertation, University College London). Retrieved June 18, 2021, from https://discovery.ucl.ac.uk/id/eprint/19321/1/19321.pdf

Guo, D. (1987). 土地改革史若干问题论纲 [Outline of the problems of land reform]. *Modern Chinese History Studies, 3*, 59–76.
Gyula, R. (2001). The formation of the industrial working class in Hungary: A lesson in social dynamics. *Review of Sociology, 7*(1), 103–113.
Hajdu, T. (1979). *The Hungarian Soviet Republic* (1st ed.). Akademiai Kiado.
Hoensch, J. K. (1988). *A history of modern Hungary: 1867–1986* (1st ed. Trans. by K. Traynor). Longman Group.
Hollos, M. (2001). *A scandal in Tiszadomb: Understanding Modern hungary through the history of three families: Understanding modern Hungary through the history of three families* (1st ed.). Routledge.
Hsu, M. W. W. (2012). *Survival through adaptation: The Chinese Red Army and the encirclement campaigns, 1927–1936* (Master thesis). Retrieved June 17, 2021, from https://www.armyupress.army.mil/Portals/7/combat-studies-institute/csi-books/ArtOfWar_SurvivalThroughAdaptation.pdf
Kaas, B. A., & Lazarovics, F. D. (1931). *Bolshevism in Hungary: The Bela Kun period* (1st ed.). Grant Richards, Fronto Limited.
Kopsidis, M. (2008). Agricultural development and impeded growth: the case of Hungary 1870–1973. In P. Lains & V. Pinilla (Eds.), *Agriculture and economic development in Europe since 1870* (1st ed., Chap. 11). Routledge.
Lenin (1921, July 17). [Assignment to secretary]. Retrieved June 17, 2021, from https://www.marxists.org/archive/lenin/works/1921/jul/17b.htm
Li, X. (2005). 中华民国史第一卷中华民国的创建与北洋政府的统治中国迈向现代社会(1912–1927) *[The history of Republic of China vol.1 the establishment of Republic of China and the governance of the Beiyang government, towards to the modern society]* (1st ed.). Nanjing University Press.
Liu, Y. (Ed.) (2006). 中华民国史第二册, 志一政治卷 *[The history of Republic of China, Vol. 2 political]* (1st ed.). Sichuan People's Publishing House.
Liu, C. (1998). 试论英国发动第一次鸦片战争的双重动因 [Analysis the two reason of Great Britain starts the opium war]. *Modern Chinese History Studies, 4*, 158–172.
Liu, C. (2011). 苏联宪法学说对中国宪法学说影响的历时性审视 [Diachronic analysis of the influence of the theory of constitution in Soviet Union on the theory of constitution of China]. *Academic Journal of Russian Studies, 1*(4), 44–52.
Low, A. D. (1963). *The soviet Hungarian Republic and the Paris peace conference* (1st ed.). American Philosophical Society.
Lowenthal, R. (1971). The Hungary Soviet and international communism. In A. C. Janos & W. B. Slottman (Eds.), *Revolution in perspective: Essays on the Hungarian Soviet Republic of 1919 (Russian & East European study)* (1st ed., pp. 173–182). University of California Press.
Marx, K. (1848). *Communism, revolution, and a free Poland*. Retrieved June 20, 2021, from https://www.marxists.org/archive/marx/works/1848/02/22a.htm
Mathe, G. (2000). The Federal Hungarian socialist soviet Republic of 1919. In A. Gergely & G. Mathe (Eds. Trans. by D. Szekely), *The Hungarian State: Thousand years in Europe* (1st ed., pp. 252–256). Korona Publishing House.
Matyas, U., & Otto, S. (1982). 匈牙利史 *[The history of Hungary]*, Original Version is Magyarorszag Tortenete (1st ed., Trans. by S. Gan, K. Gong, & H. Li). Heilongjiang People's Publishing.
Mevius, M. (2005). *Agents of Moscow: The Hungarian communist party and the origins of socialist patriotism 1941–1953* (1st ed.). Clarendon Press.
Molnar, M. (1978). *A short history of the Hungarian communist party*. Westview Press.
Palmer, F. H. E. (1903). *Austro-Hungarian life in town and country* (1st ed.). G. P. Putnam's Sons.
Pastor, P. (2003). Major trends in Hungarian Foreign policy from the collapse of the monarchy to the peace treaty of Trianon. *Hungarian Studies, 17*(1), 3–11.
Toma, P. A. (1958). The Slovak soviet republic of 1919. *The American Slavic and East European Review, 17*(2), 203–215.

References

Poloskei, F. (2000). The crisis period of the dual monarchy (1890–1918). In A. Gergely & G. Mathe (Eds. Trans. by D. Szekely), *The Hungarian State: Thousand years in Europe* (1st ed., pp. 239–240). Korona Publishing House.

Purcell, V. (1959). The opium war through Chinese eyes by arthur waley. *The Journal of the Royal Asiatic Society of Great Britain and Ireland, 91*(3–4), 151–153. Retrieved June 17, 2021, from https://www.cambridge.org/core/journals/journal-of-the-royal-asiatic-societ

Regula, J. A. (1934). *History of communist party of Poland*. Retrieved June 17, 2021, from https://www.cia.gov/readingroom/docs/CIA-RDP81-01043R001600160002-1.pdf

Schatz, J. (1991). *The generation: The rise and fall of the jewish communists of Poland* (1st ed.). University of California Press.

Serafin, M. (2015). *Socialist opposition in the Polish People's Republic, 1964–1989*. (Honours Dissertation, Northumbria University). Retrieved June 20, 2021, from https://northumbria-cdn.azureedge.net/-/media/corporate-website/documents/pdfs/departments/humanities/history/history-research/ug-dissertations/marcel-serafin-social-opposition-to-the-polish-peoples-republuic-1964-1989.pdf?modified=20190128193827

Shu, S. (2016). 共产国际指导下召开的八七会议—谨以此文纪念八七会议召开90周年 [August 7th meeting was held under the guidance of the communist international—In commemoration of the 90th anniversary of August 7th Meeting]. *Advances in Social Sciences, 5*(2), 254–259.

Simon, A. L. (2000). *Admiral Nicholas Horthy: Memoirs* (1st ed.). Simon Publications.

Skilling, H. G. (1955). The formation of a communist party in Czechoslovakia. *The American Slavic and East European Review, 14*(3), 346–358.

Suda, Z. L. (1980). *Zealots and Rebels: A history of the communist party of Czechoslovakia* (1st ed.). Hoover Institution Press.

Sugar, P. F., Hanak, P., & Frank, T. (Eds.). (1990). *A history of Hungary* (1st ed.). Indiana University Press.

Sun, J. (2003). 革命、土匪与地域社会--井冈山的星星之火 [Revolution, bandit and region community—A single spark of Jinggang mountains]. *Twenty-First Century, 80*(12), 44–56.

Sun, Y., & Tian, D. (2007). 试论1918年苏俄宪法对中国苏区法律的影响 [On the influence of constitution of Soviet Union in 1918 to the Law in Chinese Soviet]. *Journal of Inner Mongolia Agriculture University (Social Science Edition), 1*, 318–320.

Suny, R. G. (1998). *The soviet experiment: Russia, the USSR, and the successor states* (1st ed.). Oxford University Press.

Szinai, M., & Szucs, L. (Eds.). (1965). *The confidential papers of Admiral Horthy* (1st ed.) Corvina Press.

Tokes, R. L. (1967). *Bela Kun and the Hungarian Soviet Republic: The origins and role of the communist party of Hungary in the revolutions of 1918–1919* (1st ed.). Praeger.

Uhalley, S. Jr. (1988). *A history of the Chinese communist party* (1st ed.). Hoover Institution Press.

Weydenthal, J. B. D. (1986). *The communists of Poland: An historical outline* (1st ed.). Hoover Institution Press.

Wheaton, B. (1986). *Radical socialism in Czechoslovakia: Bohumir Smeral, the Czech road to socialism and the origins of the Czechoslovak Communist Party (1917–1921)* (1st ed.). Eastern European Monographs.

Wu, D. (2009). Preface. In Y. Zhang (Ed.), 中华民国史稿 *[The history of Republic of China]* (2nd ed.). Linking Publishing.

Xu, J. (2005). 论《中华苏维埃共和国宪法大纲》的历史影响 [On the historical influence of constitution of Chinese Soviet Republic]. *Social Sciences in Guizhou, 6*, 149–151.

Yang, K. (2008). 国民党的"联共"与"反共" *[Kuomintang: Unity with communists and anti-communism]*, (1st ed.). Social Sciences Academic Press.

Yang, K. (1999). 独秀与共产国际——兼谈陈独秀的"右倾"问题 [Chen Duxiu and communist international: Also on the rightism of Chen Duxiu]. *Modern Chinese History Studies, 2*, 69–88.

Yang, K. (2001). 孙中山与共产党—基于俄国因素的历史考察 [Sun Yat-sen and communist party—A historical research based on Russia]. *Modern Chinese History Studies, 3*, 1–72.

Yang, S., & Luo, Y. (1984). 中国共产党在创建黄埔军校中的作用 [The function of communist party of China during the establishment of the Republic of China Military Academy]. *Modern Chinese History Studies, 5*, 34–49.

Zhang, L. (1985). 孙中山与第一次国共合作研究述评 *[A review on Sun Yat-sen and First KMT–CCP Alliance]*. In Conference Paper, International Academic Conference on Sun Yat-Sen's Study, Zhuo county, Hebei Province, China.

Zhang, Y. (2009). 中华民国史稿 *[The history of Republic of China]* (2nd ed.). Linking Publishing.

Zhou, Z. (2011). 共产国际、国民党、共产党对第一次国共合作的认识 [The Understanding of first united front from the view of communist international, Kuomintang and communist party of China]. *Shanghai Party History and Party Construction, 4*, 12–14.

Zinner, P. E. (1963). *Communist strategy and tactics in Czechoslovakia, 1918–48* (1st ed.). Pall Mall Press.

Chapter 3
The First Written Communist Constitutions in China and the Visegrad States

Abstract In this chapter, the author will firstly introduce how the socialist states adopted the constitution and give a detailed examination of the text of the constitution separately, then a comparative work will present the major similarities and differences of the constitution, also a constitutional institute, Parliament (although, in different states, the name of this organ was different) will be paid more attention and a comparative research of this Institute will be shown in this chapter.

The last chapter gave a general picture of the birth of the communist parties in China and the Visegrad countries. Although it is not the whole picture of the parties' early activities, it demonstrates to the reader that these parties were born with a "red" spoon in their mouths.[1] They were doomed to fight capitalists and even frequently sacrifice themselves. From the early twentieth century to the Second World War, there was only one successful socialist country in the world, the Soviet Union. After the Second World War, due to the weakness of capitalism in Europe (Mannino, 1999), the Soviet Union had the chance to develop its sphere of influence in Central and Eastern Europe (Halasz, 2015). Japan lost its control over East Asia, and the CPC defeated its main rival, the Kuomintang (Chinese Nationalist Party), with the help of the Soviet Union, and then China established its own communist regime in 1949. After that, the PRC and Hungary witnessed a communist tide in the 1940s.

The PRC was established in 1949, and within five years of taking power, it controlled most of the territory in China. The Chinese government passed the Electoral Law of the PRC in 1953, officially adopting the Constitution of the PRC (Chen, 1999). After the nationwide election, the first NPC was formed. Lengthy discussions produced the first Constitution of the PRC, adopted by the first NPC. This constitution was not changed until 1975.

Hungary, Czechoslovakia and Poland adopted their own constitutions. The first Constitution of the Hungarian People's Republic was adopted in 1949. In a successful

---

The comparative studies between China and Hungary in this chapter is published in Hungarian Journal of Legal Studies.

[1] "Red", in Chinese context, it means the blood, to sacrifice one's life, it implies the revolution. Therefore, the National Flag of People's Republic of China is red.

parliamentary election, the communist Hungarian Working People's Party won 285 seats.[2] Therefore, there is no doubt that the parliament adopted a communist constitution. In Czechoslovakia, the communist constitution was adopted in 1948 and followed the Soviet Union's constitution after the Communist Party of Czechoslovakia seized power across the whole country (Skilling, 1952). In the Polish People's Republic, after a nationwide discussion, the Constitution of 1952 was adopted by the Sejm (Lasok, 1954).[3]

This chapter first introduces how the socialist states adopted their constitutions and examines the text of each constitution separately. It then presents major similarities and differences among these constitutions, also comparing their legislative bodies or parliaments (although these entities are known by different names in different states).

3.1 First Communist Constitution in China

This part focuses mainly on how the Chinese abolished the old legal system and how the CPC established a new China. It also examines the CPC's establishment of a communist regime in China and its attempt to introduce a new constitution modeled on the 1936 Soviet Union Constitution. The chapter also describes how the Chinese legislative body, which is considered the supreme organ of the state, operates, and the first elections of the NPC are discussed.

3.1.1 Adoption of the Constitution of the People's Republic of China

The PRC was established on 1 October 1949, and before the new China was founded, the CPC abolished the legal system of the Republic of China, seeking to create its own. The following section introduces how the CPC abolished the "old" legal system in mainland China and established the new constitution.

3.1.1.1 Abolition of the Republic of China's Legal System

After the second Sino-Japanese War and four years of civil war in China, the CPC won leadership of mainland China in 1949, and the Kuomintang lost its sovereign power

---

[2] Hungarian Parliamentary Election, 1949. The result of the Hungarian Parlimentary election. Retrieved June 21, 2021, from http://www.gutenberg.us/articles/hungarian_parliamentary_election_1949.

[3] Sejm, is a very important organ in Polish political life. The Polish legislative organ consists of Sejm and Senate. Sejm of the Republic of Poland, Sejm in the sytem of power. Retrieved June 21, 2021, from https://www.sejm.gov.pl/english/sejm/sejm.htm. The information of Constitution of 1952 of Polish People's Republic.

there. According to the "Abrogation of the Six Codes", published by the CPC on 22 February 1949, the so-called fake legal system guided by the Six Codes should be abolished in liberated areas. The Six Codes system also included the Constitution of the Republic of China (Ji, 2007).[4] However, after the publication of the "Abrogation of the Six Codes", the CPC and the Kuomintang government had a series of brutal battles. Before the establishment of the PRC, the CPC occupied the majority of China, and only the southern and western parts of the country were not controlled by the Party (Pepper, 1986).

Although the PRC had been established, there were still some military conflicts in mainland China. The CPC believed that it was not the right moment to launch a new Chinese legal system or People's Congress, and the Chinese People's Political Consultative Conference (CPPCC) was considered the best form for Chinese political life at that time (Xu, 2003). Therefore, as a provisional measure, the Common Program of the CPPCC (hereafter Common Program) was introduced in September 1949, the month prior to the establishment of the PRC.

The drafting of the Common Program commenced in late 1948, and the plan was to adopt it in the CPPCC, which was initiated by the Communist Party (Xu, 2003).[5]

Before the CPPCC meeting was held in Beijing, the CPC and other democratic parties held a preparatory CPPCC meeting in Beijing from 15 to 19 June 1949. Three months later, on 17 September, a second preparatory meeting was held in Beijing (Xu, 2003; Zhang & Zeng, 1979). On 21 September, the first plenary meeting of the CPPCC was held in Beijing, with 622 representatives attending (Xu, 2003).[6] After 8 days of discussion, the CPPCC passed the Common Program. It was the most important constitutional document in the formative period of the PRC, establishing the fundamental principles and policies of the government (Xu, 2003). Before the Constitution of the PRC was adopted in 1954, the Common Program was the highest power in the legal system and political arena. Even the Electoral Law of the PRC for the National People's Congress and Local People's Congresses at All Levels of 1953 (hereinafter the Electoral Law) and the first Constitution Law in China declared its inheritance of the Common Program in the preamble (Xu, 2003; Zhang & Zeng, 1979).

The new government ruled the whole country with the guidance of the Common Program from the establishment of the PRC to the adoption of the Constitution of

---

[4] The Instruction on Abrogation of Six Codes and Ensuring the Legal Principles in Liberated Area was published by Chinese Communist Party in 1949, it was considered the most important legal Instruction in the early period of Communist ruling, Six Codes include Constitutional Law, Civil Law, Criminal Law, Commercial Law, Civil Procedure Law and Criminal Procedure Law. Retrieved June 22, 2021, from http://210.73.66.144:4601/law?fn=chl327s525.txt&truetag= 2&titles=&contents=&dbt=chl. More details of Chinese Communist Party abrogated Six Codes are available at Ji's article.

[5] The old version of Political Consultative Conference (PCC) was initiated by Kuomintang and Communist Party. However, the Resolution of the PCC didn't be respected, the civil war in China broke out.

[6] Official representatives were 510, alternate representatives were 77, also invited 75 persons attend the meeting.

the PRC in 1954. In this period, China was a newly democratic country. According to the Common Program, the people's democratic dictatorships in China included not only the worker and peasant classes but also the bourgeoisie (Xu, 2003).

The Common Program included a preamble and seven chapters and contained sixty articles. The preamble consisted of a discourse on the revolutionary history and characteristics of the new state. The second chapter presented the general principles, which ensured freedom of speech, publishing, and association. In this chapter, the mandates of the organs of state power were more or less the same as they had been before. The remaining chapters addressed military, economic, cultural and education, ethnic, and foreign policies. Even the Common Program emphasized the harm of the Six Codes in Article 17. It stated that "all laws, decrees and judicial systems of the Kuomintang reactionary government which oppress the people shall be abolished. Laws and decrees protecting the people shall be enacted and the people's judicial system shall be established".[7]

3.1.1.2 Establishment of the People's Republic of China

On 1 October 1949, after the eight-year anti-Japanese war and four-year civil war between the CPC and Chinese Nationalist Party (Kuomintang), the CPC was able to apply its communist theory to the whole country (Zhou, 1999).

From 1949 to 1954, the Communist Party began the socialist transformation of China. The efforts mainly targeted the agricultural, handicraft and capitalist industries and commerce. In the countryside, land reforms occurred over more than two years, and the government gave 300 million farmers rights to their own land. At the same time, a nationwide campaign was conducted to suppress counterrevolutionaries. In the realm of foreign relations, China joined the Korean War and established diplomatic relationships with other countries (mainly socialist states) (Xu, 2003; Zhang & Zeng, 1979). The new government also abolished the legal system of the Republic of China, adopted the Constitutional Act and Common Program and sought to build a socialist legal system in China (Xu, 2003; Zhang & Zeng, 1979).

During the four years of socialist transformation, the country became increasingly stable, and the government made good progress in the economic and political arenas (Xu, 2003).

3.1.1.3 First Election of the National People's Congress in China

According to its Organic Law, the CPPCC would hold its plenary meeting every three years. However, since the socialist transformation occurred much more rapidly than

---

[7] The Common Program of the Chinese People's Political Consultative Conference (1949). English version. Retrieved June 22, 2021, from https://sourcebooks.fordham.edu/mod/1949-ccp-program.asp.

3.1 First Communist Constitution in China

originally expected, the government planned to hold the first election of the NPC in China and passed the first socialist constitution of the PRC (Xu, 2003; Zhou, 1993).

In February 1953, the Central People's Government Committee adopted the Electoral Law of the PRC. Soon after, a nationwide census and voter registration campaign took place (Xu, 2003; Zhang & Zeng, 1979). The census showed that there were 601,912,371 people living in China, and more than half had the right to vote.

According to the Electoral Law, most people above age 18 had the right to vote. Article 4, paragraph 1 stipulated that "every citizen of the People's Republic of China who has reached the age of 18, irrespective of race, gender, occupation, family background, religious belief, education, property, [or] the length of residence, has the rights to vote and stand for election".[8] In 1953, under the guidance of the Electoral Law and people's enthusiasm, a nationwide grassroots election was held in China. Nearly 278 million people participated, 85.88% of the eligible voters (Zhang & Zeng, 1979), and 5,669,144 deputies of the county-level People's Congresses were elected (Xu, 2003; Zhou, 1993).

The Electoral Law provided that the higher-level People's Congresses would be elected indirectly.[9] The deputies of the NPC were elected by the provincial People's Congress. From July to August of 1954, the deputies at the provincial levels elected 1136 deputies of the NPC; moreover, 60 deputies were elected by the military, and 30 deputies were elected by overseas Chinese (Xu, 2003).

The first election of the NPC resulted in 1226 deputies in total; 668 were Party members, and 558 were not. These results showed that the Communist Party had an open mind in this election, which ensured diversity even within the united front (Zhou, 1993).

Therefore, the legislative organ was formed when the first NPC was held in September 1954, and during the first session of the meeting of the NPC, the deputies adopted a communist constitution.

3.1.1.4 Creation of the Constitution of the People's Republic of China

When the CPC assumed the highest power in mainland China and passed the Common Program as a fundamental law, Party leadership realized that a constitution should be adopted soon (Zhang, 2016).[10] After the unification of mainland China and

---

[8] Paragraph 1, Article 4, Chapter 1, Electoral Law of the National People's Congress and Local People's Congresses of the People's Republic of China of 1953 (expired).

[9] Article 3, Electoral Law of the National People's Congress and Local People's Congresses of the People's Republic of China of 1953 (expired).

[10] Before the People's Republic of China was established, Mao Zedong had a speech on the Constitutionalism of New Democracy in 1940, in this speech, Mao said: "after the victory of Revolution and realized democracy, (The Government) publishing a fundamental law and admit it, this is Constitution." The whole speech of Constitutionalism of New Democracy (1940). Chinese version only. Retrieved June 22, 2021, from https://www.marxists.org/chinese/maozedong/marxist.org-chinese-mao-19400220.htm.

the successful socialist transformation of the country, government leadership agreed that it was time for the PRC to adopt a communist constitution.

However, two years before the constitution was adopted, Chinese leaders had their own ideas for a communist constitution. In late 1952, before the end of the first CPPCC, the Chinese delegation visited the Soviet Union for the 19th Congress of the Communist Party of the Soviet Union, and a letter from the highest Chinese leadership was sent to Stalin. The letter stated that China planned to have a socialist constitution and that the country would become a socialist society (Han, 2004). Obviously, Stalin had a very different view from that espoused in this letter; he had suggestions for the adoption of a Chinese constitution even before the establishment of the PRC. This time, he gave advice to the second most powerful person in the CCP, Liu Shaoqi. Stalin suggested that China adopt a constitution soon, since such a document formed the fundamental law in each country and its adoption would legalize the CCP's leadership in the PRC. Based on the experiences of Hungary, Czechoslovakia and Poland, the CCP would win a nationwide election and dominate the government. In response to Stalin's suggestion, the CCP decided to hold a nationwide election and prepared a new constitution (Han, 2004).

In January 1953, the Constitution Drafting Committee was formed, and not only members of the CCP but also other Democratic Party members had the chance to join (Xu, 2003).[11] Additionally, within the CCP, a Constitution Drafting Group was formed in January 1954. Mao Zedong and this group left Beijing immediately for Hangzhou. After two months, a draft constitution was completed (Xu, 2003).[12]

From 23 March to 11 June 1954, seven meetings were held by the Constitution Drafting Committee to discuss the first constitution. The committee organized 17 discussion groups; nearly 8000 people participated, and over 5900 suggestions were generated. After this thorough discussion, a draft constitution was published by the Central People's Government Committee. A nationwide discussion was soon organized in China, and it was reported that more than 150 million Chinese participated in this unprecedented exercise. There were even constitution propaganda teams organized by the local government (Xu, 2003).[13]

The eighth meeting of the Constitution Drafting Committee was held on 8 September 1954 to adopt the constitution. The draft constitution had to be approved by the Central People's Government Committee, and the meeting to do so lasted over 7 h. Finally, at the end of the meeting, the document was carefully examined and submitted to the Central People's Government Committee. The next day, the draft constitution was passed by the Central People's Government Committee and submitted to the NPC (Xu, 2003).

---

[11] There were 33 persons participated in the Constitution Drafting Committee.

[12] Although the Constitution Drafting Committee was established earlier than the Constitution Drafting Group, the first meeting of the Committee was held on 23 March of 1954, and the draft version of Constitution was finished by the Group.

[13] At the beginning time of People's Republic of China, the education level of Chinese was quite low, a propaganda team will be useful to help people familiar with Constitution.

3.1 First Communist Constitution in China

However, on the day before the meeting of the NPC, the Central People's Government Committee still made two revisions to the draft constitution, to what was considered a "must revise" regulation. The first revision, in the third paragraph of the preamble, mainly changed the characterization of the constitution. It changed the phrase "our first Constitution" to "The Constitution of the People's Republic of China", because while there had already been 8 previous constitutions published in China, this constitution was the PRC's first. The second revision was to Article 3, paragraph 3, which stated that "all nationalities have the freedom to preserve or reform their own customs and ways and religious belief." Deputies from Tibet had a different view of "reforming their religious belief", and these four words were deleted (Han, 2004).

The first NPC was held on 15 September 1954. On the afternoon of the fifth day of the congress's meeting, the deputies of the NPC decided to vote on the Constitution of the People's Republic of China, using a secret ballot. There were 1197 deputies present for the vote and only 15 absent. Voting started at 16:45 and was completed in 10 min. After one hour of counting, the result was announced: there were 1197 affirmative votes, which meant that 100% of the deputies had agreed to adopt the constitution (Han, 2004).

The deputies also passed the Organic Law of the NPC, which ensured the highest level of the constitution in the legal system of the PRC.

The next day, the People's Daily published the Constitution of the People's Republic of China, and people across the country from the cities to the countryside celebrated this very meaningful event. The adoption of the Constitution of the PRC also established the most important part of the legal system as the fundamental law in the country, and the regulations passed by the government and the NPC would be guided by the constitution.

3.1.2 Analysis of the Text and Structure of the Constitution of the People's Republic of China

The text and structure of the Chinese constitution are interesting because the document followed the model of the 1936 Soviet Union Constitution. Before the draft constitution was completed, Mao Zedong sent a telegraph to the rest of the leadership, who had stayed in Beijing, stating:

"In order to have a better discussion (on the draft Constitution) among the politburo, it is advised to read such references …:

1. 1936 Soviet Union Constitution …;
2. Russian Constitution of 1918 …;
3. The Constitution of Romania, Poland, Germany (German Democratic Republic) and Czechoslovakia, etc." (Han, 2004).

Liu Shaoqi and the rest of the leaders who had stayed in Beijing responded to this telegraph and studied not only the constitution of the Soviet Union but also those of the Eastern Bloc. As a result, the Constitution of the PRC was strongly influenced by these earlier constitutions from the Soviet Union and Eastern Bloc countries.

Because this is a comparative work, analyzing the connections among the legislative texts and identifying similarities and differences are important.[14] Therefore, the following section presents a detailed examination of the text of the Constitution of the PRC and constitutions in the Visegrad states. The similarities and differences among these states' first communist constitutions are also compared.

3.1.2.1 Analysis of the Text of the Constitution of the People's Republic of China

This was the first socialist constitution in China; it consisted of five parts, namely, a preamble and four chapters, and there were 106 articles. Additionally, like the communist countries in Eastern Europe, the Constitution of the PRC was strongly influenced by the Soviet constitution of 1936. Each level of the People's Congress and the relationship between the People's Congress and administrative organs at each level followed those of the Soviet Union (Frederick, 2008).

Because it is not practical to analyze every article of the constitution in this work, the most important text in each part of the constitution is examined here. Not every communist constitution contained a preamble. The 1936 Soviet Union Constitution and the Hungarian Constitution of 1949 featured none; however, in the Czechoslovakia Constitution of 1948[15] and the Constitution of the Polish People's Republic of 1952, like the Chinese constitution, the preamble was placed in the first section. Mao Zedong participated in the drafting of each article in the constitution, although the preamble was inspired by Mao's reading of Lenin's Declaration of Rights of The Working and Exploited People (Han, 2004; Lenin, 1918).

Preamble to the Constitution of the People's Republic of China

The preamble had six paragraphs. The first paragraph mainly reviewed the Chinese revolutionary history and decreed that China's democratic system was a people's democracy or new democracy. The second described the current situation, stating that it was a transition period, and that the main task in this period was to "bring about the socialist industrialization of the country and, step by step, to accomplish the socialist transformation of agriculture, handicrafts and capitalist industry and commerce." The

---

[14] As introduced in the Chapter One, the methodology part, contextualism is a very important method in comparative research.

[15] There is no English version of Czechoslovakia Constitution of 1948, or so called Ninth of May Constitution, the first part in the Constitution was "Prohlaseni" (Declaration), Czech version only. Retrieved June 22, 2021, from http://www.upn.gov.sk/data/pdf/ustava150-48.pdf. In Constitution of the Polish People's Republic in 1952, the first part was the Preamble as well, English version of the Polish Constitution is available. Retrieved June 22, 2021, from http://libr.sejm.gov.pl/tek01/txt/kpol/e1952a-spis.html.

third paragraph was adopted by the First NPC and noted the connection between the Common Program and the constitution. The fourth emphasized the importance of the people's democratic united front. The fifth paragraph mainly dealt with all the nationalities in the territory of China, stating that they should all be united into one great family characterized by freedom and equality. The final paragraph focused on foreign affairs, stating that the PRC "has already built an indestructible friendship with the great Union of Soviet Socialist Republics and the People's Democracies." It stated that China sought to develop equal, mutually beneficial relationships with every country in the world (Han, 2004).[16]

General Principles of the Constitution of the People's Republic of China

A section on general principles formed the first chapter in the constitution. It consisted of 20 articles and mainly dealt with the very basic regulations of the country.

This chapter contained the following six parts.

The first part mainly defined the country's form, clearly stating that the PRC was a people's democratic state and that "all power in the People's Republic of China belongs to the people."[17] The second part was Article 3, which mainly regulated the nationalities in China and stated that China was a unitary multinational state. The third part was Article 4, which mainly addressed realizing socialism: "The Constitution of the People's Republic of China in 1954 is not a complete socialist Constitution, it is a Constitution in the transition period" (Zhang & Zeng, 1979). Therefore, this constitution not only ensured the fruits of victory during the war but also provided guidelines for the future. When the constitution was adopted in 1954, socialism had not been realized in China, and the next key task was to accomplish that through socialist industrialization and socialist transformation. The fourth part mainly addressed China's economic system, and it contained 10 articles, i.e., half of the articles in the first chapter were devoted to creating China's economic system. At that time, the main economic task was transforming the economic system from capitalism to socialism. The fifth part was Article 16, which emphasized the importance of work (or labor). The last part mainly dealt with the importance of the masses of the people. It stated that the country should rely on the people, that public servants should strive to serve the people and that the armed forces of the PRC belonged to the people and would protect the fruits of the revolution.[18]

---

[16] Constitution of People's Republic of China in 1954. Englished version. Retrieved June 22, 2021, from http://e-chaupak.net/database/chicon/1954/1954bilingual.htm.

[17] Article 1 and 2, Constitution of People's Republic of China in 1954. Englished version. Retrieved June 22, 2021, from http://e-chaupak.net/database/chicon/1954/1954bilingual.htm.

[18] The first Chapter of the Constitution of People's Republic of China in 1954. Englished version. Retrieved June 22, 2021, from http://e-chaupak.net/database/chicon/1954/1954bilingual.htm.

State Structure in the Constitution of the People's Republic of China

The second chapter of the constitution concerned China's state structure and contained six sections. The first three regulated the powers and responsibilities of the PRC's central government: the NPC, the President of the PRC, and the State Council. The fourth part mainly dealt with the local-level governing organs, i.e., the local People's Congresses and the local People's Councils. The fifth part addressed the organs of self-government of national autonomous areas, and the last part covered China's judicial system, the People's Courts, and the People's Procuratorates.

On 19 May 1954, the Constitution Drafting Group discussed the first section of chapter 2, the regulations on the NPC, which was the supreme organ of state power. Each article was very detailed and was discussed by the group, and almost every article had to be compared with similar articles in the Soviet Union Constitution. Moreover, some articles were influenced by the Common Program (Han, 2004). The NPC was the "sole organ exercising the legislative power of the state", and its members were elected. However, these elections were not direct. The deputies of the NPC were elected by the provincial-level People's Congresses, with four-year terms. Additionally, as the highest organ in the state, the NPC enjoyed some privileges. Since it was only held once each year, its Standing Committee exercised some powers.

The second section regulated the chairman of the PRC. There was no such position in the Soviet Union Constitution, only the Presidium of the Supreme Soviet. However, the constitutions of Czechoslovakia and the German Democratic Republic both contained the position of president, and in China, this position was the chairman (Han, 2004).[19] According to a speech by Zhou Enlai, the leader of the central government, "China is too big, for the sake of security of the state, it is necessary to design the position of Chairman" (Han, 2004). Additionally, the chairman in China was empowered to govern the state with other central organs. Article 42, for example, stated that the chairman "commands the armed forces of the state, and is Chairman of the Council of National Defense."[20]

The third section contained the rules of the State Council. On 28 May 1954, in its third plenary session convened by Liu Shaoqi, the second powerful person in the Party, the Constitution Drafting Committee discussed the name of the central administrative organ. In the Common Program, this organ was called "政务院" (Zhengwu Yuan), and it was only one branch of the Central People's Government. The draft constitution listed three options for the name of the central government organ: the Central People's Government, the Government of the People's Republic of China,

---

[19] However, in the current Constitution of People's Republic of China, in the official English version Constitution, the same word in Chinese 主席 (Zhu Xi) is translated to President. The official English version of Constitution of People's Republic of China in 1982. Retrieved June 22, 2021, from http://www.npc.gov.cn/englishnpc/Constitution/node_2825.htm.

[20] Article 42, the Constitution of People's Republic of China. English version. Retrieved June 22, 2021, from http://e-chaupak.net/database/chicon/1954/1954bilingual.htm.

3.1 First Communist Constitution in China

and "国务院" (Guowu Yuan). However, the State Council was given more power than in the regulation in the Common Program (Han, 2004).[21]

The fourth section concerned the local People's Congresses and People's Councils. The constitution established three levels of administrative divisions in the PRC: the central government level, the province level and the county level. The province level included provinces, autonomous regions and directly-controlled municipalities. At the county level, there were autonomous zhou,[22] counties, autonomous counties, and cities.[23]

The fifth section in the chapter addressed the organs of self-government of national autonomous areas. On 29 May 1954, the fourth plenary session of the Constitution Drafting Committee was held, mainly discussing the organs of self-government of national autonomous areas, the judicial system and the fundamental rights and duties of citizens. In the Common Program, chapter six regulated nationality policy. In the constitution, seven articles regulated the privileges of the organs in the national autonomous areas. However, these privileges would follow the constitution and other laws published by the central legislature. The first article in this section stated that "local people's councils throughout the country are local organs of state administration under the co-ordinating leadership of the State Council and are subordinate to it." The next article stated that "the organization of the organs of self-government of autonomous regions ... should conform to the basic principles governing the organization of local organs of state as specified in Chapter Two, Section IV of the Constitution." Article 69 provided that the administrative organs should also follow the regulations in "Chapter Two, Section IV of the Constitution." (Han, 2004)[24] Although the organs in the national autonomous areas enjoyed privileges since most of these areas were remote, the economy and education in these areas were less developed, and these privileges would have helped those of other nationalities in China experience better development.

The sixth section of chapter 2 dealt with the PRC's judicial system. The first of two parts was about the People's Court, which was designated as the country's judicial

---

[21] The Central People's Government in Common Program is more combination of the Standing Committee of National People's Congress and State Council, and the State Council is only the executive branch in the Central People's Government. Nevertheless, in the Constitution, the State Council or so-called Central People's Government means the central administration organ. The Common Program of the Chinese People's Political Consultative Conference (1949). English version. Retrieved June 22, 2021, from https://sourcebooks.fordham.edu/mod/1949-ccp-program.asp.

Paragraph 1, Article 4, Chapter 1, Electoral Law of the National People's Congress and Local People's Article 47, the Constitution of People's Republic of China. English version. Retrieved June 22, 2021, from http://e-chaupak.net/database/chicon/1954/1954bilingual.htm.

[22] Autonomous zhou in Chinese 自治州, it is an autonomous prefecture in China. In Chinese administrative system, zhou is a city level prefecture.

[23] Article 53, the Constitution of People's Republic of China. English version. Retrieved June 22, 2021, from http://e-chaupak.net/database/chicon/1954/1954bilingual.htm.

[24] Article 66, 67, and Chapter Six of Common Program. The Common Program of the Chinese People's Political Consultative Conference (1949). English version. Retrieved June 22, 2021, from https://sourcebooks.fordham.edu/mod/1949-ccp-program.asp.

authority, and the second about the People's Procuratorate, which was considered the procuratorial authority. The President of the Supreme People's Court and the Chief Procurator of the Supreme People's Procuratorate had four-year terms, which was in accord with the term of the NPC. The regulation on the People's Court stated that "the people's courts administer justice independently and are subject only to the law" (Han, 2004).[25] The People's Court responded and was accountable to only the People's Congress on its level. However, there was no rule regarding the justice of the Supreme People's Procuratorate; on the local level, the "local people's procuratorates at various levels exercise their functions and powers independently and are not subject to interference by local organs of state" (Han, 2004).[26] Additionally, the local People's Procuratorates were under the leadership of two organs, the same-level People's Congress and the higher-level People's Procuratorate.

Fundamental Rights and Duties of Citizens in the Constitution of the People's Republic of China

Chapter three stipulated the fundamental rights and duties of citizens of China. It contained 19 articles. In the first part, Articles 85–99 mainly regulated the rights of citizens of the PRC. In the second part, Articles 100–103 stipulated the duties of citizens. In the rights section, Articles 100–103 not only stated the rights of the masses but also emphasized the rights of elderly men and women, minors and overseas Chinese (Han, 2004).[27]

The Constitution of the PRC used three different words relating to the masses: "people", "citizen" and "voter". However, there were some differences among these words. "People" was more of a political concept, and an article by Chairman Mao asked, "Who are the people? At the present stage in China, they are the working class, the peasantry, the urban petty bourgeoisie, and the national bourgeoisie. These classes, led by the working class and the Communist Party, unite to form their own state and elect their own government" (Mao, 1949). "Citizen" was more of a legal concept, referring to a person with Chinese citizenship; the same article by Mao referred to the "landlord class and bureaucrat-bourgeoisie, as well as the representatives of those classes, the Kuomintang reactionaries and their accomplices." These groups apparently did not belong to the "people" but were still Chinese citizens. The concept of a "voter" was also different. Article 86 provided that citizens who reached

---

[25] Article 78, Constitution of People's Republic of China. English version. Retrieved June 22, 2021, from http://e-chaupak.net/database/chicon/1954/1954bilingual.htm.

[26] Article 83, Constitution of People's Republic of China. English version. Retrieved June 22, 2021, from http://e-chaupak.net/database/chicon/1954/1954bilingual.htm.

[27] Article 85–102, Constitution of People's Republic of China. English version. Retrieved June 22, 2021, from http://e-chaupak.net/database/chicon/1954/1954bilingual.htm.

the age of 18 had the right to vote, and "insane persons and persons deprived by law of the right to vote and stand for election" did not (Han, 2004).[28]

National Flag, National Emblem, and Capital in the Constitution of the People's Republic of China

This was the last chapter of the constitution. It contained three articles, and the first declared the "red flag with five stars" the national flag of the PRC. Red indicated the revolution and sacrifice, the five stars symbolized the unity of Chinese nationalities, and the large star was the CPC. The second article established the national emblem of the PRC, and the last article declared Beijing its capital city. However, the constitution did not establish a national anthem (Han, 2004).[29]

3.1.2.2 Analysis of the Structure of the Constitution of the People's Republic of China

This part briefly examines the structure of the Constitution of the PRC and presents the main idea of each of its sections. Then, the similarities and differences in the structures of the constitutions of China and the Visegrad states are discussed.

The structure of the 1954 Constitution of the PRC was much simpler than those of the Visegrad states' communist constitutions. It consisted of a preamble and four chapters. The preamble focused on three topics. First, it reviewed the revolutionary history; second, it presented the main task in the present; and third, it addressed the nation issue and the relationship with the so-called People's Democratic States. Chapter one contained the general principles, essentially the most basic and important principles in the constitution. Chapter two focused on the state structure. Chapter three addressed the fundamental rights and duties of citizens. The last chapter regulated, as in other communist constitutions, the capital city, national flag, and national emblem. It did not address the national anthem.[30]

---

[28] Article 86, Constitution of People's Republic of China. English version. Retrieved June 22, 2021, from http://e-chaupak.net/database/chicon/1954/1954bilingual.htm. The differences of "people", "citizen" and "voter" please see Han's book.

[29] Article 104, 105 and 106, Constitution of People's Republic of China. English version. Retrieved June 22, 2021, from http://e-chaupak.net/database/chicon/1954/1954bilingual.htm.

[30] Constitution of People's Republic of China. English version. Retrieved June 22, 2021, from http://e-chaupak.net/database/chicon/1954/1954bilingual.htm.

3.2 First Written Communist Constitutions in the Visegrad States

As noted earlier, there were only 3 countries in the Visegrad area: Hungary, Poland, and Czechoslovakia. In this section, the author discusses the first communist constitutions in these states individually and then conducts a comparative analysis of the constitutions of China and the Visegrad countries.

3.2.1 Hungarian People's Republic

Hungary became a people's republic in 1949 after the socialist party took the majority in the parliament. This part explores how the socialist constitution was adopted in Hungary and analyzes its text.

3.2.1.1 Adoption of the 1949 Constitution of the Hungarian People's Republic

Hungary, located in Central-Eastern Europe, was historically a great power, especially after the Austro-Hungarian Compromise of 1867. Long ago, Hungary had an unwritten constitution, the Golden Bull, which was issued in 1222 (Ferenc & Lorman, 2019). However, the first written constitution, the Constitution of the Hungarian People's Republic, was adopted by the National Assembly of Hungary in 1949 (Solyom-Fekete, 1980).

There is a famous ancient saying in China: "Take history as a mirror and you will understand why dynasties rise and fall." [以史为鉴, 可以知兴替] (Liu, Later Jin of Five Dynasties) This could apply to the history of Hungary. Hungary had a very short experience as a Soviet Republic. After the First World War, with the "help" of Soviet Russia, the Hungarian Communist Party founded the Hungarian Soviet Republic. However, this republic lasted only 133 days (Apor, 2009).

History always presents a similar plot to the audience. After the Second World War, Hungary was "liberated" by the Red Army in 1945 (Zhelitski, 1997). Although Hungary was independent, it was essentially controlled by the Allied Control Council. Although it was not large, the Communist Party was one of the most active parties in Hungary. In November 1945, the Smallholders Party won a parliamentary election, taking 245 seats, accounting for 57% of the total (Zhelitski, 1997). However, through nationwide propaganda, the Communist Party of Hungary gradually won support from the masses. In the parliamentary election of 1947, in favor of the amended Electoral Law (Act 12 of 1947) and financial support, the Communist Party distributed over 4 million election posters and 10 million leaflets and brochures throughout the country. On election day, the "certified lists of names" "helped" the Communist Party win the election. On 5 September 1947, the election results were released by the central electoral committee, and the Communist Party took 100 seats, becoming the largest party in the parliament (Izsak, 2002). In the 1949 election, the Hungarian Working People's Party gained 285 seats.[31]

By controlling the parliament, the Hungarian Working People's Party began the socialist transformation of the entire country. In 1947, as many studies have noted, to lead the country from capitalism to socialism, the Communist Party-controlled Council of Ministers organized a Constitution Drafting Committee. The committee soon submitted a socialist constitution to the Hungarian National Assembly, without any delays in the national legislative organ, and the National Assembly adopted the Constitution of the Hungarian People's Republic of 1949. Additionally, like other socialist countries in Central-Eastern Europe and beyond, the 1949 Hungarian Constitution was strongly influenced by the 1936 Soviet Constitution (IBP USA, 2013). As William Solyom-Fekete writes in an article, "the 1949 Constitution was a slavish imitation of the Soviet-type constitutions, with some variations resulting from the historical and political differences between the Soviet Union and Hungary." (Solyom-Fekete, 1980).

The 1949 Constitution incorporated numerous regulations from the 1936 Soviet Constitution. It ensured that the socialist system applied in the whole society. Although it was amended significantly after its adoption, for example, in 1972 and 1989, it remained valid until 2012.[32]

3.2.1.2 Analysis of the Text and Structure of the 1949 Constitution of the Hungarian People's Republic

The 1949 Constitution of the Hungarian People's Republic consisted of a preamble and 11 chapters. However, the author divides it into seven parts here for ease of analysis. The first part was the preamble, like most communist constitutions at that time; the second part included chapters one and two, the Hungarian People's Republic and the Social Structure, which mainly presented the essential principles; the third part, from chapters three to seven, mainly contained provisions on the state structure from the central government to local authorities. The next part of the constitution covered the fundamental rights and duties of citizens, which were stipulated in chapter eight; chapter nine, Fundamental Electoral Principles, could be viewed as the fifth part of the constitution. The sixth part was chapter ten, on the emblem, flag and capital of the Hungarian People's Republic. The seventh and final part was chapter

---

[31] The Hungarian Working People's Party was formed in 1948 through a merge of the Hungarian Communist Party and the Social Democratic Party. The date of the number of seats of each party in the election was available in gutenberg website. Hungarian Parliamentary Election, 1949. Retrieved June 22, 2021, from http://www.gutenberg.us/articles/hungarian_parliamentary_election_1949.

[32] Even after the Revolutions of 1989, the Hungarian Constitution had a serious of crucial amendments. The socialist system had been abandoned, from some scholars' opinion that the new de facto Constitution was adopted after the Revolutions of 1989. Since in the content, a western standard Constitution had been adopted. However, from a legal perspective, the new version Constitution was officially adopted in 2011.

eleven, the final provision. As the author divides the 1949 Constitution into seven parts, the following introduction of its text is also presented in six parts rather than 11.

The first part of the constitution was the preamble. Preambles could also be found in the communist constitutions of the other Visegrad countries and the PRC. The preamble was quite short (compared with those in the other four states). It reviewed how the Soviets had "helped" the Hungarians defeat the German fascists and the so-called great landowners and capitalists. It also clearly declared the leadership of the working classes and farmers in the new People's Republic. At the end, the preamble stated that due to the changes in the economic and social structure, the People's Republic was adopting the new constitution and indicated the future development of the country (Peaslee, 1974).[33]

The second part contained the general principles of the constitution, and it included the first two chapters. Chapter one defined the Hungarian People's Republic. It asserted that Hungary was a People's Republic and that all the power of the state belonged to the working people. It was a dictatorship of the proletariat. Chapter two, titled Social Structure, had 6 articles. It focused on the economic structure of the "new" society; the capitalist system would be gradually eliminated by the government and a socialist system created in its place. Article Four stipulated that the bulk of the means of production would be owned by the public; however, it also allowed private ownership of means of production. The next paragraph of Article Four stated that the power to direct the national economy belonged to the working people and noted the task of building a socialist economic system to replace capitalism. Article Five discussed the importance of the state national-economic plan. The next article decreed that all the natural and public resources belonged to the working people but would be managed by the state (government). Article seven was related to the agrarian problem. The last two articles in this chapter dealt mainly with labor (Peaslee, 1974).

The third part of the 1949 Constitution included chapters three to seven and mainly addressed the state structure. This part can be divided into three sections: the first on central power, the second on local power and the third on judicial power.

The first section, regarding central power, included chapters three and four. Chapter three stated that the highest organ of state authority was the parliament. The parliament enjoyed various state powers, such as legislative power, determining the state budget, and electing the Presidential Council and the Council of Ministers. Parliamentary terms would be four years, although this was not always the case in reality. Along with the parliament, the Presidential Council, which was selected by the parliament at its first sitting, was another important organ of state authority since the position of president was not referenced in the 1949 Constitution. The Presidential Council enjoyed some of the power of a president or head of state, such as appointing diplomatic representatives, receiving letters of credence on foreign diplomatic representatives, and ratifying international treaties. The Presidential Council's

---

[33] The Preamble of Constitution of the Hungarian People's Republic, published in Budapest 1953, supplied by Ministry of Foreign Affair. Hungarian Version of Constitution of Hungarian People's Republic was published in Magyar Kozlony (Hungary Gazette) in 20 August 1949, Budapest.

3.2 First Written Communist Constitutions in the Visegrad States

term would expire when the parliament elected a new one. Members of the Council of Ministers would not be elected as members of the Presidential Council. The other organ of central power was the highest organ of state administration, the Central Government or Council of Ministers. This was an executive organ at the highest level. The Council of Ministers consisted of a Chairman, Deputy Chairman, Minister of State and Ministers of various ministries, and the members of the Council of Ministers were elected by the Presidential Council. There were 26 ministries in the entire central government. To develop the socialist economy, some ministries were created, such as the Ministry of State Farms and Forests and the Ministry of Home Trade. The Council of Ministers was empowered to issue decrees and decisions that did not conflict with the laws of the People's Republic or decrees of the Presidential Council. Because Hungary was a centralized state, the central authority and administration were empowered to annul or modify regulations made by the lower state power (Peaslee, 1974).

Local organs of state power were regulated in chapter five. The main administration in the local-level government was local councils, and councils at different levels governed their own administrative areas. Local councils were empowered to pass rules and regulations in their own areas, which were not to infringe on any law or decree from higher authorities. Additionally, they could modify the regulations made by the lower-level council in their own administrative areas each year. Members of the local councils were elected by voters after nomination by the Patriotic People's Front. The term of the councils was four years. The executive committee was the executive organ of the local council and was accountable to the same-level council that elected it and to the executive committee of the superior council body (Antal, 2010).

The judiciary was addressed primarily in chapters six and seven. Chapter six focused on the courts. The Supreme Court was the highest court in the People's Republic. All the judges were appointed. According to the communist system, the courts of the Hungarian People's Republic were to "punish the enemies of the working people" (Antal, 2010). Public prosecutors were another important part of the judiciary. Their main task was enforcement of the law. The Chief Public Prosecutor was elected by and accountable to the parliament; all other public prosecutors were appointed by the Chief Public Prosecutor.

The fourth part of the constitution concerned the rights and duties of citizens. Like in other communist states, citizens enjoyed rights to education, labor and rest and freedom of religious worship. However, most of the rights were limited to be in accordance with the communist system, and the working class enjoyed more rights than others. Article 48, paragraph 1 stipulated that "the Hungarian People's Republic ensures the rights to education for every worker." The previous article stated that "the Hungarian People's Republic protects the health of the workers and assists them in the event of sickness or disability". Even freedoms of speech, press and assembly would be "in accord with the interests of the workers" (Antal, 2010).[34]

---

[34] Paragraph 1, Article 55 of the Constitution of Hungarian People's Republic in 1949.

The electoral system was also important in the practices of the communist political system. Therefore, chapter nine focused on elections. The electoral provisions in the 1949 Hungarian Constitution almost provided for universal suffrage, except that the "excluding provision" in Article 63, paragraph 2 stated that "enemies of the working people… are excluded from the suffrage by law" (Antal, 2010).[35]

Chapter ten established the coat of arms, flag and capital of the Hungarian People's Republic, with the coat of arms and flag characterized by communist aesthetics.

The last chapter contained the final provisions. It included two articles dealing mainly with the time that the constitution would enter into force, law enforcement, and the supreme importance of the constitution to the state power and the citizens (Antal, 2010).

3.2.2 Czechoslovak Republic

Czechoslovakia adopted its new constitution after the end of the Second World War. This section examines how the Nazis occupied the Czech part and the satellite state, Slovakia, established a new country and adopted a constitution influenced by the Soviet Union and its own constitutional tradition.

3.2.2.1 Adoption of the Ninth of May Constitution of the Czechoslovak Republic

The two World Wars brought significant changes to Czechoslovakia. After the First World War, Czechoslovakia was established in 1918 with the support of the Great Powers (Glaser, 1961).[36] During the Second World War, the Czech part became the Bohemia-Moravia Protectorate, and the Slovakian part became independent and established the Slovak Republic; however, both parts of Czechoslovakia were considered "puppets" of Nazi Germany. During the war, Benes and other Czechoslovakian politicians organized the Czechoslovak government in exile in London. At the end of the war, the Red Army, the military force of the Soviet Union, crossed the eastern border of Slovakia. Later, in May 1945, with the help of the masses of Prague, the Red Army liberated the city. Czechoslovakia officially fell into the Soviet Union's sphere of influence, although United States forces penetrated the western border of Bohemia earlier than Soviet Union forces (Glaser, 1961).

The liberated Czechoslovakia did not completely or voluntarily join the Soviet orbit at the very beginning. Benes and most of the government ministers were not

---

[35] Paragraph 2. Article 63 of the Constitution of Hungarian People's Republic in 1949.

[36] How Masaryk, Benes and other Czechoslovakia elites created Czechoslovak Republic could refer to Kurt Glaser's book.

great fans of communism, preferring the Western orbit (Glaser, 1961).[37] However, propaganda from communist politicians soon drew people's attention. It became increasingly popular, especially in the Czech regime.

With support from the Soviet Union, the leader of the Communist Party of Czechoslovakia, Premier Gottwald, and his comrades initiated the so-called coup d'état, and noncommunist ministers were exiled. The Communist Party enjoyed great power in the government. To ensure the legitimacy of the government, the communists drafted a new constitution and brought it to the parliament. On 9 May of 1948, with 100 percent affirmative votes (Glaser, 1961),[38] Benes refused to sign it and resigned on June 7. Gottwald, the Premier and the Chairman of the Communist Party, signed it and precisely one week later became the new president of Czechoslovakia.

Since it was adopted on 9 May 1948, the constitution was known as the "Ninth of May Constitution"; however, it was not an exact copy of the 1936 Soviet Union Constitution. It was "an elaborate hybrid, a combination of Western parliamentarism with sovietism" (Taborsky, 1961). Even the communists explained that the 1948 Constitution included two components. The first was the 1920 Constitution, since some of the provisions in the old constitution still met the present conditions (in 1948), and the other parts were based on the "achievement of national and democratic revolution of 1944 and 1945" (Taborsky, 1961). Although the influence of the Soviet Union was not mentioned in this official commentary, we can easily see elements from the 1936 Soviet Union Constitution in the text and structure of the Ninth of May Constitution.

3.2.2.2 Analysis of the Text and Structure of the Ninth of May Constitution of the Czechoslovak Republic

In this part, the author examines the text and structure of the Czechoslovakian Ninth of May Constitution. Like other constitutions in the Visegrad States and China, the Czechoslovakian constitution had its own characteristics, although all the constitutions were strongly influenced by the 1936 Soviet Union Constitution.

The Ninth of May Constitution had three parts: the declaration or preamble (depending on the translation; in the Czech language, it is Prohlášení), the fundamental articles, and the detailed provisions. The last part included ten sections. Unlike the other constitutions in the area, the Czechoslovakian constitution put the section on the rights and duties of citizens in front of the state structure, also because, as its name implied, Czechoslovakia consisted of two nations, Czechs and Slovaks (Glaser, 1961; Marcus, 2000).[39] At the very beginning of Czechoslovakia, the leaders of the state

---

[37] In July 7, 1947, the government of Czechoslovak Republic even sent a delegation to Paris, since the Marshall Plan conference was held here. However, the pressure from Kremlin forced Czechoslovakia withdrew from the Marshall Plan.

[38] There were 246 representatives attended the Parliament meeting, 54 representatives were absence.

[39] In the beginning period of the country, Czechoslovakia's second nation should be German, in the census of 1926, it showed the whole country had 6.5 million Czechs, 3.3 million Germans and

"invented" the nation of Czechoslovakia and enshrined it in the 1920 Constitution,[40] and the declaration in the Ninth of May Constitution stated that "the Czechs and Slovaks, two brotherly nations." Therefore, the Ninth of May Constitution contained a section on Slovak national organs.[41]

The first part of the Ninth of May Constitution was the declaration, which can also be divided into four sections. The first section declared that Czechoslovakia would build a socialist state. To defend the achievement of national and democratic revolution, the people's democratic order—"we"—initiated action in February 1948. In the next section, "we" reviewed the history of Czechoslovakia, which had begun a thousand years earlier. Then, it reviewed how the Czechs and Slovaks fought the German Hapsburg Dynasty and established the state, how they fought Nazi Germany with the help of the Allies, and especially how the Soviet Union liberated Prague on 9 May 1945, exactly three years before the Ninth of May Constitution was adopted in Parliament. This section contained another notable statement, which the author mentioned previously. Czechs and Slovaks were officially recognized as two nations, unlike in the first constitution of the Czechoslovak Republic in 1920, which "invented". Czechoslovakia as a unitary nation. Glaser, in his book Czechoslovakia, a critical history, states that the Ninth of May Constitution made "the following propositions, none of which is true: That there is a 'Czechoslovak nation'" (Glaser, 1961). The third section of the declaration established "our" goals of building a people's democratic state and realizing socialism. The last section described the structure of the remaining sections. Moreover, the declaration emphasized that the state was a Slav state, within the so-called Slav family and Slav power. Pan-Slavism deeply influenced this constitution, and this kind of political ideology also played a very important role in the minority policies in Czechoslovakia, with numerous minorities having to leave the country.

As the final section of the declaration indicated, the second part of the constitution was the fundamental articles. This part consisted of 12 articles, which included the most important principles and provisions, basic political issues, citizens' rights and duties, Slovakia, the judiciary, the economy and essentially all other basic societal matters. Since the Ninth of May Constitution was a hybrid of the 1920 Constitution and a Soviet-style constitution, there is no doubt that bourgeois thought and communist ideology coexisted in the same articles.

The final part of the Ninth of May Constitution contained the detailed provisions; as the last section in the declaration stated that "we have expounded them (the Fundamental Article, i.e., the second part in the Constitution) in detail." This part consisted

---

2.5 million Slovaks, since the anti-German policy, especially after the second world war, more and more German left the country. However, according to the census of Czechoslovakia in 1950, there were only 165,000 German still stay in this country.

[40] In the Preamble of the Constitution of Czechoslovak Republic in 1920, it declared "We, the Czechoslovak nation…" Constitution of Czechoslovak Republic in 1920. English version. Retrieved June 23, 2021, from https://archive.org/details/cu31924014118222.

[41] Constitution of the Czechoslovak Republic in 1948 (Czechoslovak Ministry of Information, 1948).

3.2 First Written Communist Constitutions in the Visegrad States

of 10 sections and 178 articles in total. It listed the principal rules of society, from politics to the judiciary to the economy.

The author divides this section into five parts. The first part contained the rights and duties of citizens. The second was the political part. The third covered the judiciary. The fourth addressed the economy, and the final part was general, with concluding and transitional provisions.

Unlike other constitutions presented in this work at that time, the Ninth of May Constitution placed the chapter on citizens' rights and duties before that on the state structure, which was an "invention" since neither the 1920 Constitution of the Czechoslovak Republic nor the 1936 Soviet Union Constitution was ordered in this way.[42] Although we examine these provisions on the rights and duties of citizens with current standards, the regulations presented in this chapter were well organized and almost fully covered people's most important rights. However, because this constitution was a combination of the 1920 Constitution of the Czechoslovak Republic and the 1936 Soviet Union Constitution, the constitution-makers in Czechoslovakia added some socialist ingredients to the rights and duties of citizens. For example, Article 20 provided that citizens enjoyed the freedom to present their ideas to the public, and the following paragraph stated that "this right may be restricted by law only with a view to the public interest and to the cultural needs of the people." In the chapter on citizens' rights and duties, the phrase "People's Democratic Order" may draw people's attention. This phrase appeared in the constitution 17 times in total, and we found 7 instances in this chapter. The vague term "People's Democratic Order" largely restricted citizens in realizing their rights. Moreover, to ensure citizens' realization of their rights in the "right" way, Article 37, paragraph 1 included the following provision: "Statements and acts that constitute a threat to the independence, entirely and unity of the State, the Constitution, the Republican form of government and the People's Democratic Order, are punishable according to law" (Taborsky, 1961).[43]

The following part addressed how the state would function. At the central or highest level, the state had three major organs: the National Assembly, the President of the Republic, and the Government. The National Assembly was the legislative organ; it had two sessions, Spring and Autumn, which were summoned by the President of the Republic. The Presidium of the National Assembly was its standing committee. The position of President of the Republic was unique in this area at that time as the Hungarian People's Republic and the Polish People's Republic did not include it in

---

[42] In 1920 Constitution of Czechoslovak Republic, Section Five, Rights, Liberties and Duties of the Citizens was followed the Judicial Powers, Constitution of Czechoslovak Republic in 1920. English version. Retrieved June 23, 2021, from https://archive.org/details/cu31924014118222. In the 1936 Soviet Union Constitution, The Fundamental Rights and Duties of Citizens was in Chapter 10, the English version of Constitution of the Union of Soviet Socialist Republics. Retrieved June 23, 2021, from https://constitutii.files.wordpress.com/2013/01/1936-en.pdf.

[43] Constitution of Czechoslovak Republic in 1920. English version. Retrieved June 23, 2021, from https://archive.org/details/cu31924014118222. More detailed analysis of the rights and duties of citizens in the Ninth of May Constitution is available in Taborsky's book.

their constitutions.[44] The government was led by the prime minister, and it was an executive organ in the state. However, Czechoslovakia was a unitary state in 1948. Slovaks, as the second nation in the state, "brothers" of the Czechs, enjoyed some special rights that were accorded by the Ninth of May Constitution. Two main organs, the Slovak National Council and the Board of Commissioners, governed the territory of Slovakia. However, the performance of those powers was not to conflict with the constitution or other laws.[45] At the local level, the governing organ was the National Committee, and a lower-level National Committee was subordinate to a higher-level committee.[46]

The next part covered the judiciary. The Ninth of May Constitution used democratic words to decorate the clauses in this chapter; however, as mentioned previously, when in exercising their power, judges were to abide not only by the law but also by the "People's Democratic Order".[47]

The economic system was also regulated in the constitution. Nationalization of the main economic enterprises started in 1945 and finished before the adoption of the constitution; therefore, it was no wonder that state-run enterprises played a main role in the economic system. The Uniform Economic Plan penetrated people's daily lives. However, the Ninth of May Constitution failed to regulate the land as national property (Taborsky, 1961).

The final part contained general, concluding, and transitional provisions. It regulated the capital city, the coat of arms and the enforcement of the constitution, since some of the former constitutional acts may no longer have been in force.

3.2.3 Polish People's Republic

The invasion of Poland marked the beginning of the Second World War. In the battle against Nazi Germany and the Axis powers, Poland was within the Soviet sphere of influence. Therefore, it was not surprising that the Poles adopted a socialist constitution. This part addresses how the Polish communist party took over the Polish

---

[44] Constitution in most Socialist Republic followed the 1936 Soviet Union Constitution at that time, there wasn't President position in the 1936 Constitution, therefore most Socialist Republic Constitutions were not included the position of President. In Czechoslovakia case, when the Ninth of May Constitution was drafted, Benes was the President, he and his successor Gottwald enjoyed a great power and reputation in the State. Also, the Ninth of May Constitution was a hybrid of 1920 Constitution of Czechoslovak Republic and 1936 Soviet Union Constitution, it was not doubt, some political traditions was reserved in the Ninth of May Constitution.

[45] Article 109, Constitution of Czechoslovak Republic in 1948, published by Czechoslovak Ministry of Information, 1948.

[46] Paragraph 2, Article 131, Constitution of Czechoslovak Republic in 1948, published by Czechoslovak Ministry of Information, 1948.

[47] Article 143, Constitution of Czechoslovak Republic in 1948, published by Czechoslovak Ministry of Information, 1948.

Parliament and adopted a Soviet-style constitution. It also examines the text of the Constitution of the Polish People's Republic.

3.2.3.1 Adoption of the 1952 Constitution of the Polish People's Republic

Poles are very proud of their long and rich constitutional history. The first constitution of Poland, also the first modern constitution in Europe, was published on 3 May 1791. In some scholars' opinions, the 1791 Constitution could be compared with the United States Constitution and French Constitution, which was adopted four months after the Polish Constitution (Banaszak et al., 2012; Cholewinski, 1998).

After the First World War, Poland gained sovereignty in 1918 and was considered an independent state, and the country was ruled as an authoritarian regime. In 1935, as advocated by the de facto leader, Polish statesman Pilsudski, Poland adopted a new constitution. The presidential system was introduced into Polish political life. It limited the powers of the Polish Parliament. However, one month after the constitution was adopted, statesman Pilsudski passed away. The rest of the leadership eagerly pursued the highest position in Poland. However, since there was no similarly charismatic politician, the 1935 Constitution did not perform very well (Brzezinski, 1998). Four years after its adoption, the Second World War broke out. Soon, Poland was controlled by Nazi Germany, and the Polish government went into exile in France first and then in Great Britain (Brzezinski, 1998).

Finally, with the help of the Allies, Poland was liberated. As in other countries in this area, the Soviet Union's military, the Red Army, was the main force to liberate it. In the late summer of 1944, in Lublin, a city located in eastern Poland, a Soviet Union-sponsored organization was formed, the Polish Committee of National Liberation (Polska Komitet Wyzwolenia Narodowego—PKWN) and announced its manifesto. It denied the legitimacy of the 1935 Constitution in Poland, and based on the 1936 constitution-based government in exile, the 1935 Constitution was not recognized by the PKWN. Other political or military organizations at that time were brutally attacked by the Soviet Union's puppet in Poland. For instance, the Polish Home Army was one of the largest military forces in Poland, and with the attack of communists in Poland, it was disbanded in early 1945 by its commander (Micgiel, 1997).[48]

Soon, the PKWN enjoyed major power in the liberated territory of Poland, although some parts of the state were still controlled by Nazi Germany. On the last day of 1944, the PKWN changed its name to the provisional government of the Polish Republic, and Lublin became the center of liberated Poland. The next year, Polish people, along with other nations, witnessed the failure of the Axis Powers, and Poland again gained its independence. However, at that time, Poles could not fully determine the fate of their state by themselves. With their victory in the Second World War, the greatest powers among the Allies held several meetings and carved

---

[48] In the spring of 1944, Home Army had more than 350,000 soldiers, Communist's military force only counted 10,000–20,000 soldiers.

out their spheres of influence, and the Visegrad states had no independent choice. The Potsdam and Yalta Agreements "regulated" the area, and it was doomed to choose the path of socialism.

The Polish Workers' Party, a political coalition led mainly by the Polish Communist Party, won the elections in the Sejm (Polish Parliament) in 1947. In the same year, the "Small Constitution" was adopted by the Sejm and declared itself the successor to the 1921 constitution. The Small Constitution did not last long. Before the next Sejm election in 1952, the Sejm paid great attention to drafting a new constitution. Similarly to the constitution-drafting process in the PRC, a nationwide discussion was organized. Eleven million Poles were involved, 2822 suggestions were sent in by the masses, and a more communist-style constitution was finally adopted in the summer of 1952 (Brzezinski, 1998; Lasok, 1954).

3.2.3.2 Analysis of the Text and Structure of the 1952 Constitution of the Polish People's Republic

The 1952 Constitution of the Polish People's Republic mostly copied the 1936 Soviet Union Constitution. In Brzezinski's opinion, "the 1952 Constitution… retaining much of the original language of that document and reflecting of major inputs by Soviet constitutional theorists" (Brzezinski, 1998).

In this part, the author reviews in detail the text and structure of the 1952 Constitution of the Polish People's Republic. Since it was also strongly influenced by the 1936 Soviet Union Constitution, similarly to the constitutions of other socialist states in this area, its structure had no obvious differences from the 1949 Constitution of the Hungarian People's Republic and the Ninth of May Constitution of the Czechoslovak Republic. The 1952 Constitution of Poland consisted of a preamble and ten chapters. The preamble was the foreword of the document, which was called the Constitution. The ten chapters could be divided into six parts. The first two chapters mainly addressed the structure of the Polish People's Republic. Chapter one covered the political structure, and chapter two the social and economic structure. The second part regulated state power, following the Soviet style. The constitution distributed state power between the central and local levels. Chapter three concerned state authority at the central level, chapter four state administration at the central level, and chapter five state authority at the local level. The third part regulated the judiciary. The next part listed the fundamental rights and duties of citizens. Part five addressed the principles of electoral law. The final part contained other provisions that can be divided into two parts: first, regulations on the coat of arms, colors, and capital of the Polish People's Republic; and second, procedures for amending the constitution.

In the following section, the author analyzes the text of the 1952 Constitution of the People's Republic of Poland.

The first part was the preamble, which was a declaration. It enshrined the leadership of Polish working people, with its first sentence stating that the Polish People's

Republic was a republic of working people. It declared the state a socialist state. Similarly to the preambles to the constitutions of the other Visegrad states, it followed the rule of "review the fighting history of the Communist Party in the Revolution period". The preamble also devoted nearly half its space to describing how the working people and peasants in Poland were under the leadership of the Communist Party, which, with the help of the Soviet Union, was establishing a People's Republic. It reviewed the interwar period history; in particular, the preamble used one paragraph to reference the 1944 Manifesto of the Polish Committee of National Liberation, which played an important role in the state of the people's democracy in Poland. In addition to reviewing the revolutionary history of Polish working people and farmers, the preamble addressed four purposes of adopting the new constitution. The first was "to consolidate the People's State." People's State and People's Republic were the most common names used for the socialist states. The 1952 Polish constitution was adopted to officially establish a socialist system in the country. The second purpose was "to accelerate the political, economic and cultural development of the Fatherland"; the third was "to strengthen the patriotic feelings, the unity and solidarity of the Polish Nation,"—i.e., Poles united by patriotism would benefit the leadership and governance of the Polish working class; and the final one "to strengthen friendship and co-operation between nations", which stipulated the foreign policy of new sovereignty.[49]

The next part of the 1952 Constitution consisted of chapters one and two, which listed the principles of the political, social, and economic structures. Six articles addressed the political structure of the Polish People's Republic. The first and most important rule was that the "Polish People's Republic is a State of People's Democracy." People's democracy was a very important ideology in the Communist Party ruling-state, and it was the first stage in moving toward a fully communist regime (Brzezinski, 1998). Working people were nominally leaders or owners of the Polish People's Republic; therefore, the provisions on the political structure ensured the leadership of working people in Poland.

Chapter two included regulations on the social and economic structure. Establishing a socialist system was the constitution's goal. It ended the dominant position of capitalism in the social and economic areas and created a socialist social and economic system. Planned economic policy was the main characteristic of the new system; therefore, Article 7 used words such as "national economic plan" and "planned economic policy". Moreover, the state controlled foreign trade: "The State has the monopoly of foreign trade." In agrarian policy, the constitution recognized the legitimacy of individual farms of working farmers and expressed the intention to help them avoid "capitalist exploitation", while the establishment of cooperative farms gained special, comprehensive support from the state. Moreover, the Polish People's Republic recognized and protected legal private property. The end of the chapter emphasized the importance of labor.

---

[49] Constitution of Polish People's Republic in 1952, the English version is available in the official website of the library of Sejm in Poland. Retrieved June 23, 2021, from http://libr.sejm.gov.pl/tek01/txt/kpol/e1952a-spis.html.

The third part of the constitution regulated state power. Chapters three and four did so at the central level, and chapter five at the local level. The Sejm was the supreme organ of state authority. Chapter three stipulated the power of the Sejm (Seym in the English translation) and its standing organization, the Council of State. There were 14 articles in this chapter, which ensured the highest position of the Sejm. The Sejm was entitled to pass laws and adopt national economic plans and annual state budgets. Each Sejm served a term of four years and would hold at least two sessions. When the Sejm was adjourned, the Council of State would exercise state power (Brzezinski, 1998).

Chapter four regulated the supreme organs of state administration, the central government. The Council of Ministers was the supreme executive and administrative organ of state authority, and the Sejm was empowered to appoint and recall any members of the government and Council of Ministers. The Chairman, Vice Chairman and other committee leaders formed the core of the executive organ. The position of President of the Republic was abolished. This was common in communist constitutions because the Soviet Union promoted "democratic centralism", which favored state leadership by a group of people rather than a single charismatic leader.

Chapter five outlined how local-level state authorities would exercise state power through People's Councils. People's Councils had terms of three years. However, one term of the Sejm was four years. In practice, there were 49 People's Councils in the People's Republic, and each was in charge of all-around governance of its territory. However, any decree by a People's Council was to be in accordance with the higher-level People's Council and the central authority, the Sejm.

Part four related to the judiciary. Two institutions were created by the constitution: the courts and the Public Prosecutor's office. There were four different courts: the Supreme Court, Voivodeship (provincial level) Courts, District Courts and Special Courts. Article 52 declared that "judges are independent and subject only to the law". However, the courts were given the responsibility to "protect the achievements of the Polish working people, safeguard the people's rule of law." The Public Prosecutor was charged with enforcing the law, and the Public Prosecutor General was the highest organ and appointed and recalled by the Council of State (Brzezinski, 1998; Lasok, 1954).[50]

The fundamental rights and duties of citizens were enumerated in chapter seven. Citizens of the Polish People's Republic enjoyed many rights guaranteed in the constitution (on paper), such as freedom of speech, press and association, which were rights typically granted in Western democracies. However, these individual rights were usually followed by conditions; for example, Article 72 granted freedom of association but then stated: "The setting up of, and participation in, associations

---

[50] Constitution of Polish People's Republic in 1952, the English version is available in the official website of the library of Sejm in Poland. Retrieved June 23, 2021, from http://libr.sejm.gov.pl/tek01/txt/kpol/e1952a-spis.html.

3.2 First Written Communist Constitutions in the Visegrad States 69

the aims or activities of which are directed against the political or social system or against the legal order of the Polish People's Republic are forbidden."[51]

Chapter eight provided the principles of electoral law; the election of state authorities from the local to the central levels would be "universal, equal, direct and carried out by secret ballot." Citizens were entitled to vote after reaching 18 years of age. People who were insane or were deprived by a court decision of their public rights lost the right to vote.

The final part of the constitution regulated the coat of arms, colors and capital of the Polish People's Republic and the procedure for amending the constitution. The coat of arms and colors followed the Polish tradition. The amendment procedure was stricter than other laws. To amend the constitution, least half of the deputies had to be present in the Sejm, and over two-thirds of the present deputies had to support the amendment (Brzezinski, 1998; Lasok, 1954).[52]

3.3 Comparative Analysis of the Structure and Text of the First Written Communist Constitutions of China and the Visegrad States

In the mid-twentieth century, after the Second World War, the PRC and the Visegrad states established socialist systems and adopted their first communist constitutions. Although all these constitutions were strongly influenced by the 1936 Soviet Union Constitution, they each had some individuality (Da, 2019). In this part, the author employs a comparative analysis approach to the text and structure of these first communist constitutions. By examining the differences and similarities in how the states structured their constitutions and employed the constitutional provisions, we can better understand the historical background of the constitution-making process and the development of the constitutions in the entire communist period in each state.

3.3.1 Comparative Analysis of the Structures of the First Written Communist Constitutions of China and the Visegrad States

After the destructive Second World War, newly independent states found that there were two possible roads to follow: capitalism or socialism. The Soviet Union was

---

[51] Paragraph 3, Article 72, Constitution of Polish People's Republic in 1952, the English version is available in the official website of the library of Sejm in Poland. Retrieved June 23, 2021, from http://libr.sejm.gov.pl/tek01/txt/kpol/e1952a-spis.html.

[52] Article 89, 90, 91, Constitution of Polish People's Republic in 1952, the English version is available in the official website of the library of Sejm in Poland. Retrieved June 23, 2021, from http://libr.sejm.gov.pl/tek01/txt/kpol/e1952a-spis.html.

the first and largest socialist state in the world at that time. Through communist party propaganda, coalitions of socialist groups gradually won the leading position in each state, socialism spread nationwide, and communist constitutions were adopted by the legislatures. At almost the same time, in East Asia, the CPC fought two wars, the Anti-Japan War and the Civil War. The CPC won these wars and established a socialist regime. To legitimate the CPC's leadership, the PRC's first communist constitution was adopted in 1954.

Although China and the Visegrad states established socialist regimes and adopted communist constitutions and all these constitutions were patterned after the 1936 Soviet Union Constitution, different social conditions and histories in these countries led to differences in these constitutions.

In terms of structure, constitutions in the Visegrad states seemed more "willing" to follow the pattern of the 1936 Soviet Union Constitution, except for the Union Republic part.[53] There were 13 chapters in the 1936 Soviet Union Constitution. The first two chapters stated the principles of the republic and then addressed the central-level state power. Provisions on local-level state power were contained in the following chapter. The next chapter stipulated the rules of the judiciary. Chapter ten contained the fundamental rights and duties of citizens. Chapter eleven provided the principles of the electoral system. The final two chapters addressed the coat of arms, flags, capital and procedures for amending the constitution.[54]

The constitutions of the Visegrad states more or less followed this structure. For example, the 1952 Constitution of the Polish People's Republic "copied" it, except for the chapters related to the Union Republic. The structure of the 1954 Constitution of the PRC was much simpler than those of its brother states in the Visegrad area. There were only four chapters and a preamble in the 1954 Chinese constitution; however, it was not simpler or cruder than the constitutions in the Visegrad states. The state structure addressed in the Chinese constitution included the central- and local-level state powers, the judiciary, and even the organs of self-government in national autonomous areas.[55] However, the constitution of the PRC lacked two parts present in the 1936 Soviet Union constitution and the constitutions of the Visegrad states: provisions on the electoral system and the process of amending the constitution. However, the 1954 Chinese constitution did list some principles of the electoral system in the NPC and fundamental rights and duties of citizens.

---

[53] When the first Communist Constitution was adopted in Czechoslovakia in 1948, the Republic was still a unitary State, until the 1960 Constitution of Czechoslovakia was adopted, Czechoslovakia became a Federal State.

[54] Constitution of the Union of Soviet Socialist Republics 1936, English version. Retrieved June 23, 2021, from https://constitutii.files.wordpress.com/2013/01/1936-en.pdf.

[55] Similar regulation could be found in 1936 Soviet Union Constitution, however since Soviet Union was a federal State, autonomous areas in Soviet Union were called "Republic", China, as a unitary State, the highest-level autonomous area was equal a province. Ninth of May Constitution of Czechoslovak Republic regulated the Slovak national organs in Chapter Five, since Slovak was the second nations in the State. However, according to the Ninth of May Constitution, Czechoslovakia was still a unitary State.

Due to the popularity of "democratic centralism" in socialist states, the state leadership preferred leading by group; therefore, the 1936 Soviet Union Constitution and most socialist constitutions had no position of President of the Republic. However, the Ninth of May Constitution of the Czechoslovak Republic and the 1954 Constitution of the PRC contained this position.[56] Czechoslovakia was more influenced by capitalism, and the good personal reputations of Presidents Masaryk and Benes made the presidential position more important in Czechoslovakia than in its neighbors (Taborsky, 1961).[57] China, however, was the major power against the Axis Powers on its battlefields in the Second World War. The CPC won not only China's Civil War but also the support of the masses. CPC leader Mao Zedong enjoyed the highest respect of the entire society. Therefore, when the 1954 Constitution was adopted, he became the first Chairman of the PRC (Li, 2010; Xu, 2003).[58]

3.3.2 Comparative Analysis of Text of the First Written Communist Constitutions of China and the Visegrad States

Here, the author analyzes the texts of the first communist constitutions in the socialist states in the Visegrad area and China. It is difficult to compare the texts word for word due to their numerous provisions. Therefore, this part focuses on the preamble and the sections on the fundamental rights and duties of citizens and the supreme organ of state power.

3.3.2.1 Comparative Analysis of the Preambles to the First Written Communist Constitutions of China and the Visegrad States

The 1936 Soviet Union Constitution did not include a preamble; however, the three communist constitutions of the Visegrad states and the 1954 PRC constitution did.

Except for the Constitution of the Hungarian People's Republic, the Visegrad constitutions gave significant space to the preambles. As the first section of these constitutions, regardless of its length, the preamble was the political declaration of the constitution. It legitimated the sovereignty of the state and the leadership of the country's working class. Since the Soviet Union was the "big brother" of the socialist

---

[56] Chapter Three, Ninth of May Constitution of Czechoslovak Republic and Section Two, Chapter Two, Constitution of People's Republic of China provided the provisions of President (Chairman) of the Republic.

[57] During the drafting process of Ninth of May Constitution, Benes was still the President of Czechoslovak Republic.

[58] Mao Zedong and other leaderships of Chinese Communist Party participated in the drafting process of Constitution, in order to perform the State power more efficiency and security, Mao suggested to set up the position of Chairman, he even mentioned that in the Constitution of Czechoslovakia and German Democratic Republic were provided the position of President.

world, all of the constitutions mentioned it in their preambles. The constitutions' text provides a sense of each state's relationship with the Soviet Union. In the Chinese case, it was mentioned in the last paragraph of the preamble: The "Soviet Union" and other "People's Democracies" were friends of the PRC, and the relationship between China and the Soviet Union was equal.

However, the Hungarian preamble stated that "the armed forces of the great Soviet Union liberated our country from the yoke of the German fascists" in the first sentence. In the Czechoslovakian case, after reviewing the revolutionary history of Czechoslovakia, the constitution acknowledged the importance of the "Union of Soviet Socialist Republics" to Czechoslovakia's liberation during the Second World War. A similar statement on the Soviet Union could also be found in the preamble to the 1952 constitution of the Polish People's Republic: "The historic victory of the Union of Soviet Socialist Republics over fascism liberated Polish soil."[59]

Due to the Soviet Union's different levels of "importance" during the liberation period of the Second World War, the constitutions showed different attitudes toward it. For the Visegrad states, according to the preambles, the Soviet Union was a savior; however, for China, it was more like a good friend. Because of these differences in the relationships, the Soviet Union always oversaw reforms in the Visegrad states, while China split with the Soviet Union in the 1960s.

3.3.2.2 Comparative Analysis of the Fundamental Rights and Duties of Citizens in the First Written Communist Constitutions of China and the Visegrad States

Stipulating the fundamental rights and duties of citizens was a fad among socialist states, led by the 1936 Soviet Union Constitution. As a People's Republic, China also followed this trend, and its 1954 Constitution contained a chapter on these rights and duties. The constitutional drafting committees in the Visegrad states followed suit.[60]

The fundamental rights and duties of citizens were similar in all the constitutions in both scope and structure. For the most part, the rights and duties in the 1936 Soviet Union Constitution could also be found in the constitutions of the Visegrad states and China; even the 1949 Constitution of the Hungarian People's Republic and the

---

[59] Constitution of the People's Republic of China in 1954. Bilingual version. Retrieved June 23, 2021, from http://en.pkulaw.cn/display.aspx?cgid=52993&lib=law. Constitution of Hungarian People's Republic in 1949, English version was published in Budapest, 1953 and supplied by Ministry of Foreign Affairs. Constitution of Czechoslovak Republic in 1948, English version was published in Prague, 1948 by Czechoslovakia Ministry of Information. Constitution of Polish People's Republic in 1952, English original version was published in Warsaw, 1953, reproduction by permission of the Buffalo and Erie county public library.

[60] In Chinese Constitution in 1954, Chapter Three; in Hungarian Constitution in 1949, Chapter Eight; in Czechoslovakia Constitution in 1948, Chapter one of detailed provisions of the Constitution; Polish Constitution in 1952, Chapter Seven regulated the fundamental rights and duties of citizens.

3.3 Comparative Analysis of the Structure and Text of the First …

1952 Constitution of the Polish People's Republic followed the Soviet structure. For example, the first four fundamental rights in the Soviet Union were the rights to work, leisure, assistance for workers in sickness and disability and education. The Hungarian and Polish constitutions followed this order. All the constitutions protected freedom of speech, press, and assembly; asserted the equality of men and women, and required citizens to defend the state. There is no doubt that these constitutions' provisions on citizens' fundamental rights and duties were strongly influenced by the 1936 Soviet Union Constitution.

However, because of the unique social conditions and histories of each state, their constitutions did display some differences in fundamental rights and laws. The 1936 Soviet Union Constitution stated that "citizens of the U.S.S.R. are ensured the right to unite in public organizations–trade unions".[61] The constitutions in the Visegrad states also provided these rights to their citizens. The only exception was the Constitution of the PRC, and there was no similar provision on the right to organize trade unions. However, the Trade Union Law of the PRC was passed in 1950. Public sources do not explain why the 1954 Chinese Constitution deleted this right. However, obviously, trade unions did not play an important role in the history of the PRC compared with in its brother states in Visegrad.[62] Additionally, since the Constitution of the PRC did not have a chapter on the electoral system, universal suffrage was guaranteed in the chapter on citizens' fundamental rights and duties.

Citizens of Czechoslovakia enjoyed more constitutional rights than their socialist comrades in the Visegrad states and China. There was a section of fundamental rights of citizens on personal freedom; according to the provision, Czechoslovakian citizens would not be subject to illegal prosecution, arrest, or custody. The Czechoslovakian constitution was more advanced than those in the other Visegrad states and China. One reason for this advanced position was that Czechoslovakia was more economically developed; the year that the Ninth of May Constitution was adopted, Czechoslovakia was already an industrialized country (Myant, 1989). Moreover, the Ninth of May Constitution used a different structure for the fundamental rights and duties of citizens, appearing to follow that of the 1920 Constitution of the Czechoslovak Republic combined with the 1936 Soviet Union Constitution.[63]

---

[61] Article 126, Constitution of the Union of Soviet Socialist Republics 1936, English version. Retrieved June 23, 2021, from https://constitutii.files.wordpress.com/2013/01/1936-en.pdf.

[62] Trade Union in Hungary, Czechoslovakia and Poland played a very important role during the reform period, the most obvious example was Polish Trade Union, Solidarity in 1980s.

[63] Constitution of the Czechoslovak Republic (1920), English version. Retrieved June 23, 2021, from https://archive.org/details/cu31924014118222.

3.3.2.3 Comparative Analysis of the Supreme Organs of State Power in the First Written Communist Constitutions of China and the Visegrad States

However, the beginnings of the communist constitutions asserted that all the power of the state belonged to the (working) people.[64] Apparently, it was unrealistic to guarantee that everyone could exercise state power in practice; therefore, the highest organ in the state, acting on behalf of the (working) people, would exercise state power. This organ, however, would not be the parliament, since, according to the political philosophy of Marxism-Leninism, "the Commune was to be a working, not a parliamentary, body, executive and legislative at the same time" (Lenin, 1932).

Each socialist state "created" a supreme organ to exercise state power on behalf of the (working) people, although the name of this organ varied by country. In the Soviet Union, it was the Supreme Soviet of the USSR; in the PRC, it was the NPC; in the Hungarian People's Republic, it was referred to by the constitution as the "Országgyűlés" (sometimes translated as National Assembly, sometimes as Parliament); in the Czechoslovak Republic, it was the "Národní shromáždění" (National Assembly); in the Polish People's Republic, following this pattern, it was the "Sejm". These names alone show some of the constitutional drafters' leanings during the process of constitution-making. The communist constitutions in the Visegrad states used their traditional names for their parliaments, even though their masters of communism, Marx and Lenin, declared that parliamentarism should be abolished. In China, the NPC was not a traditional name inherited from the former ruling government[65]; its first use was in the Constitution of the Chinese Soviet Republic, a regional government in China in the 1930s. The Visegrad states maintained parliamentary systems for a long time; however, in China, the history of parliamentarism was shorter, and it was always interrupted by brutal wars.

Although the supreme organ of the state power was to play the same role as parliament, it undertook the role of legislature, passed the annual state budget, elected some officers on different committees, etc. Since the supreme organ of state power in each state only held short sessions each year,[66] a resident organization was needed for daily political life. This organization had almost all the power that the supreme organ of state power held, except for some ultimate powers, such as amending the constitution.

Moreover, in Czechoslovakia and China, the de facto head of state, the President of the Republic, shared some power with the supreme organ of the state power. In Czechoslovakia, since the Ninth of May Constitution was a hybrid of the 1936 Soviet Union Constitution and the 1920 Constitution of the Czechoslovak Republic,

---

[64] In 1936 Soviet Union Constitution, 1949 Hungarian Constitution and 1952 Polish Constitution, "State power belongs to working people". In 1954 Chinese Constitution and 1948 Czechoslovakia Constitution, "State power belongs to the people".

[65] National Assembly was officially regulated in 1947 Constitution of Republic of China, Constitution of Republic of China 1947.

[66] In Visegrad States, it was usually twice per year, in China, it was once per year.

the president's power, which was regulated in the Ninth of May Constitution, was almost the same as that in the 1920 Constitution. In China, the 1954 Constitution also established the position of Chairman of the Republic, although it was intended as a figurehead.

In each state, the supreme organ of state power consisted of deputies, who would be elected. The constitution and the electoral law in each state provided that these elections would be universal, equal, and carried out by secret ballot. Not every country provided for direct elections of the deputies of the supreme organ. In China, NPC elections were indirect, with deputies elected by the provincial-level People's Congress. Deputies from different electoral districts even represented different proportions of inhabitants. According to the 1953 Electoral Law, "in the proportion of one Deputy to 800,000 inhabitants; in Municipality and the city with 500,000 inhabitants, in the proportion of one Deputy to 100,000 inhabitants."[67] This seems unfair because NPC deputies represented different proportions of inhabitants in different electoral districts. Deng Xiaoping, the chief architect of the reform and opening-up policy, stated, "such regulations seem unfair … it guarantees the Deputies to each nation, each class shall correspond with their social status." In 1953, the proportion of urban residents of China's total population was 10.6% (Li, 2007). Most working-class people lived in urban areas, and the constitution asserted, "the People's Republic of China is a people's democratic state led by the working class"[68] To guarantee the leadership of the working class, China's Electoral Law contained such odd provisions.

3.4 Conclusion

This chapter introduces the first communist constitutions of China and the Visegrad states. After the Second World War, the Great Powers divided up Europe into political spheres. The Soviet Union enjoyed overwhelming influence in Eastern Europe, including the Visegrad area. In the mid-twentieth century, states in this region established their socialist sovereignties and created communist constitutions. Almost at the same time, in East Asia, people in the PRC witnessed a similar process in their state with the "help" of the Soviet Union.

The constitution is the fundamental law in modern states, and examining a state's constitution can reveal its ultimate system. The first communist constitutions in China and the Visegrad states were clearly in the Soviet style; however, the different social conditions of each state, especially in economics and politics, made each constitution unique. Using comparative analysis in this chapter, the author concludes that the Visegrad states were much more heavily supervised by the Soviet Union than China and that as a result, the constitutions in this region were more influenced by the 1936 Soviet Union Constitution. However, states in Visegrad had longer histories with

---

[67] Electoral Law of People's Republic of China 1953.

[68] Constitution of People's Republic of China 1954.

the modern concept of democracy, and in some ways, their constitutions were more "open" than the Chinese one and performed better in practice.

References

Antal, T. (2010). Local soviets and councils in the Ex-socialist European states with special regard to Hungary (1950–1990). *Hungarian Studies, 24*(1), 135–166.

Apor, P. (2009). *Fabricating authenticity 1919 and the Hungarian communists between 1949 and 1959* (Doctoral dissertation, Debrecen University, Doctoral School of History and Ethnography, Debrecen, Hungary). Retrieved June 22, 2021, from https://dea.lib.unideb.hu/dea/bitstream/handle/2437/89593/tezis_angol.pdf;jsessionid=47AC29698439DD6C0B4795CC7024B186?sequence=6

Banaszak, B., et al. (2012). *Constitutional law in poland* (1st ed.). Wolters Kluwer

Brzezinski, M. (1998). *The struggle for constitutionalism in Poland* (1st ed.). St. Martin's Press.

Chen, A. (1999). *Restructuring political power in China: Alliances and opposition, 1978–1998* (1st ed.). Lynne Rienner Publishers.

Cholewinski, R. (1998). The protection of human rights in the new polish constitution. *Fordham International Law Journal, 22*(2), 236–291.

Da, L. (2019). The first written communist constitutions in China and Hungary and the influence of the 1936 Soviet constitution: A comparative perspective. *Hungarian Journal of Legal Studies, 60*(2), 209–225.

Ferenc, H., & Lorman, T. (Eds.). (2019). *A history of the Hungarian constitution: Law, government and political culture in Central Europe* (1st ed.), I.B. Tauris.

Frederick, T. C. (2008). Establishment and consolidation of the new regime. In R. Macfarquhar & J. K. Fairbank (Eds.). *The Cambridge history of China, Vol. 14, The People's Republic, Part 1: The emergence of revolutionary China 1949–1965* (1st ed.). Cambridge University Press.

Glaser, K. (1961). *Czechoslovakia: A critical history* (1st ed.), The Caxton Printers, Ltd.

Halasz, I. (2015). The institutional framework and methods of the implementation of soviet legal ideas in the Czechoslovakia and Hungary during Stalinism. *Journal on European History of Law, 6*(2), 29–37.

Han, D. (2004). *1954年宪法与新中国宪政 [The 1954 constitution and the constitutionalism of New China]* (1st ed.). Hunan People's Publishing House.

Izsak, L. (2002). *A political history of Hungary, 1944–1990* (Andrew T. Gane tr, 1st ed.), Eotvos University Press.

Ji, P. (2007). 废除《六法全书》的历史公案[The historical Koan of abrogation of six codes] *Hong Kong Fax, 4*, 1–56.

Lasok, D. (1954). The Polish constitution of 1947 and 1952: A historical study in constitutional law (Doctoral dissertation, LSE). Retrieved June 22, 2021, from http://etheses.lse.ac.uk/112/1/Lasok_The_Polish_Constitutions_of_1947_and_1952.pdf

Lenin. (1918). *Declaration of rights of the working and exploited people*. Retrieved June 22, 2021, from https://www.marxists.org/archive/lenin/works/1918/jan/03.htm

Lenin, V. I. (1932). *State and revolution*. International Publishers.

Li, B. (2007). 逐步实行城乡按相同人口比例选举人大代表[*Gradually achieving the deputy election to national people's congress with the same proportion in rural and urban area*]. National People's Congress website. Retrieved June 23, 2021, from http://www.npc.gov.cn/npc/xinwen/rdlt/rdjs/2007-11/05/content_374368.htm

Li, G. (2010). 存与废、虚与实: 新中国国家主席制度的变迁 [Existing or abolishing, virtual and actual: The Changes of the chairman system of People's Republic of China]. *Beijing Daily* (6 September 2010). Retrieved June 23, 2021, from https://m.sohu.com/n/367756564/

References

Liu, X. (Later Jin, Five Dynasties). *An old book of Tang, Wei Zheng Zhuan*. Retrieved June 22, 2021, from http://www.guoxue.com/shibu/24shi/oldtangsu/jts_075.htm

Mannino, V. V. (1999). *Cold war: When did it start? Why did it start?* (Bachelor thesis, Air University).

Mao Z. (1949, June 30). *On the people's democratic dictatorship: In commemoration of the twenty-eighth anniversary of the communist party of China*. From Selected Works of Mao Zedong. English version is available. Retrieved June 22, 2021, from https://www.marxists.org/reference/archive/mao/selected-works/volume-4/mswv4_65.htm

Marcus, L. P. (2000). The carpathian germans. In S. Wolff (Ed.), *German minorities in Europe: Ethnic identity and cultural belonging* (1st ed., pp. 97–108). Berghahn Books.

Micgiel, J. (1997). Bandits and reactionaries: The suppression of the opposition in Poland, 1944–1946. In N. Naimark & L. Gibianskii (Eds.), *The establishment of communist regimes in Eastern Europe, 1944–1949* (1st ed., pp.93–110). Westview Press.

Myant, M. (1989). *The Czechoslovak economy 1948–1988: The battle for economic reform*. Cambridge University Press.

Peaslee, A. J. (1974). *Constitutions of nations, Volume III- Europe* (Revised 3rd ed.), Springer.

Pepper, S. (1986). The KMT-CCP conflict, 1945–1949. In J. K. Fairbank & A. Albert Feuerwerker (Eds.), *The cambridge history of China, Volume 13, Republican China 1912–1949, Part 2* (1st ed., pp. 723–788). Cambridge University Press.

Skilling, H. G. (1952). The Czechoslovak constitutional system: The soviet impact. *Political Science Quarterly, 67*(2), 198–224.

Solyom-Fekete, W. (1980). Hungary. In B. Simons William (Ed.), *The constitutions of the communist world* (1st ed., pp. 191–214). Springer.

Taborsky, E. (1961). *Communism in Czechoslovakia, 1948–1960*. Princeton University Press.

IBP USA. (2013). *Hungary country study guide, Volume 1 strategic information and developments* (2013 ed.), International Business Publications.

Xu, C. (2003). 中华人民共和国宪法史 *[Constitution history of People's Republic of China]* (1st ed.). Fujian People's Publishing House.

Zhang, J., & Zeng, X. (1979). 中国宪法史略 *[History of the constitution of China]* (1st ed.), Beijing Publishing House.

Zhang, J. (2016). 中国宪法史 *[The history of the Chinese constitution] (Revised ed.)*. China Legal Publishing House.

Zhelitski, B. (1997). Postwar hungary, 1944–1946. In N. Naimark & L. Gibianskii (Eds.), *The establishment of communist regimes in Eastern Europe, 1944–1949* (1st ed., pp. 73–92). Westview Press.

Zhou, H. (1999). 中华人民共和国国史通鉴 *[The history of People's Republic of China]*, vol. 1, no.1, (1st ed.). Red Flag Publishing House.

Chapter 4
Development of the Constitutions of China and the Visegrad States in the Reform Period

Abstract In this chapter, the author will introduce the development of constitution in each State during the reform period, then a comparative analysis of the constitutions in each State will be presented. Besides the constitution in the paper, the author will also compare how the supreme organ of the State power in each State operates in practice, and the last part will be a short conclusion.

In the last chapter, the author described how the constitutional drafters "produced" their work, that is, the constitution of each state, and compared the structure and text of the states' constitutions.

In this chapter, the author discusses the development of constitutions in each state during the reform period and then compares them. The author also compares how the supreme organs of state power operated in practice, ending with a short conclusion.

First, the timing of the reform period should be clarified. In this monograph, this period is viewed as beginning in the mid-1950s in the Visegrad states. In the PRC, it came much later. Here, the author identifies the turning point of the reform period as 1976, the year that the Cultural Revolution ended in China. The author considers the end of the reform period to be the late 1980s, more specifically, before the Revolutions of 1989 in Eastern Europe. "Reform" as a noun means "an improvement, especially in a person's behavior or in the structure of something."[1] Until the collapse of the socialist systems in the Visegrad states, all the changes in society and amendments to the constitutions in each state—the 1956 Revolution in Hungary, the Prague Spring in 1968, Solidarity in Poland in the 1980s, and the collapse of the Cultural Revolution in China in 1976—took place within the socialist framework. Several significant reforms occurred in the socialist regimes.

Two states established new constitutions under communist party rule, the PRC and Czechoslovakia. In Hungary and Poland, although the new constitutions were not drafted by the constitutional committees, some notable amendments were passed by the supreme organ of the state.

---

[1] "Reform", Retrieved June 23, 2021, from http://dictionary.cambridge.org/dictionary/english/reform.

In the following section, the author introduces the development of each state's constitution separately. The Constitution of the PRC is discussed first, and then the Visegrad states are introduced as a group and their constitutional development discussed individually.

4.1 Development of the Constitution of the People's Republic of China in the Reform Period

China's first communist constitution was published in 1954. However, this constitution was short lived. Right after its promulgation, it performed quite well and was followed by the state leadership, CPC and government (Han, 2004; Xu, 2003).[2] However, the "rule of law" did not last long in China. Han Dayuan's book divides the implementation of the constitution into three periods: in the first, from 1954 to 1956, the constitution was fully honored by the state authorities, although the honeymoon between the ruling Party and the constitution or law lasted only two years. After this "harmonious period", conflicts emerged between the ruling government and the constitution from 1957 to 1965, the second period. Constitutional provisions were badly weakened by the ruling Party during this period. The Party introduced numerous movements, and the entire state became fanatical about building a socialist society. This fever simmered for ten years, from 1966 to 1976. With the Cultural Revolution, the 1954 Constitution was completely invalidated, and the whole state was ruled by men (Han, 2004).

During the reform period, the PRC adopted two constitutions in 1978. The second version, the Constitution of the People's Republic of China, was adopted in 1975 as the "achievement" of the Cultural Revolution. However, without introducing the 1975 Constitution, constitutional development in China could not be fully studied. Therefore, the author discusses the 1975 Constitution of the PRC in the reform period.

---

[2] Some leadership of the government and National People's Congress expressed their opinions on the implementation of the Constitution of China in public, for example, in 1955, the vice chairman of the Standing Committee of National People's Congress, Peng Zhen addressed the importance of Constitution in the performance of State power; in the next year, one of the leader of the Chinese Communist Party, Dong Biwu, President of the Supreme People's Court of China made a report in the 8th National Congress of the Communist Party of China, emphasized the importance of law, especially the Constitution. Not only the leaderships declared the importance of Constitution, in the few years after the 1954 Constitution was published, Chinese Constitution was well implemented. Take an example, when the Constitution was promulgated, State organs in the central level were immediately elected according the provisions and principles of 1954 Constitution.

4.1.1 1975 Constitution of the People's Republic of China

Before the reform period commenced in China, the country sustained massive damage from various movements and the Cultural Revolution and sank into chaos, not only in the economic and political arenas but also in the legal system. The country's legal education system ceased functioning as well. Therefore, the 1954 Constitution did not fulfill its functions. In reality, the state functioned without rule of law (Xu, 2003).[3] In this context, the second Constitution of the PRC was passed by the Fourth NPC in 1975, an epilogue to the Cultural Revolution.

During the Cultural Revolution, Mao came up with the idea of drafting a new constitution, since the 1954 Constitution clearly did not fit the current situation. He hoped to change the state structure and eliminate the position of the Chairman of the People's Republic of China; in March 1970, drafting started.

The 1975 Constitution was supposed to be a socialist constitution and would be promulgated in 1970 when the Fourth NPC was held that year. However, events did not unfold as planned, and a series of incidents[4] postponed the convening of the NPC. Therefore, drafting of the constitution was postponed for nearly five years until the Fourth NPC was held in 1975.

On 17 January 1975, the Fourth NPC, with 2864 deputies (2885 in total), passed the 1975 Constitution, which was the second constitution of the PRC.

The 1975 Constitution was much simpler than the 1954 Constitution in words, with only approximately 4000 characters, and articles, with 30 compared with the 106 in the 1954 document. It was clearly less complex and "seasoned with a revolutionary flavor" (Kim, 1981), and it was largely devised by Mao Zedong.[5]

However, the 1975 Constitution followed the basic structure of the 1954 Constitution. It contained a preamble and sections on the general principles; state structure; fundamental rights and duties of citizens; and national flag, national emblem, and capital.[6]

The preamble was the first part of the constitution and included punctuation; it accounted for almost 20% of all the characters in the constitution. It had 8 paragraphs and could be divided into two parts. The first reviewed China's revolutionary history and how the CPC led the people to success in socialist construction after the

---

[3] Highest leader of the Communist Party, also Chairman of People's Republic of China gave a speech in 1958, and he mentioned that "rule of law or rule of man, it seems that mainly rely on (rule of) man, law is only the reference of governing."

[4] Such as the Lin Biao Incident, Lin Biao was the vice Chairman of the Communist Party and official successor of Mao, and Lin's successor position was even regulated in the Party Constitution and the drafting of the 1975 Constitution. The Conflict between Mao and Lin made Lin fled from the Country, Lin died from air crash.

[5] During the drafting period, Mao Zedong brought up his opinion, the Constitution should be simplified and easy to memorize. There was another version of drafting Constitution with 60 Articles, and Mao thought it was too complicated.

[6] Constitution of People's Republic of China, 1975. Chinese version only. Retrieved June 23, 2021, from https://constitutions.albasio.eu/wp-content/uploads/costituzioni/CHN_Constitution_1975_ZH_(Simplified_Chinese).pdf.

establishment of the PRC. The second part was full of political declarations, most of which could be found in the Constitution of the CPC (Xu, 2003).[7]

The general principles was the second part of the 1975 Constitution and included 15 articles. Considering that the entire constitution contained only 30 articles, the overwhelming proportion of general principles demonstrated that the 1975 Constitution was not a normal constitution. It was a political slogan-style constitution.

The first article declared the PRC a socialist state, in contrast to the 1954 Constitution, which declared a "People's Democratic State". The 1975 Constitution officially declared that the Communist Party-ruled state would now be socialist. Article 2 then enshrined the CPC's leadership. It is rare for a constitution to proclaim one political party's ruling role. However, the 1975 Constitution not only gave CPC leadership an important place in the constitution but emphasized it in different places in the document.[8]

The election procedure for each level of the People's Congress was also specified in this section. Article 3 proclaimed that the deputies would be selected by democratic consultation. This seriously weakened the suffrage of citizens.

Regarding the ownership of means of production, the only two listed in the constitution were the people as a whole and collective ownership. The ownership of individual working people and capitalist ownership referenced in the 1954 Constitution were removed (Kim, 1977).

The third part addressed the state structure. The structure of this part was similar to that in the 1954 Constitution, only without a section on the Chairman of the PRC. Since one of the main reasons for creating a new constitution was that Mao Zedong did not want to retain the office of Chairman, it is clear why that section was omitted.

The NPC was still the supreme organ of state power. However, it was led by the CPC (Kim, 1977). This implied that the CPC occupied the highest position in the entire nation. Moreover, this part contained an odd regulation related to the NPC's power. The "National People's Congress is accorded the power… to perform the power which the National People's Congress considers it should have." It seemed that the NPC would enjoy power without limits. The State Council was still the executive organ of the central government.

At the local level, the constitution contained an outcome of the Cultural Revolution, the People's Commune. This was the standing committee of the local People's Congress and the executive organ of local state power. People's Communes were to exist even in the autonomous areas. The last part of state structure concerned the judiciary.

References to the independence of the judiciary and People's Procuratorate system in the 1954 Constitution were deleted, the public security bureau took the role of prosecutor, and the judiciary would mobilize people to criticize severely anti-revolutionary criminal cases.

---

[7] Constitution of Communist Party of China, 1973. Chinese version only. Retrieved June 23, from http://cpc.people.com.cn/GB/64162/64168/64562/65450/4429427.html.

[8] Take an example, there were four places in the Preamble mentioned "the leadership of Chinese Communist Party".

Fundamental rights and duties of citizens were contained in the 1975 Constitution, but it specified fewer rights and duties than the 1954 document. There were 19 articles in the 1954 Constitution, while the 1975 Constitution had only four. Surprisingly, the 1975 Constitution listed a new citizen right, the right to strike. It also listed citizens' duties before their rights. This implied a mentality that citizens should perform their duties rather than enjoy their rights.

The last part of the constitution addressed the national flag, national emblem, and capital. It was similar to the 1954 Constitution. The five-star red flag was the national flag, and the national emblem was "Tiananmen under the light of five stars, framed with ears of grain, and with a cogwheel at the base." The capital was Beijing.[9]

4.1.2 1978 Constitution of the People's Republic of China

In 1976, the Cultural Revolution ceased, and the Gang of Four was captured and prosecuted by the judiciary.[10] Since the highest leadership was changed, the Cultural Revolution-style constitution no longer fit China's political and economic system. Therefore, a new constitution was needed by the ruling Party. Mao Zedong and Zhou Enlai, the most powerful people in China, passed away in 1976. Hua Guofeng became the most powerful person in the Communist Party, and he insisted on following Mao's ruling policies from the Cultural Revolution period. For this reason, the 1978 Constitution did not correct the mistakes of the 1975 Constitution; rather, it continued them.

The 1978 Constitution was not drafted by the Constitutional Drafting Committee but instead by the CPC's Politburo. The draft was read by the 2nd Plenary Session of the 11th Central Committee of the CPC in 1978. In the same year, the 5th NPC was held in Beijing, and the new constitution was passed and promulgated (Xu, 2003).

The 1978 Constitution was a compromise between the 1954 and 1975 constitutions. Its structure followed the tradition, with a preamble and four chapters. The number of articles, 60, also implied balance.

The 1978 Constitution had the "longest" preamble, consisting of 8 paragraphs with 1119 characters in total. Similarly to the preceding constitution, the first two paragraphs reviewed the revolutionary history. In the second paragraph, the Cultural Revolution was still treated as a Party achievement, and it declared that the "People's Republic of China has become a Socialist State with the preliminary of prosperity." There were three particularly noteworthy features. The first was a declaration that Chairman Mao was the founder of the state. The second was a statement that the Cultural Revolution was an achievement of the Party. The third was a stated intent to "liberate Taiwan, unite the State" as a main task for the state (Heer, 1978).[11]

---

[9] Article 30, Constitution of People's Republic of China, 1975.

[10] Gang of Four was considered as the leadership of Cultural Revolution, included Jiang Qing, wife of Mao Zedong, Zhang Chunqiao, Wang Hongwen and Yao Wenyuan.

[11] Constitution of People's Republic of China, 1978.

The first chapter of the constitution was the general principles, which consisted of 19 articles. Most of these remained unchanged from the preceding constitution. However, there were still some significant changes. First, the 1978 Constitution deleted the provision on democratic consultation-based elections of NPC deputies. Second, regarding political articles, although most of the Cultural Revolution-style articles were retained, the expression "see truth from the facts" appeared in Article 16. Later, this expression was used frequently in the debate over whether reform and opening were needed (Heer, 1978).[12] Third, in the socioeconomic articles, the 1978 Constitution restored the statement, "the State protects the rights of citizens to own lawfully earned incomes", which was contained in the 1954 Constitution.[13] Fourth, in the cultural and education articles, the 1978 Constitution deleted a provision on "speaking out freely, airing views fully, holding great debates and writing big-character posters". This Cultural Revolution-period slogan was replaced by the "hundred flowers campaign" policy to encourage the flourishing of culture (Xu, 2003).

Since the 1978 Constitution followed the structure of the previous constitution, chapter two still addressed the state structure. Because the most powerful person in the Party, Hua Guofeng, insisted on following Mao's policy, the office of Chairman of the PRC was not restored.

The NPC was considered the supreme organ of state power, and "under the leadership of the Chinese Communist Party", which was present in the 1975 Constitution, was deleted. However, the election of deputies still followed the democratic consultation principle with secret ballots. The constitution listed the powers given to the NPC, and most could be traced back to the 1954 Constitution, except for that related to the Chairman of the PRC. This is understandable since there was no such position in this constitution. For the same reason, the Chairman of the Standing Committee of the PRC took some of the responsibilities of the Chairman of the PRC.[14]

The State Council continued to play its role as the executive organ of the supreme organ of state power and the central government. Compared with the 1975 Constitution, the State Council gained more power to rule the country; however, some powers that were accorded in the 1954 Constitution were still not restored.

For the local-level People's Congress and Revolutionary Committee, the 1978 Constitution reestablished three levels of local state power: provincial, county and commune. The city level, which was established in the 1975 Constitution, was eliminated, and the township level in the 1954 Constitution became the commune level in the 1978 Constitution. The Revolutionary Committee was one of the vestiges of the Cultural Revolution. This again shows that the 1978 Constitution did not overcome the harm of the Cultural Revolution; therefore, it was not successful.

Regarding government in areas occupied by ethnic minorities, the 1978 Constitution gave two powers of self-government to the national autonomous areas: making

---

[12] Constitution of People's Republic of China, 1978.

[13] In the 1975 Constitution, it was regulated as "The State protects the rights of citizens to own lawfully-labor incomes…".

[14] Constitution of People's Republic of China, 1978.

regulations and using their own language. As in the 1954 Constitution, two powers remained absent: arranging public finance and organizing the public security bureau.

The section on the judiciary reestablished the People's Procuratorate system; however, the relationship between the higher- and lower-level Procuratorates was different from that in the 1954 Constitution. In the 1978 Constitution, the higher Procuratorate supervised the lower one instead of the Party leadership.

People enjoyed more rights in the 1978 Constitution than in the 1975 Constitution. However, two regulations should be noted. The first stated that "citizens enjoyed the right of striking and employ the way of 'speaking out freely, airing views fully, holding great debates and writing big-character posters'" The right to strike was first granted in the 1975 Constitution, and the second right came from a famous slogan from the Cultural Revolution. This again shows that the Cultural Revolution continued to play an important role in China. In the duties part, family planning became a duty of every Chinese citizen.

The last chapter of the 1978 Constitution on the national flag, emblem and capital remained the same as in the 1954 Constitution.

4.1.3 1982 Constitution of the People's Republic of China

Hua's[15] rule did not last long, and Deng Xiaoping gained esteem among the core leadership in China. Whether China continued to maintain the vestiges of the Cultural Revolution was openly debated in the media. In May 1978, an article titled "Practice is the Sole Criterion for Testing Truth" was first published in Theoretical Trends, an internal journal of the Party. Later, a national newspaper, Guang Ming Daily, reproduced the whole article, generating national attention.[16] The same year, the 3rd Plenary Session of the 11th Central Committee of the CPC created one of the most important policies in the history of the PRC, the reform and opening-up policy. This indicated that the leadership of the Communist Party had changed its attitude toward the Cultural Revolution. Deng Xiaoping, later the core figure of the second generation of the Communist Party, ensured his primacy in the state.

In 1982, the 5th Plenary Session of the 5th NPC was held in Beijing, and the most important activity in this session was promulgating the 1982 Constitution. There were 3421 deputies in the NPC, and 3040 attended this session. After a secret ballot, the result was finally announced: 3037 deputies voted in favor, 0 opposed it, and 3 abstained (Xu, 2003).

Before the 1982 Constitution was adopted, the 1978 Constitution was revised. There were two main revisions passed by the NPC, which occurred in the second

---

[15] Hua Guofeng, former Chairman of Chinese Communist Party and former Prime Minister of State Council.

[16] The article "Practice is the Sole Criterion for Testing Truth" is issued on May 10, 1978. Retrieved June 23, 2021, from https://www.chinadaily.com.cn/china/19thcpcnationalcongress/2011-05/10/content_29715401.htm.

and third sessions of the 5th NPC. These two revisions abolished the influence of the Cultural Revolution. The process by which the constitution was revised is also interesting. For example, the second revision was initiated by the Central Committee of the CPC. After it was passed by the committee, this document was sent to the Standing Committee of the NPC, since according to the law, the Central Committee of the CPC did not have the power to submit a bill. The Standing Committee of the NPC passed the resolution and submitted it to the third session of the 5th NPC. Finally, deputies in the session passed the Resolution of Constitution.[17]

The 1982 Constitution finally returned the country to the right track. According to Chiu, "on paper, the 1982 Constitution is far better than any of its predecessors in establishing a certain degree of 'rule of law' in China." (Chiu, 1985).

The 1982 Constitution is also the current constitution. It has 5 parts: a preamble and 4 chapters. The basic structure of the chapters changed only slightly. The fundamental rights and duties of citizens were moved to the second chapter, before state structure.

The preamble contains thirteen paragraphs and four main narratives. The first part consists of 6 paragraphs and mainly reviews the revolutionary history of China. Paragraph seven declares that the essential task of the state will be achieved through four modernizations. The next paragraph emphasizes the importance of class struggle. Paragraph nine deals mainly with the unity of the state and the Taiwan issue. These three paragraphs address the three tasks of the state, which should be carried out by the people with the leadership of the CPC. The following three paragraphs state the three conditions to realize these tasks: patriotic united fronts, harmonious nations, and peaceful global environments. The last paragraph in the preamble emphasizes the need to respect the constitution (Xu, 2003).

Chapter one of the 1982 Constitution is the general principles, which consist of 32 articles. Compared with the 1975 Constitution, which contained only 30 articles, the 1982 Constitution is more detailed. The first article of the constitution is clearly very important. It declares that the PRC is a socialist state, which has been ensured since the 1975 Constitution. In addition, it declares for the first time that the "socialist system is the basic system of the People's Republic of China". Therefore, the whole constitution is based on this primary system. In the political arena, there are no significant changes; however, regarding the economy, some new terms are presented. Article 11 states that the private economy is a component of the socialist public economy. Article 18 provides that foreign enterprises' legal interests are protected by law, and so they have been since 1978. The reform and opening-up policy was established in the state, and attracting foreign investment and developing the Chinese economy became state policy. In culture and education, "building of a socialist society with an advanced culture and ideology" was a new expression in the constitution.[18] One of the potential negative influences of the reform and opening-up was that with the opening of China's door, "bad" influences and ideology would come in. To protect socialist

---

[17] In this resolution, National People's Congress decided to abolish one right of citizens, right to speaking out freely, airing views fully, holding great debates and writing big-character posters, since it was considered as the most famous vestiges from Cultural Revolution.

[18] Article 24, Constitution of People's Republic of China, 1982.

culture and ideology, the constitution emphasizes the importance of socialist culture and ideology. Moreover, Article 19 promotes the nationwide use of Putonghua[19]; the same article states that "the State… universalizes compulsory primary education." Such provisions raised the education level in China and promoted the development of the Chinese economy. During the drafting of the constitution, the reunion of Hong Kong and Macau with mainland China was negotiated, and the special administrative region was established and regulated in the constitution.

This was the first time that the fundamental rights and duties of citizens became the content of the second chapter in the constitutional history of the PRC. This arrangement shows that the government values the rights of citizens. Additionally, the 1982 Constitution ended an argument on the meaning of citizen. According to the text, "all persons holding the nationality of the People's Republic of China are citizens of the People's Republic of China."[20]

Compared with the 1954 Constitution, the current constitution almost restored the rights of citizens granted in the first PRC constitution, except for the freedom of residence and movement. These rights were granted in Article 90 of the 1954 Constitution but disappeared in the 1982 Constitution (Chiu, 1985). It is understood that at that time, the hukou system limited the freedom of residence and movement in China.[21] Additionally, two significant rights of citizens are missing from the current Constitution. The first is the right to strike, which was guaranteed in the 1975 and 1978 constitutions. Neither the NPC nor its Standing Committee provided a reason for this change; in the author's opinion, the government wanted a stable environment for the development of the economy. The second right is that to free speech, air views fully, hold great debates and write large-character posters. As noted above, this right was granted in the 1978 Constitution and considered a vestige of the Cultural Revolution. It was rescinded in 1980.

However, the 1982 Constitution provided some new rights to Chinese citizens. The most significant is in Article 38, which protects citizens' dignity, since during the Cultural Revolution, there were many cases of former leaders and intellectuals being insulted and slandered by the Red Guards.[22] There were also some new duties to perform. For example, citizens must defend the honor and interests of the motherland.

The third chapter covers the state structure, which follows the structure of the preceding constitution. The most significant changes were the restoration of the

---

[19] Putonghua, the standard language in People's Republic of China.

[20] Article 33, Constitution of People's Republic of China, 1982. Before the 1982 Constitution settled this argument, there were different define of citizen. Some of them argued only the person who reached the age of 18 shall be considered as citizen; some of them think that only the person who enjoyed the political rights shall be considered as citizen.

[21] Hukou (household) system is a traditional system in China, government use this system to rule the citizens. Every citizen in China should register in the local government; anyone who wants to resident in other places, especially from rural area to urban area should get the permission from the government. However, now the regulation of Hukou system is much loose.

[22] Red guards were mobilized in the Cultural Revolution period, and usually consisted of students. They insulted the privileged people in the name of revolution.

position of President[23] of the PRC and the creation of a new body, the Central Military Commission (Jones, 1985).

Compared with the previous constitution, the 1982 Constitution contains very detailed provisions on the state structure. Article 64 provides the procedure for modifying the constitution. Article 70 enumerates the specific committees to be established by the NPC. The question of who is in charge of the Chinese military was also resolved in this constitution: The newly established institution is considered the leader of the national military. At the local level, the role of the commune as the local governor was eliminated, and the township became the lowest state power. The regulations of the judiciary are more reasonable; on paper, the People's Courts and the People's Procuratorates are independent and only obligated to the law.

In general, the provisions on the state structure in the 1982 Constitution are much more reasonable than those of previous constitutions and provided favorable conditions for the development of the Chinese economy.

The last chapter of the 1982 Constitution concerns the national flag, national emblem, and capital. It is the same as that of the 1954 Constitution.

4.1.4 Conclusion

In modern countries, the constitution is usually considered the most important legal document in the state. Only after extreme changes in society does a state change its constitution. However, during the eight short years from 1975, the second constitution of the PRC, to the current constitution, which was promulgated in 1982, the world saw three constitutions adopted in the PRC. On the one hand, this shows the dramatic changes that occurred during those years; on the other hand, it also shows that the Communist Party did not take these constitutions very seriously in that period.

The current constitution has been in force since 1982 and amended four times. The continuous constitution demonstrates the stable environment of the PRC. It is also one of the most important reasons that China's economy has been able to grow so dramatically.

---

[23] In Chinese, this position's name is the same, 主席 (Zhu Xi). However, the English version makes the difference. In the 1954 Constitution, it translated as chairman, and in the 1982 Constitution, it translated as president. Not only in the Constitution, in English context, Mao Zhu Xi translated as Chairman Mao, the current leader in China, Xi Zhu Xi usually translated as President Xi.

4.2 Development of the Constitutions of the Visegrad States in the Reform Period

As mentioned in the last chapter, the countries in the Visegrad area established their socialist regimes and promulgated Soviet Union-style constitutions in the late 1940s and beginning of the 1950s.[24]

However, this harmonious socialist scenario did not last as long as the communist leaders expected. In 1953, Stalin, the main designer of the 1936 Soviet Union Constitution (Getty, 1991),[25] passed away. His successor, Nikita Khrushchev, obviously did not agree with Stalin's ruling policies in the Soviet Union. Three years later, the 20th Congress of the Communist Party of the Soviet Union was held in Moscow. The secret speech that Khrushchev gave during this meeting, in which he criticized Stalin, was later released. The shocking news of this decisive speech soon spread from east to west, and all the socialist states and their communist leaders had to respond (Mitrovits, 2014).[26]

In the Visegrad states, the Communist Party also had to deal with de-Stalinization. After the death of Stalin, socialist doctrine from the Soviet Union no longer seemed as strict, and the states in the Eastern Bloc had the chance to practice their own socialist model. At that time, there were two models of socialism, the Soviet Union model and Yugoslavia model. In the Soviet Union's view, it was impossible to allow the Eastern socialists to abandon the Soviet Union model. However, some states in the Visegrad area reformed their societies, and such experimental reforms occurred not only in the economic but also in the legal arenas. Here, the author presents how the constitutions developed in Hungary, Czechoslovakia, and Poland (Mitrovits, 2014).

During the whole reform period, which the author defines as from the mid-1950s to 1988, only Czechoslovakia promulgated a new constitution, and the other two states only passed constitutional amendments. Therefore, the author presents how the constitutional amendments developed in the Hungarian People's Republic and Polish People's Republic and the development of the Czechoslovakian constitution.

---

[24] Czechoslovakia adopted its communist Constitution in 1948; Hungary published its Constitution in the next year; in 1952, the last country in Visegrad States, Poland promulgated its Constitution.

[25] 1936 Soviet Union Constitution, also known as the Stalin Constitution. In many articles, authors refer to Stalin Constitution as 1936 Constitution. For example, in Getty's article, he mentioned both terms "Stalin Constitution" and "1936 Constitution".

[26] In People's Republic of China, when Khrushchev's speech came to China, the leadership had many discussions on it. In Visegrad States, it also caused some debates.

4.2.1 Development of Constitutional Amendments in the Hungarian People's Republic in the Reform Period

Hungary adopted a socialist system in 1949, when the communist constitution was publicly promulgated. It should be acknowledged that the Soviet Union used more influence to "help" the Hungarians choose socialism than Hungary's neighbor, Czechoslovakia (Mitrovits, 2014).[27] Such differences later came up with the different reactions of the states' ruling parties to de-Stalinization, or, more broadly, during the entire reform period.

In the Hungarian People's Republic, several constitutional amendments were adopted by the National Assembly during the reform period. Among them, the amendments of 1972 and 1983 were notable for their significant changes, especially the 1972 amendment (IBP Antalffy, 1981; USA, 2013).[28]

Act 1 of 1972, published in the Hungarian Gazette on 26 April 1972, consisted of a preamble and 10 chapters. It dramatically changed the 1949 Hungarian Constitution, most significantly by officially declaring the Hungarian People's Republic a socialist state. Hungary was not the earliest to do this among the Visegrad states but still earlier than the Polish People's Republic, which officially announced itself a socialist state in 1976, nearly four years later.

At that time, the Hungarian People's Republic had been ruled by the leader of the Hungarian Socialist Workers' Party, Janos Kadar, since 1956 (Romsics, 2010).[29] The whole regime was stable until Kadar lost his position in May 1988.

The 1972 amendment was adopted on 26 April 1972.[30] Compared with the 1949 Hungarian Constitution, which heavily "copied" the 1936 Soviet Union Constitution, the new constitution contained more Hungarian historical continuity (Romsics, 2010). This feature characterized the preamble as well.

At 5 paragraphs, the preamble to the 1972 Constitution was longer than its 1949 predecessor. The first paragraph addressed Hungary's 1000-plus-year history, which was full of suppression and struggle between the rulers and the populace. The narrative of Hungarian history was a new addition. Referencing the country's revolutionary history rationalized the socialist regime with Hungarian historical revolutionary continuity. However, the Soviet Union's "liberation" of the entire state during

---

[27] In Czechoslovakia, the Communist Party was much more employed the democratic tactics to seize power, nevertheless, in Hungarian case Soviet Union had to put more sources interfering in the establishment of socialist regime in Hungary.

[28] There were 49 Constitutional amendments of the 1949 Constitution of Hungarian People's Republic, however, if we only calculate the Constitutional amendments in reform period, until 1988, there were 20 amendments adopted by the National Assembly. Alkotmany modositasok 1949–2009 (Constitutional amendments 1949–2009). Retrieved June 23, 2021, from http://www.sze.hu/~smuk/DoktoriIskola/Alkotm%E1ny/ALK_m%F3dos%EDt%E1sok_1949-2009.doc.

[29] After the Soviet Union's intervention, Revolution of 1956 in Hungary was fall. Nagy Imre left his office and Kadar started his regime in Hungary nearly 32 years.

[30] 1972 Constitutional amendment of Hungarian People's Republic, Hungarian version. Retrieved June 23, 2021, from http://www.sze.hu/~smuk/DoktoriIskola/Alkotm%E1ny/Alk_egyseges_3.pdf.

4.2 Development of the Constitutions of the …

the Second World War also needed to be taken into account, and the next paragraph reviewed how Soviet Union had "helped" Hungary establish the socialist regime. The Hungarian socialist revolutionary tradition also contributed to the establishment of the new state. The history of the 1919 Hungarian Soviet Republic was introduced in the third paragraph.[31]

The 1972 amendment also changed the structure of the constitution from that of the 1949 document. As noted in the last chapter, the 1949 Constitution had 11 chapters, and the 1972 amendment combined the first two chapters into one. Therefore, there were only 10 chapters in the constitution as amended in 1972.[32] The following three chapters covered the National Assembly and the Presidential Council, the Council of Ministers, and the Local Councils. Chapters two, three and four employed more concrete titles than the 1949 Constitution. Nevertheless, the differences in the text of the constitution were not very notable. The rest of the chapter titles in the 1972 amendment followed those in the 1949 Constitution.

The first chapter of the 1972 amendment was dramatically changed. It contained 18 articles, and some new provisions were added. Article 2 officially declared the Hungarian People's Republic an effective socialist state. Also notable, Article 3 announced the leadership of Marxist-Leninist parties in society. The Patriotic People's Front was recognized as an important movement to solve political, economic, and cultural problems. Moreover, unlike the 1949 Constitution, which focused on the economy, the drafters of the 1972 amendment seemed to draw a more comprehensive picture of the social structure, focusing not only on the economy but also social and cultural areas.[33]

The following three chapters focused on state power from the central to the local levels. The supreme organ of state power gained more power. Since there were only two sessions each year for the National Assembly, a standing organ, the Presidential Council, exercised more power than the National Assembly. The Council of Ministers was the executive organ, and the 1972 amendment specified its powers. The Local Council was the local state power. The 1949 Constitution divided the Hungarian territory into four levels: county, district, city, and community. However, the district level was entirely abandoned in 1984 (Antal, 2010).

The courts and the prosecutor's office constituted the judicial system of the Hungarian People's Republic. The Chief Prosecutor was still elected by the National Assembly; however, the term of office changed from six to four years.

The greatest improvement in the rights and duties of citizens came with changing the term "workers" to "citizens". For example, Article 46 of the 1949 Constitution stated that "the Hungarian People's Republic guarantees to the workers the right to rest and to enjoy holidays." A similar provision was included in the 1972

---

[31] Constitutional amendment of Hungarian People's Republic, Hungarian version. Retrieved June 23, 2021, from http://www.sze.hu/~smuk/DoktoriIskola/Alkotm%E1ny/Alk_egyseges_3.pdf.

[32] The first two Chapters in the 1949 Constitution were Hungarian People's Republic and Social structure. In 1972 Constitutional amendment, the first Chapter was Hungarian People's Republic and Social Structure.

[33] For example, regulations on protecting the family, supporting the people indeed and developing science, etc. were stipulated in the Chapter one in 1972 Constitutional amendment.

amendment: "The Hungarian People's Republic guarantees to the citizens the right to rest."[34] Giving certain rights only to certain classes violated the principle of equality. Therefore, the 1972 amendment accorded rights to all Hungarian citizens, marking great progress in the history of the Hungarian constitution in the socialist era.

The section on the electoral system abolished the provision that "enemies of the working people and persons suffering from mental disease are excluded by law from the right to vote."[35] On paper, every citizen of the Hungarian People's Republic finally enjoyed equal suffrage.

The emblem and national flag were changed from those in the 1949 Constitution in amendments in the 1950s, and these changes were continued in the 1972 amendment.

As Hungarian political scientist Istvan Kovacs stated, as quoted by the Hungary Country Guild Study, that "the 1972 amendments brought into harmony the wording of the Constitution and the socialist transformation of the country between 1949 and 1972." (IBP USA, 2013) In the 1972 amendment, the Hungarian People's Republic officially declared itself a socialist state and ensured the fruits of all the constitutional amendments from 1950 to 1972. This suggests that Hungary was seeking its own "socialist road" instead of copying the "Soviet socialist road".

After the 1972 amendment, the Hungarian National Assembly passed another important amendment in 1983. It established a legal organ, the Constitutional Council, which was to protect the constitution in case of any constitutional violation (Csink & Schanda, 2015).[36]

4.2.2 Development of the Constitutional Documents of Czechoslovakia in the Reform Period

Among the countries in the Visegrad area, Czechoslovakia was the earliest to adopt a communist constitution, and its economy was also in first place in the region.[37] During the reform period, several amendments were adopted; however, the most important constitutional document in this period was the 1960 Constitution and its 1968 amendment. The 1960 Constitution officially declared Czechoslovakia a socialist state; the notable amendment, passed eight years later, changed Czechoslovakia from a unitary to a federal state.

In the following section, the author introduces the 1960 Constitution and its 1968 amendment. The Constitution of the Czechoslovak Socialist Republic was adopted by the National Assembly of Czechoslovakia on 11 July 1960. Before it was adopted,

---

[34] Constitution of Hungarian People's Republic 1949 and Amendment to the 1949 Constitution of Hungarian People's Republic, 1972.

[35] Paragraph 2, Article 63, Constitution of Hungarian People's Republic 1949.

[36] Article 1, Amendment to Constitution of Hungarian People's Republic 1983.

[37] According to the table of Maddison project, GPD per capita among Czechoslovakia, Hungary and Poland in communist period, Czechoslovakia was always the first place. The Maddison-Project. Retrieved June 23, 2021, from http://www.ggdc.net/maddison/maddison-project/home.htm.

drafting preparation for the constitution was completed in the state.[38] The significant meaning of this constitution can be found in the preamble and the first chapter. The preamble to the 1960 Constitution solemnly declared that "socialism has triumphed in our country". Chapter one announced that "the Czechoslovak Socialist Republic is a socialist state founded on the firm alliance of the workers, farmers and intelligentsia, with the working class at its head."[39] Therefore, the 1948 Czechoslovakian Constitution, as a framework for the transition from capitalism to socialism, finally achieved its historical task and officially abolished capitalism. Czechoslovakia became the first country in the region to enter the socialist system.

The 1960 Constitution consisted of a preamble and nine chapters. In contrast to the 1948 Constitution, socialism was central to the new constitution. As in other socialist states, the preamble not only was used as political propaganda but also set goals for the future. It was divided into three parts. The first part declared that "we" had achieved the goal of transitioning from a capitalist to a socialist state and that this movement would continue to reach the goal of "an advanced socialist society and gathering strength for the transition to communism." Additionally, it stated Czechoslovakia's diplomatic policy of seeking friendship with other socialist states. The second part of the preamble reviewed the history of the state since 1945 and how the working people had led the transition to a socialist state. The final part exhorted the state to continue socialist construction and achieve the higher goal of a communist state. To encourage people, it also described the wonderful life in communist society, "from each according to his ability, to each according to his needs."[40]

The 1960 preamble abandoned the democratic character of its predecessor. More Marxist-Leninist doctrines were introduced. It appeared to be a standard preamble for a socialist state. In the 1948 Constitution, the preamble began, "We, the Czechoslovak people." However, that in the 1960 Constitution was revised to "We, the working people of Czechoslovakia." The classic statement in Marxism-Leninism was also contained in the preamble. For example, the guiding principle of socialism, "from each according to his ability, to each according to his work," and the principle of communism were cited in the previous paragraph.

The 1948 Constitution had a unique structure among those of socialist states in the region. The 1960 Constitution abandoned this unique character, and its structure was much more similar to other socialist states' constitutions. The first chapter concerned the social order. It established the principles of the state, and the term "working people" replaced "people", which appeared frequently in the 1948 Constitution. For instance, the 1960 Constitution declared that all the power of the Republic belonged to working people, while the 1948 Constitution stated that state power would belong to the people. Of course, as a socialist state, most people in Czechoslovakia were

---

[38] The drafted version Constitution firstly presented to the central committee of the Party in April of 1960, then, a nationwide discussion was held in May and June, finally it submitted to the National Assembly, and adopted. See Skilling (1962).

[39] Constitution of Czechoslovak Socialist Republic 1960 (English version, third edition was published by Orbis, Prague, 1964).

[40] Ibid.

"working people"; however, the 1960 Constitution officially established that the minority who did not belong to the "working people" were subordinated to the majority "working people".

The second chapter enumerated the rights and duties of citizens, which still seemed numerous. However, the narrative of these provisions was full of the socialist character. "Working people", as the leaders of the state, enjoyed the rights guaranteed by the constitution. However, citizens were to exercise these rights in accordance with socialist interests.

While the political institutions in the 1960 Constitution were fully retained, the new constitution made some slight changes. Since the power of the President of the Republic was reduced, the National Assembly, which was recognized as the supreme organ of state power, expanded its power. For instance, it could not only pass the new constitution but also supervise its implementation. Meanwhile, the powers of the President of the Republic were reduced. The provision in the 1948 Constitution allowing the president to dissolve the National Assembly was now eliminated (Skilling, 1962). In the government, the most important change was a socialist premise introduced to the public. The activities of the government were to fit the purpose of "fulfilment of the economic and cultural tasks of socialist construction, the raising of the standard of living of the working people, strengthening of the country's security, and pursuance of a peaceful foreign policy."[41] Slovakia was still considered an autonomous area; therefore, the Slovakia National Council, the national organ of state power, enjoyed some privileges granted by the constitution. The central government reduced the powers of the Slovakian national organ as a whole from those in the 1948 Constitution. However, the 1960 Constitution strengthened the power of the Slovakian National Council. In the former constitution, there were three national organs in Slovakia. However, the 1960 Constitution abolished the Board of Commissioners, and the Slovakia National Council became the core organ in Slovakia. At the local level, the national committee was designed as an administrative organ. The 1960 Constitution expanded the power of the national committees (Skilling, 1962). However, as a socialist constitution, it focused more on its socialist character. Again, it used the term "working people" instead of "people".

Czechoslovakia's judiciary followed the Soviet pattern. It consisted of two organs: courts and prosecutors' offices. The 1960 Constitution specified that judicial organs should serve the socialist system. Moreover, judges at different levels would be elected by the National Assembly or national committee. Judgeships were no longer permanent positions.

The entire chapter on the economic system was deleted in the 1960 Constitution, and specific provisions on the national flags and emblems were included.

The 1960 Constitution was later amended several times, until the split of Czechoslovakia in 1992. Among these amendments, the most important was the

---

[41] Article 68, Constitution of Czechoslovak Republic 1960.

4.2 Development of the Constitutions of the …

Act of 143 in 1968 (hereafter referred to as the 1968 amendment) (Simons, 1980).[42] It officially declared that Czechoslovakia was a federal state.

After tanks were sent to Prague by the Soviet Union and the communist military organization the Warsaw Pact in August 1968, the most important reform in Czechoslovakia, "Prague Spring", ultimately failed. The same year, the National Assembly of the Czechoslovakia Socialist Republic adopted a new constitutional amendment on October 27, in which unitary Czechoslovakia became a federal state.

The most important provisions in the 1968 amendment also focused mainly on the conditions at the federal level, such as introducing a bicameral legislature and allowing each state to have its own National Assembly. In addition, a constitutional supervisor organ, the Constitutional Court, was introduced in the 1968 amendment (Cutlert & Schwartz, 1991).

The 1968 amendment consisted of one declaration and eight chapters. The declaration noted the 50 years of cooperation between the two nations and the voluntary federation between them. Following the history of the Czechoslovakian constitution, it is interesting to see how the narrative of the relationship between Czechs and Slovaks changed so dramatically. In the first constitution, which was adopted in 1920, Czechs and Slovaks were considered one nation, and now, in 1968, the constitution recognized that they were different nations.

The 8 chapters in the 1968 amendment focused mainly on state power and constitutional courts. It should be acknowledged that the Czech region always had the dominant position in the country regardless of politics and economics. Therefore, the federation provisions in the amendment greatly expanded Slovakia's political power.

On paper, the Czech Republic and the Slovak Republic shared the same power in the country. The Czech Republic governed the Czech territory, and the Slovak Republic governed the Slovakian territory. Prague was the capital city of the federal country, and it was also the capital of the Czech Republic. However, the capital city of Slovakia was Bratislava, the current capital of Slovakia.

The federal assembly was the supreme organ of the federal state. However, to protect Slovakia's ability to govern in Slovakian territory, there were two houses created at the federal level: the House of the People and the House of Nations. The first house consisted of 200 deputies, who were elected by a proportion of the population. The Czech region therefore had more deputies due to its larger population. The House of Nations consisted of 150 deputies and was divided into two parts for each nation. Seventy-five deputies would be elected from the Czech Republic, and the remaining 75 would be elected from the Slovak Republic.

Another constitutional institution created by the 1968 amendment was the Constitutional Court. As Article 86 of the 1968 amendment stated, "the Constitutional Court

---

[42] In reform period, there were six amendments adopted by the National Assembly, then new amendments adopted in 1989–92. Although, Act of 143 in 1968 was considered as the most important amendment, the other amendments still did a great change, for example, Act of 144 in 1968 mainly focus on the right of minorities in Czechoslovakia. Act of 143 in 1968, English version. Retrieved June 23, 2021, from http://czecon.law.muni.cz/content/en/ustavy/1968/.

of the Czechoslovak Socialist Republic is a judicial organ for the protection of constitutionality." At the federal level, the Constitutional Court consisted of 12 members, four of whom were substitutes. With the same consideration, to protect the rights of Slovakia, the 1968 amendment provided for four judges; two substitutes would be elected by the citizens of the Czech Republic, and the remaining members would be citizens of Slovakia. Additionally, each republic would organize a Constitutional Court.

The 1968 amendment divided state power into two republics. Slovakia enjoyed more power now according to the amendment. However, in practice, the federal government still controlled the entire state through the Communist Party. The Constitutional Court, which was supposed to protect constitutionality, was not set up (Cutlert & Schwartz, 1991).

4.2.3 Development of Constitutional Amendments in the Polish People's Republic in the Reform Period

The last country in the region was the Polish People's Republic, which adopted its communist constitution in 1952, and by 1989, 17 amendments had been passed by the Sejm, Poland's highest state organ (Brezezinski & Garlicki, 1995). Beginning in the 1970s, amendments to the 1952 Constitution slightly expanded citizens' civil rights, and more socialist characteristics were also introduced to the constitution. Among these significant changes, the 1976 amendment was the most important. It officially made the Polish People's Republic a socialist state, as its neighboring states had done earlier.

In the following section, the author introduces the 1976 amendment and how it changed the structure and text of the 1952 Constitution.

The 1976 amendment made numerous changes to the 1952 Constitution. It was believed that nearly one-third of the provisions changed after the 1972 amendment.[43] This amendment consisted of a preamble and 11 chapters. Compared with the 1952 Constitution, an additional chapter was included.[44] Moreover, the new version of the constitution included more articles.

The largest change in the 1976 amendment was that it officially declared the Polish People's Republic a socialist state. This was declared in the first article of the amendment's first chapter, which covered the political system. This chapter also introduced new elements to the populace. First, the Polish United Workers' Party ensured its leading position in the state. It was the "guiding political force of society

---

[43] Poland, The Constitution of 1952. Retrieved June 23, 2021, from http://www.country-data.com/cgi-bin/query/r-10729.html.

[44] Chapter 4 in the 1976 amendment introduced a new organ to masses, supreme board of control. Amendment to Constitution of Polish People's Republic, 1976, English version. Retrieved June 23, 2021, from http://libr.sejm.gov.pl/tek01/txt/kpol/e1976.html.

4.2 Development of the Constitutions of the …

in building socialism." The mechanism of the National Unity Front was established for the purpose of consolidating the leading power of the Party.

In the section on state power, the 1976 amendment followed the structure of the 1952 Constitution. The highest organ of state power was the Sejm (or Diet). The Council of Ministers and its individual members were the highest administrative organs in the state, and they were appointed by the Sejm. At the local level, there were People's Councils at different levels. The Court and Public Prosecutor's Office constituted the judicial system in Poland. In addition, the 1976 amendment created a new organ to supervise state administration at the central and local levels.

However, the state power section also made some changes. For example, the number of deputies of the Sejm was set at 460. The Council of State, the standing organ of the Sejm, was entitled "to watch over the constitutionality of laws" (Garlicki, 1988). The Supreme Board of Control, the new organ, was to supervise the state administration activities and monitor activity in the non-socialized and socialized economies, and it was subordinated to the supreme organs of state authority and administration. A new member of the Council of Ministers was established, the Chairman of the Supreme Board of Control. The terms of the People's Councils were no longer unlimited and would instead be regulated by law. The Court and the Public Prosecutor's Office were still seen as protectors of the achievement of a socialist system. However, judges would be appointed by the Council of State rather than elected.

In the section on citizens' rights and duties, there was one notable new right and duty: the right to benefit from the natural environment and the duty to protect it. This environmental provision was a creative element of the 1976 amendment. It showed the advancement of Polish legislative technique, although the environment was the object and not the subject.

The principle of electoral law remained unchanged in these two constitutions. In the section on the coat of arms, colors, national anthem and capital, the national anthem of the Polish People's Republic was changed to Mazurek Dąbrowskiego (Polish is not yet lost). Moreover, this section now contained a provision on respect for and special protection of the coat of arms, colors, and national anthem.[45]

In addition to the 1976 amendment, several other amendments were adopted by the Sejm. For instance, the Supreme Board of Control was transferred from the Council of Ministers to the Sejm to reduce the influence of the Polish United Workers' Party over the Sejm in 1980. Two important organs were created in the 1982 amendment—the Constitutional Tribunal and the State Tribunal—with the purpose of implementing the rule of law. In 1987, another important organ was introduced to the masses, the People's Ombudsman. Moreover, several times, the provision on martial law was halted and again put into force by the amendments.[46]

---

[45] Constitution of Polish People's Republic 1952. English version. Retrieved June 23, 2021, from http://libr.sejm.gov.pl/tek01/txt/kpol/e1952a-spis.html. The 1976 amendment of the Constitution of Polish People's Republic. English version. Retrieved June 23, 2021, from http://libr.sejm.gov.pl/tek01/txt/kpol/e1976.html.

[46] Poland, The Constitution of 1952. Retrieved June 23, 2021, from http://www.country-data.com/cgi-bin/query/r-10729.html.

4.2.4 Conclusion

With the development of socialist construction, states in the Visegrad region declared the establishment of socialist states in their constitutional documents in succession. While the first communist constitutions in these states heavily followed the 1936 Soviet Union Constitution, the development of the constitutions in these countries reached different levels. Each state sought its own path of socialist construction, and the same was true of their constitutional development. In the beginning, an increasing number of provisions with socialist characteristics were included in the constitutional documents, and as the Visegrad states developed in the reform period, the influence granted to the Communist Party over state power in the constitutions gradually weakened. Organs to monitor constitutionality were established in each state and regulated in constitutional amendments.

In general, the development of constitutions in the Visegrad states in the reform period could be characterized as on a path to the Western-style constitutional tradition or as hearkening back to their historical traditions. Countries in the region had historically tended to practice and follow the European legal system. This constitutional development in the reform period ultimately caused the 1989 Revolutions and the collapse of socialism in the region.

4.3 Comparative Analysis of the Development of the Constitutions of China and the Visegrad States in the Reform Period

In this last part, the author compares the development of constitutions in China and the Visegrad states in the reform period. During this period, the most significant change in these countries was that they all successively declared themselves socialist states in their constitutions.[47] With this establishment of socialist systems, an increasing number of provisions of a socialist character were included in constitutional documents. However, there were still differences between China and the Visegrad states and even within the Visegrad region itself. Therefore, in the following section, the author analyzes the similarities and differences among China and the Visegrad states.

---

[47] People's Republic of China announced it in the 1975 Constitution, Czechoslovakia announced it in the 1960 Constitution, Hungarian People's Republic adopted the amendment to Constitution which included the socialist state provision in 1972 and Polish People's Republic adopted the similar provision of amendment to Constitution in 1976.

4.3.1 Similarities

The reform period defined in this work began in the mid-1950s and ended in 1988, one year before the Revolutions of 1989. Over 30 years, constitutional development in each state presented one trend. That is, each state sought to eliminate the influences from the Soviet Union and establish its own road to socialism.

In the last chapter, the author discussed the influence of the 1936 Soviet Union Constitution on each state's first communist constitution. Each state more or less copied the structure and people's democracy-style provisions of the 1936 Soviet Union Constitution, and the Soviet Union was treated as the big brother in the socialist family.

However, the harmonious atmosphere in the socialist community did not last long. With the de-Stalinization movement in the mid-1950s, countries increasingly sought their own way to develop socialism. This trend in each state caused deep changes in society, and ultimately, these changes were ensured by the supreme organ of state power and even formalized in constitutional amendments in some countries, such as China. Czechoslovakia actually adopted a new constitution.

The friendship between China and the Soviet Union ended at the beginning of the 1960s (Hao, 2003). In the Visegrad states, different grassroots revolutions against the hegemony of the Soviet Union took place in the reform period, and some Party leaders had different ideas for developing socialism from the Soviet Union.[48] Such conflicts with the Soviet Union ultimately reflected the ruling policies of the Party in each state. Developing its own road to socialism gradually became the consensus in each state. Although the Visegrad states were generally controlled by the Soviet Union, some changes still occurred in the reform period. In China, developing its own socialist system inevitably caused changes. Some of the more significant changes ultimately became constitutional provisions in each state.

In China, after the break with the Soviet Union, a series of movements were instigated by the CPC; among them, the Cultural Revolution had the strongest influence. Two constitutions, in 1975 and 1978, were results of the Cultural Revolution to some extent. The 1975 Constitution obliterated the normal political system and civil rights of Chinese citizens, and the 1978 Constitution reintroduced some of these but retained the vestiges of the Cultural Revolution.

In the Visegrad states, developing their own socialist roads also caused changes, albeit differently from in China. Some democratic traditions were restored to the political field to protect constitutionality and citizens' civil rights. For instance, the Hungarian People's Republic used the term "citizen" instead of "worker", Czechoslovakia created its Constitutional Court in the 1968 Constitutional amendment, and

---

[48] During the reform period, revolutions happened all the time in the Visegrad states. In Hungary, 1956 Revolution was suppressed by Soviet Union. In the same year, an uprising broke out in Poznan, a city in Poland, and finally failed because of the suppression of the government. In Czechoslovakia, Prague spring failed after the Soviet Union and Warsaw Pact's tank enter the capital of Czechoslovakia in 1968.

a similar provision (on the Constitutional Tribunal) could be found in the 1982 Constitutional amendment in Poland.

Another notable similarity was that each state declared itself a socialist state and enshrined this in its constitutional documents. As a result, some socialist-style provisions were also adopted by supreme organs of state power in each state.

The 1975 Constitution of the PRC first announced that "China is a socialist state". Although it contained only 30 articles, some socialist principles still existed. Article 9 stated, "the state shall carry out… 'from each according to his ability, to each according to his work' socialist principle".[49]

In Hungary, the 1972 amendment kept the socialist principle "from each according to his ability, to each according to his work", taken word for word from the 1936 Soviet Union Constitution.[50]

The same phenomenon occurred in Poland; the 1952 Polish Constitution contained the same socialist principle in Article 14, and the 1976 amendment kept it.

The Czechoslovakian constitution even went slightly further. The 1948 Constitution did not contain such socialist principles. However, the 1960 Constitution specified the path of socialist construction. At the socialist level, the principle was "from each according to his ability, to each according to his work". At the higher level, that is, the communist level, the principle was "from each according to his ability, to each according to his needs", since with economic development, the materials in society could meet people's needs (Marx, 1970).[51]

During the reform period, the ruling party in each state also legitimated its leading position by enshrining it in the constitution. In China, Article 2 of the 1975 Constitution declared, the "Chinese Communist Party is the leadership core of all Chinese people". Article 3 of the 1972 Hungarian amendment stated, the "Marxist-Leninist workers' Party is the dominant power". Czechoslovakia and the Polish People's Republic had similar declarations in their constitutional documents. The 1960 Czechoslovakian Constitution called the Communist Party of Czechoslovakia the guiding force in society and the state (Article 4). Article 3 of the 1976 amendment to the Polish constitution stated that "the Polish United Workers' Party shall be the guiding political force of society in building socialism" in the Polish People's Republic.

---

[49] Article 9, Constitution of People's Republic of China, 1975.

[50] This socialist principle original came from 1936 Soviet Union Constitution, in the Article 12 of Chapter One, and it copied by the Constitution of Hungarian People's Republic in 1949 (Paragraph 4, Article 9), and it kept in the 1972 amendment (Paragraph 4, Article 14).

[51] This idea of communist principle can be found in Marx's Critique of the Gotha Program.

4.3.2 Differences

Because China and the Visegrad states were socialist states, there were some similarities in their constitutions during the reform period. They followed the Marxist-Leninist doctrines and enshrined those principles in their constitutions. The communist parties legitimated their ruling position in the constitutions and sought their own roads to socialism.

However, there were still some differences since each country had its own history, economy, politics, and leadership. Over 30 years of constitutional development in China and the Visegrad states, each state adopted numerous constitutional documents, and it is almost impossible to analyze all those changes in a few paragraphs. Therefore, in the following section, the author analyzes the main constitutional developments in the political and economic arenas. The societal context in each state during the reform period is presented first.

The PRC developed its own constitutional practices according to its social movements. Many movements initiated by the Communist Party, including the Great Leap Forward and the Cultural Revolution (CIA, 1967; Palese, 2009),[52] led to political fanaticism in the entire state. This fanaticism finally cooled after the 3rd Plenary Session of the 11th Central Committee of the CCP at the end of 1978.[53] After this meeting, a new constitution was adopted in 1982, and the road to socialism in China was gradually normalized.

The situation in the Visegrad states was different. Although many protests and even revolutions occurred during the reform period in each state, the Soviet Union was still supreme in this area. The Warsaw Pact was established to neutralize the threat from NATO (CIA, 1965).[54] However, the constitutional development in the region took a more democratic direction.

In the political arena, although the Visegrad states joined the Soviet group, the development of their constitutions was more democratic than in China. For instance, during the reform period, new institutions were introduced in their constitutional amendments to protect constitutionality in each state.

---

[52] Great Leap Forward (大跃进) a social movement started in 1958 in order to accelerate the development of economy in China, and failed in 1961. Cultural Revolution officially initiated in 1966 and it was considered as the most tragic moment during the reform period.

[53] 3rd Plenary Session of the 11th Central Committee of CCP (十一届三中全会), held in 1978, during this meeting, reform and opening-up policy established and "two whatevers" policy abolished.

[54] In Hungary, mainly university student participated in the 1956 Revolution, In Czechoslovakia, the famous Prague spring failed in the late summer of 1968, Polish had Poznan uprising in 1956 and development of trade union latterly became the solidarity movement in 1980s. Warsaw Pact established in 1955 in Warsaw. NATO, North Atlantic Treaty Organization established in 1949 by US and Countries in Western Europe. The official website of NATO. Retrieved June 23, 2021, from .https://www.nato.int/nato-welcome/index.html#events.

In Hungary, a Constitutional Council was created in Act 2 in 1983 to protect constitutionality.[55] In Czechoslovakia, an organ to protect the constitution was established in the 1968 amendment to the 1960 Constitution, with chapter six creating the Constitutional Court in the Federal Republic.[56] However, until the Revolutions of 1989, this organ was never truly established due to the failure to adopt the implementing laws (Visser, 2014). Similarly, in Poland, the Constitutional Tribunal was created in 1982. However, since the implementing law was not adopted until 1985, this constitutional organ did not begin operating until that year (Blokker, 2014).

In China, the development of the constitution was much more complicated. After three years of implementation, the 1954 Constitution was gradually invalidated in the mid-1950s, and after that, the state was ruled by men for almost 20 years (Xu, 2003). After the Cultural Revolution and the 3rd Plenary Session of the 11th Central Committee of the CCP, the principle of rule of law became the consensus among the leadership. The 1982 Constitution restored the political structure established in the 1954 Constitution.[57] Therefore, during the reform period, China's constitution did not achieve great progress in the political arena.

Regarding the economy, states in the Visegrad region had long histories of practicing capitalism before joining the Eastern Bloc. All were very tolerant of private property in their constitutions. In Hungary, the 1972 amendment stated that the "Hungarian People's Republic recognizes and protects private property".[58] The Czechoslovakian Constitution protected "the citizen's personal ownership of consumer goods, particularly articles of personal and domestic use, family houses, as well as savings derived from labor."[59] The Polish constitution stated that "the Polish People's Republic shall recognize and protect—on the basis of the law—individual property and the right to inherit land, buildings and other means of production owned by peasants, craftsmen and home-workers."[60] The Chinese government treated private property more strictly than before. The 1975 and 1978 constitutions contained the same provision on private property: "The state protects lawful income, saving, house and ownership of other consumer goods." In the 1982 Constitution, the term "consumer goods" was changed to "lawful property". During the reform period, there

---

[55] Act of 2, 1983 or 1983 amendment. It adopted in December 27 of 1983. This Act was Published by Hungarian Gazette (Magyar Kozlony) in the same day.

[56] Act of 143 of Constitution of Czechoslovak Socialist Republic of 1968. English version. Retrieved June 23, 2021, from http://czecon.law.muni.cz/content/en/ustavy/1968/.

[57] The 1975 and 1978 Constitution were more like utopian experiments in socialist China, it damaged the political tradition which established in the 1954 Constitution. With the enthusiasm finally cooled down, the 1982 Constitution reconstructed the political system in China by restoring the 1954 Constitution's political tradition.

[58] Article 11, Amendment to Constitution of Hungarian People's Republic, 1972.

[59] Paragraph 1, Article 10, Constitution of Czechoslovakia, 1960.

[60] Article 17, Amendment to Constitution of Polish People's Republic, 1976.

was a clear boundary between personal consumer goods and personal means of production. The latter only belonged to the state or group (Fan, 2004).[61]

In addition, collective farms in rural areas in China were "better" developed than in the socialist states in the Visegrad region. At the end of 1958, over 99% peasants had joined the rural People's Commune (Xinhua News Agency, 2009). Even in the 1975 Constitution, the rural People's Commune was considered the integrated organ of administration and economic management, and land was considered owned by the state or collective.[62] However, in the Visegrad states, rural land policies were more tolerant. It was possible for peasants to own land (Swain, 1996).

During the reform period, each country's constitution changed significantly. Some of the changes were similar, as all the states declared themselves socialist by adopting new constitutional documents. However, some differences can be identified in the states' constitutional development. The development of China's constitution during the reform period was more like an irrational social experiment, ultimately returning to the original 1954 Constitution. However, the development of constitutions in the Visegrad states inclined toward democracy.

4.4 Comparative Analysis of the Supreme Organs of State Power in China and the Visegrad States

As noted several times in the previous section, the Soviet Union was the big brother of the socialist states, and its political structure affected other socialist states, including China and the Visegrad states.

According to the Soviet Union's Constitution (1936 and 1977 versions), "the highest organ of state authority of the U.S.S.R. is the Supreme Soviet of the U.S.S.R."[63] China and the Visegrad states followed this political model and created similar organs in their constitutions. In the following section, the author discusses and compares the development of the supreme organ of state power in each country.

---

[61] Amendment to Constitution of People's Republic in 2004 changed this provision, "Citizens' lawful private property is inviolable." It showed that as an individual, it allowed to own means of production.

[62] Article 7, Constitution of People's Republic of China, 1975. And the provision of land until the current Constitution in China still regulated as only owned by state or collective.

[63] Article 30, Constitution of USSR, 1936. The 1977 Constitution of USSR regulated the same regulation in Article 108. English version of 1936 USSR Constitution. Retrieved June 23, 2021, from https://www.departments.bucknell.edu/russian/const/1936toc.html. Also, The 1977 Constitution of USSR is available. English version. Retrieved June 23, 2021, from http://www.departments.bucknell.edu/russian/const/1977toc.html.

4.4.1 Development of the National People's Congress of the People's Republic of China

When the PRC was established, its founding fathers designed a Soviet Union-style political system and enshrined it in the constitutional document the Common Program.[64] The document stated, that "the supreme organ of the state authority is National People's Congress." After the first NPC election, the NPC deputies passed the Constitution of the PRC in 1954.

The first section of chapter two of the 1954 Constitution officially ensured the position of the NPC as "the supreme organ of the state authority". In addition, it was the "only legislative authority in the country". The term of the NPC was four years, and there was one regular meeting each year. The NPC exercised its power by holding the meeting, at which it was empowered to amend the constitution and enact laws, elect or decide certain important officers in the state, such as Chairman and Premier, and remove these officers. On the economy, it could create and oversee the national economic plan, the state budget and financial reports. The permanently acting body of the NPC was the Standing Committee. It was empowered to interpret the laws and install or remove certain important officers, such as the Vice President of the Supreme People's Court, and handle foreign relations. In special situations, it could decide to mobilize the military or declare martial law in some areas or the entire state.[65]

The 1975 Constitution severely damaged the political system due to the influence of the Cultural Revolution. However, the NPC was still considered the supreme state organ on paper. The "supreme organ of state authority" was under the leadership of the CPC. The term of the NPC was extended to five years. Since the position of Chairman of the PRC was eliminated, the NPC would appoint the Premier according to the advice of the CPC's Central Committee. The Standing Committee was the permanently acting body of the NPC, but its powers were reduced.[66]

The 1978 Constitution partially restored the powers of the NPC and its Standing Committee as included in the 1954 Constitution. However, there were still some differences. For instance, NPC deputies were elected by democratic consultation. The NPC would supervise the enforcement of the constitution and the law. The Standing Committee would interpret not only the law but also the constitution.[67]

The current Constitution developed the structure of the NPC, which was created by the 1954 Constitution. The provisions in the new Constitution are more accurate. For example, the Standing Committee shall "enact and amend statutes with the exception of those which should be enacted by the National People's Congress", and the power to supervise the enforcement of the Constitution is transferred to the Standing Committee. Additionally, the current Constitution pays more attention to

---

[64] Paragraph 2, Article 12, Common Program 1949.

[65] Section 1, Chapter 2, Constitution of People's Republic of China, 1954.

[66] Section 1, Chapter 2, Constitution of People's Republic of China, 1975.

[67] Section 1, Chapter 2, Constitution of People's Republic of China, 1978.

NPC deputies; deputies cannot be prosecuted related to their speeches and votes during meetings, which provides the legal conditions for the deputies to fulfill their duties and exercise their rights.[68]

4.4.2 Development of the National Assembly of the Hungarian People's Republic

After its election in 1949, the National Assembly adopted a new Constitution since the Communist Party had won. In the Soviet-style Constitution, the National Assembly was the supreme organ of state authority in the Hungarian People's Republic.[69] Its term was four years. Two regular meetings would be held each year. The National Assembly had the powers to enact laws; elect some officers; and make decisions on war, and peace and amnesty. On the economy, it would devise the national economic plan and state budget. In special situations, the National Assembly could dissolve itself or prolong its term.

Since the Constitution of Hungary did not provide for a position of President of the State, the Presidential Council, the permanently acting body of the National Assembly, had some powers of the head of state, such as "appointing diplomatic representatives and receiving the letters of credence of foreign diplomatic representatives." Twenty-one members constituted the Presidential Council—one president, two vice presidents, one secretary and 17 members—and they would be elected by the National Assembly. Since the National Assembly was not a permanently acting body, the Presidential Council took a more active role in the political life of the People's Republic. When the National Assembly was not in session, the Presidential Council could exercise its powers, except for amending the Constitution.[70] In reality, the Presidential Council became the de facto legislative organ by publishing the decree. It could also be considered the constitutional protection organ because Article 20, paragraph 2 stated that the "Presidential Council may annual or modify by law, regulation or measure, in the case of infringe of the Constitution."

The electoral procedures for deputies of the National Assembly were also specified in the 1949 Constitution; Hungarian citizens were entitled to vote and could be elected as members of the National Assembly. The elections would be universal, equal, and direct and conducted by secret ballot. However, "enemies of the working people" would be excluded from suffrage.[71]

---

[68] Section 1, Chapter 2, Constitution of People's Republic of China, 1982.

[69] Orszaggyules, this Hungarian word literally means "country assembly". However, since the different translation, in some English version of Constitution of Hungarian People's Republic, it translated as National Assembly, in other version, it translated as Parliament.

[70] Article 20, Paragraph 4, Constitution of Hungarian People's Republic, 1949.

[71] Article 63, Paragraph 2, Constitution of Hungarian People's Republic, 1949.

4.4.3 Development of the National Assembly of the Czechoslovak Republic

The 1948 Constitution of the Czechoslovak Republic is considered the country's first communist constitution. However, as noted in the previous chapter, it was more like a hybrid of the 1920 Constitution and the Soviet Union Constitution. Therefore, more Czechoslovakian political traditions remained in the 1948 Constitution.

In the 1948 Constitution, the National Assembly was only considered the supreme organ of legislative power,[72] unlike in other countries in the region or China, where it enjoyed more power and was regarded as the supreme organ of state power. The term of the National Assembly was six years, and there were two general sessions each year: the spring session in March and the autumn session in October. Deputies were protected by the constitution while they fulfilled their mandate. Czechoslovakia kept the position of President of the Republic, who could summon or dissolve the National Assembly. The most important task of the National Assembly was passing laws. It could also enact the state budget law and audit the state account. The Presidium was the permanently acting body for the National Assembly and consisted of 24 members. When the National Assembly was not in session, the Presidium could exercise some of its powers.[73]

The 1948 Constitution changed significantly in 1960, when it officially declared Czechoslovakia a socialist state. In the 1960 Constitution, the National Assembly was considered "the supreme organ of state power".[74] It contained three hundred deputies with four-year terms. There were two regular sessions each year. Compared with the 1948 Constitution, the 1960 Constitution gave more powers to the National Assembly, since it was no longer the only legislative organ. The President of the Republic would be elected by the National Assembly and take responsibility for it. The National Assembly would have the power to declare war. The Presidium of the National Assembly was also expanded, and its 30 members would be elected by the National Assembly.

The Constitution of the Czechoslovak Republic changed dramatically again in 1968 when the socialist state became a federal state. In the new constitution, the Federal Assembly became "the supreme organ of state power", and it consisted of two houses, the House of the People and the House of Nations.[75] There were 300 members of the House of the People and 150 of the House of Nations. Both houses had four-year terms and held two regular sessions each year, in spring and autumn. In general, the decisions of the Federal Assembly would receive approval from each house.[76] When the Federal Assembly was not in session, the Presidium of the Federal Assembly would take charge, and each House had its own deputies to the Presidium.

---

[72] Article 5, Constitution of Czechoslovak Republic, 1948.

[73] Chapter 2, Constitution of Czechoslovak Republic, 1948.

[74] Article 39, Paragraph 1, Constitution of Czechoslovak Republic, 1960.

[75] Article 29, Constitution of Czechoslovak Socialist Republic, 1968.

[76] In general, a simple majority of deputies of House of People represented in enough, however, in House of Nations case, a simple majority of deputies should meet the condition: both deputies

Twenty members of the Presidium would be elected by the House of the People and twenty members by the House of Nations.[77]

4.4.4 Development of the Sejm of the Polish People's Republic

The Polish People's Republic adopted its constitution in 1952. It made the Sejm "the supreme organ of state authority". The numbers of deputies were not fixed; instead, every 60,000 inhabitants could elect one deputy to the Sejm for a term of four years. Each year, the Sejm would hold at least two sessions. In addition to enacting laws and adopting national economic plans and state budgets, the Sejm would elect some important officers. The Council of State was the permanently acting body for the Sejm, and its members would be elected by the Sejm. The Council of State would interpret laws and appoint officers. Since there was no position of the President of the Republic, some powers of the head of state were undertaken by the Council of State, such as appointing and recalling Polish ambassadors to and from other states, receiving letters of credence and recalling diplomats from other states to the Polish People's Republic.[78]

The constitutional regulations on the Sejm changed several times. For instance, the 1976 amendment, fixed the number of deputies to the Sejm at 460. Another notable change was that the Council of State would "watch over the constitutionality of laws."[79]

4.4.5 Similarities in the Development of the Supreme Organs of State Power in China and the Visegrad States

The most obvious similarity of the supreme organs of state power among these socialist states was that they were not purely legislative. Although the name of this organ in each Visegrad state was unchanged after the state adopted a Soviet-style system, it was endowed with more political and economic powers. The founding father of socialism, Marx, stated that, in his opinion, "parliamentary cretinism... had destroyed all the conditions of parliamentary power with their own hands." (Marx, 1937). Therefore, the first socialist state abandoned the capitalist parliament and established its own supreme organ of state power.

---

of Czech Socialist Republic and Slovak Socialist Republic shall be simple majority. Article 40, Constitution of Czechoslovak Socialist Republic, 1968.

[77] Article 56, Constitution of Czechoslovak Socialist Republic, 1968.

[78] Article 25, Constitution of Polish People's Republic, 1952.

[79] Article 30, Paragraph 3, Amendment to Constitution of Polish People's Republic, 1976.

The constitution of each state also regulated the term of the so-called supreme organ and the session for each year, particularly when each state announced that it was now socialist in the constitution. In China, the term of the NPC was five years, and it had one regular meeting each year.[80] In the Visegrad states, the Hungarian People's Republic kept its four-year term for the National Assembly. There were at least two meetings each year. In its first Soviet-style constitution, Czechoslovakia followed the previous constitutional provision. The term for the National Assembly was six years, and the National Assembly held two regular sessions each year; after the 1960 Constitution was passed and the state became socialist, the term was reduced from six to four years. In the Constitution of the Polish People's Republic, the Sejm's term was four years, and there were at least two sessions each year.

Of the powers of the supreme organ of state power, the ultimate one was legislation. In addition, there were some similarities among the states. This supreme organ also dealt with economic policies. In China, the NPC would "adopt the national economic plans, examine and approve the state budget and the financial report".[81] In the Visegrad states, the Hungarian People's Republic gave it similar tasks, and a socialist-style national economic plan and state budget would be decided by the National Assembly.[82] In Czechoslovakia, after the state announced its choice of a Soviet-style system, the National Assembly was given more tasks than it was used to. In addition to enacting the State Budget Act and auditing the state account, it would review the reports of the Uniform Economic Plan, which were mainly implemented by the government.[83] The Polish People's Republic also adopted similar provisions and stated that the Sejm would adopt the national economic plan and state budget.[84]

Since the supreme organ of state power in each state only held regular sessions one or two times per year, a permanently acting body was created in the constitutions. Typically, this organ would undertake most of the tasks of the supreme organ of state power when the supreme organ was not in session. However, there were some powers that the supreme organs would not share with their permanently acting body. For instance, revising the constitution or adopting a new one would be the exclusive power of the supreme organ of state power.

---

[80] The 1952 Constitution regulated the term of National Assembly for four years then it extended to five years since the second Constitution.

[81] Article 27, Constitution of People's Republic of China, 1954.

[82] Article 10, Paragraph 3, Constitution of Hungarian People's Republic, 1949.

[83] Article 163, Constitution of Czechoslovak Republic, 1948.

[84] Article 19, Constitution of Polish People's Republic, 1952.

4.4.6 Differences in the Development of the Supreme Organs of State Power in China and the Visegrad States

China and the Visegrad states joined the socialist community after the Second World War, and they then copied the Soviet political system and enshrined it in their constitutions. There were some differences in the states' supreme organs of state power because the states' realities and historical backgrounds were so different, especially when we consider the Visegrad states as one group and China as its own entity.

Chinese people used a parliamentary system for the first time in 1910 when the Qing Dynasty established the Advisory Council. Soon, with the dynasty's collapse in 1911, this parliamentary organ ceased to exist. The Republic of China later summoned its first parliamentary session in 1913, but it was interrupted by numerous wars (Zhang, 1984). Countries in the Visegrad region had much longer histories with parliaments, especially Hungary, whose first representative parliament gathered on 4 July 1948 and exercised its powers during the communist period (Hermann, 2005). Therefore, the practices of the supreme organs of state power in China and the Visegrad states differed dramatically. In China, the first Soviet-style constitution only lasted several years, and the entire country was governed without the instruction of laws, and, in addition, the NPC almost dissolved in the Cultural Revolution period (Tang, 2014). In contrast, the states in the Visegrad region continued the practice of supreme organs of state power during the communist period.

There was another difference between China and the Visegrad states in the election of deputies to the supreme organ of state power. In China, the 1953 Electoral Law provided that every 800,000 inhabitants would elect one deputy to the NPC; however, in urban areas, every 100,000 inhabitants would elect one deputy. This provision was changed in 1995, and each rural People's Congress deputy represented four times more people than each urban deputy. Finally, the Electoral Law of 2010 realized the equality of all votes in rural and urban areas. The same number of inhabitants now elects one deputy to the NPC (Zhao, 2012). However, the principle of equality of all votes was protected in the constitutions of the Visegrad region from the very beginning.

4.5 Conclusion

In this chapter, the author examined the development of constitutions in China and the Visegrad states during the reform period and compared them. In addition, the author analyzed the development of the "supreme organ of state power" in each state by examining the changes in constitutional provisions in each state.

The most significant change in the states' constitutions during the reform period was the "announcement of a socialist state". Based on this premise, each state revised its constitution and adopted a more socialist-style provision. The most notable example was Czechoslovakia. Its first Soviet-style constitution, adopted in 1948, was considered a "hybrid of the 1936 Soviet Constitution and the 1920 Czechoslovakia Constitution". Many components of the 1948 Constitution retained the features of the 1920 Constitution, such as its structure. The National Assembly was only defined as a "supreme organ of legislative power". Citizens enjoyed more rights than those in neighboring states and China. However, after the country declared itself a socialist state, the structure and provisions of the constitution became more similar to those of the other Visegrad states.

During the reform period, each state sought its own road to develop its socialist system, and the outcomes of the development of the socialist construction were also regulated in each country's constitution. These constitutional revisions demonstrate how fruitful or fruitless socialist construction was in each state. The PRC was an extreme case here; its first Soviet-style constitution was only in force for several years, and then the whole country sank into a so-called class struggle for nearly twenty. The outcome of the Cultural Revolution, the 1975 Constitution, supports the author's argument; the entire constitution had 30 articles, compared with 106 in its predecessor. The People's Commune was not only the economic organ but also the administrative organ at the local level.

The supreme organs of state power in each state shared some similarities since they operated in similar systems. However, due to the different economic and cultural conditions and historical backgrounds in each state, some differences existed, especially between China and the Visegrad states. Because China lacked experience with the parliamentary system, the People's Congress system did not function well during the Cultural Revolution.

References

Antal, T. (2010). Local Soviets and councils in the Ex-socialist European States with special regard to Hungary (1950–1990). *Hungarian Studies, 24*(1), 135–166.

Antalffy, G. (1981). Main features of state and constitutional development in the Hungarian People's Republic. In G. Antalffy & R. Harsfalvi (Eds.), *New traits of the development of state and legal life in Hungary*. Szegedi Nyomda

Blokker, P. (2014). *New democracies in crisis: A comparative constitutional study of the Czech Republic, Hungary, Poland, Romania and Slovakia* (1st ed.). Routledge

Brezezinski, M. F., & Garlicki L. (1995). Polish constitutional law. In S. Frankowski & P. B. Stephan III (Eds.), *Legal reform in post-communist Europe: The view from within* (1st ed., pp. 21–50). Kluwer Academic Publishers.

Chiu, H. (1985). The 1982 constitution of People's Republic of China and the rule of law. *Review of Socialist Law, 11*(1), 143–160.

CIA. (1965). *Eastern Europe and the Warsaw Pact* (National Intelligence Estimate. No. 12-65). Retrieved June 23, 2021, from https://www.cia.gov/readingroom/docs/DOC_0000273191.pdf

CIA. (1967). *The Chinese cultural revolution* (National Intelligence Estimate. No. 13-7-67). Approved for release date: May 2004. Retrieved June 23, 2021, from https://www.cia.gov/library/readingroom/docs/DOC_0001095914.pdf

Csink, L., & Schanda, B. (2015). The Constitutional Court. In Varga, A. Z., Patyi, A. & Schanda, B. (Eds.), *The basic (fundamental) law of Hungary: A commentary of the new Hungarian Constitution* (revised ed., pp. 185–196). Clarus Press.

References

Cutlert, L., & Schwartz, H. (1991). Constitutional reform in Czechoslovakia: E Duobus Unum? *The University of Chicago Law Review, 58*(2), 511–553.

Fan, Y. (2004). 公民的合法的私有财产不受侵犯——财产权入宪的意义 [Citizens' lawful private property is inviolable: The meaning of property right in the constitution]. *Qiushi, 15*, 44.

Garlicki, L. (1988). Constitutional developments in Poland. *Saint Louis University Law Journal, 32*(3), 713–736.

Getty, J. A. (1991). State and society under Stalin: Constitutions and elections in the 1930s. *Slavic Review, 50*(1), 18–35.

Han, D. (2004). *1954年宪法与新中国宪政 [The 1954 Constitution and the Constitutionalism of New China]* (1st ed.). Hunan People's Publishing House.

Hao, C. (2003). 试论苏南冲突和中苏交恶的共同特点 [On the similarities between the Tito-Soviet Split and Sino-Soviet Split]. *International Forum, 5*(1), 26–32.

Heer, P. D. (1978). The 1978 constitution of the People's Republic of China. *Review of Socialist Law, 4*(1), 309–322.

Hermann, N. (2005). Revolution and war of independence. In I. G. Toth (B. Adams, S. Kereszy, & A. Palko, Ed. and Trans.), *A concise history of Hungary: The history of Hungary from the early middle ages to the present* (1st ed.). Corvina Books Ltd.

IBP USA. (2013). *Hungary Country study guide, Volume 1 Strategic information and developments* (2013 ed.). International Business Publications.

Jones, W. C. (1985). The constitution of the People's Republic of China. *Washington University Law Review, 63*(4), 707–735.

Kim, C. (1977). The 1975 constitution of the People's Republic of China. *Hastings International and Comparative Law Review, 1*(1), 1–35.

Kim, C. (1981). Recent developments in the constitutions of Asian Marxist-Socialist States. *Case Western Reserve Journal of International Law, 13*(3), 483–500.

Marx, K. (1937). The Eighteenth Brumaire of Louis Bonaparte. Chapter Five. Translated and published by Progress Publishers. Retrieved June 23, 2021, from https://www.marxists.org/archive/marx/works/1852/18th-brumaire/index.htm

Marx, K. (1970). Critique of the Gotha Program. In Marx/Engels Selected Works (Vol. 3, pp. 13–30). Published by Progress Publishers. Retrieved June 23, 2021, from https://www.marxists.org/archive/marx/works/download/Marx_Critque_of_the_Gotha_Programme.pdf

Mitrovits, M. (2014). *The first phase of de-stalinization in East-Central Europe (1953–1958), a comparative approach* (Postdoctoral research study, National Science Research Program, Hungary). Retrieved June 23, 2021, from http://real.mtak.hu/30824/1/The_First_Phase_of_De_Stalinization_in_East_Central_Europe_u.pdf

Palese, A. (2009). *The Great Leap Forward (1958–1961): Historical events and causes of one of the biggest tragedies in People's Republic of China's history* (Bachelor thesis, Lund University) Retrieved June 23, 2021, from http://lup.lub.lu.se/luur/download?func=downloadFile&recordOId=1671693&fileOId=1671694

Romsics, I. (2010). *Hungary in the twentieth century* (2nd ed.), Corvina Books Ltd.

Simons, W. B. (Ed.) (1980). *The constitutions of the communist world*. Sijthoff & Noordhoff Publisher

Skilling, H. G. (1962). The Czechoslovak constitution of 1960 and the transition to communism. *The Journal of Politics, 24*(1), 142–166.

Swain, N. (1996). Getting land in Central Europe. In R. Ray Abrahams (Ed.), *After socialism: Land reform and social change in Eastern Europe* (1st ed., pp. 193–215). Berghahn Books.

Tang, D. (2014, September 17). 人大制度四大发展阶段 [Four development period of people's congress system]. *Outlook Weekly*. Retrieved June 23, 2021, from http://www.npc.gov.cn/npc/zt/qt/jndbdhcllszn/2014-09/17/content_1878887.htm

Visser, M. D. (2014). *Constitutional review in Europe: A comparative analysis* (1st ed.). Hart Publishing.

Xinhua News Agency. (2009, August 10). 共和国的足迹——1958年: "急急忙忙往前闯"[*The footprint of the Republic, 1958: Rush Forward*]. Retrieved June 23, 2021, from http://www.gov.cn/test/2009-08/10/content_1387664.htm

Xu, C. (2003). 中华人民共和国宪法史 *[Constitution history of People's Republic of China]* (1st ed.), Fujian People's Publishing House.

Zhang, Y. (1984). 民国初年的国会 (一九一二——一九一三) [Parliament in the early period of Republic of China (1912–1913)]. *Journal of Institute of Modern History, 13*, 83–196.

Zhao, X. (2012). 论全国人大代表的构成 [The formation of the deputy to National People's Congress]. *Peking University Law Journal, 24*(5), 973–989.

Chapter 5
Development of Constitutions in China and the Visegrad States in the Transformation Period

Abstract In this chapter, the author will analyze the development of constitution between China and the Visegrad States during the transformation period. Here, the author defined the transformation period which started from 1989, and finished until the new constitution adopted. However, the maturation time was hardly to be defined in an exact time point. Therefore, here the author roughly defined it the second half of 1990s. Besides, the implementation of constitution required a special organ guarantee the constitutionality in the state. Therefore, in this chapter, the author will also examine the constitutional review system in each state and make a comparative analysis.

In the last chapter, the author introduced and compared the development of constitutions in each state during the reform period and performed a comparative analysis of the supreme organs of state power in China and the Visegrad states. Although during the reform period, each country declared the establishment of a socialist system in its constitution, and some similar provisions could be found in the states' constitutions, their numerous differences caused different results, especially when we consider the Visegrad states as a group and compare the development of constitutions in China and the Visegrad countries.

In this chapter, the author analyzes the development of constitutions in China and the Visegrad states during the transformation period. Here, the author defines the transformation period as beginning in 1989 and ending when new constitutions were adopted. However, this maturation time can hardly be pinpointed. Therefore, here, the author roughly defines it as the second half of the 1990s.[1] During this period, the Revolutions of 1989 occurred in Eastern Europe; the same year, Beijing, the capital of the PRC, witnessed the Tiananmen Incident, which prompted the Communist Party to reform its ruling policies in the entire country. In addition, the implementation of constitutions required a special organ to guarantee constitutionality in the

---

[1] The transformation period in different states were different. Like Czech Republic and Slovakia, new Constitution adopted in 1993, Poland had its new Constitution in 1997, and in Hungarian case, 1949 Constitution officially out of valid until 2011, even though, a series of radical modifies had been made National Assembly. And in Chinese case, socialist Constitution still entered into force, with four amendments.

© The Author(s), under exclusive license to Springer Nature Singapore Pte Ltd. 2021
L. Da, *Development of the Constitutions in China and the Visegrad States*,
https://doi.org/10.1007/978-981-16-5636-1_5

state. Therefore, in this chapter, the author also examines the constitutionality review system in each state and performs a comparative analysis.

5.1 Development of the Constitution of China in the Transformation Period

In the history of the twentieth century, 1989 was a year of marvels. That year, China and the Visegrad states experienced pivotal moments, and the results of these turning points still affect each country now.

In this chapter, the author introduces the first two amendments to the current Constitution of the PRC. It has been amended five times. The first amendment was adopted in 1988 and the last in 2018. As Deng Xiaoping Theory states, "China is at the primary stage of socialism, and will remain so for a long time to come" (Deng, 1993; Zhang, 2014).[2] Based on this theory, the current Constitution is a socialist constitution, and the next-level document should be a communist constitution. However, here, the author analyzes the development of constitutions in the Visegrad states from 1989 to the second half of the 1990s. Therefore, the author explores the development of the current Constitution of the PRC by examining its first three amendments, which were adopted in 1988, 1993 and 1999.

5.1.1 First Amendment to the Current Constitution of China

Six years after the adoption of the Constitution of the PRC in 1982, its first amendment was passed by the NPC in 1988. Only two articles were revised, and they focused mainly on the economy.

The first article of the amendment regulated "the private sector of the economy". With the reform and opening-up policy, China's economy has grown rapidly, especially the private sector. According to statistics, in 1987, the private sector constituted 5.6% of the gross industrial output of the entire state, while in 1978, the percentage was almost zero (Xu, 2003). Since the private sector is increasingly important to the state economy, the 7th NPC adopted the first article of amendment to the Constitution of the PRC, which states that "the State permits the private sector of the economy to exist and develop within the limits prescribed by law. The private sector of the economy is a complement to the socialist public economy. The state protects the

---

[2] De Xiaoping, the second generation of leadership core in China, after his death in 1997, his thoughts were introduced as Deng Xiaoping Theory and adopted by the 15th National Congress of the Communist Party of China.

lawful rights and interests of the private sector of the economy and exercises guidance, supervision and control over the private sector of the economy".[3] Therefore, the private sector of the economy is officially protected by the Constitution.

Another modification of the Constitution related to "land". Because China is a socialist state, land in mainland China is owned by the state or collectives. People were previously only allowed to use the land but not to own it. The household responsibility system was another creative policy of the 1980s. It was first adopted in Xiaogang, a small village in Anhui Province (Wu & Zhang, 2008). Soon it spread to the entire country. In 1987, almost 98% of households in the countryside had adopted this system, which indicated that "rural people's communes, agricultural producers' co-operatives" were extinct (Xu, 2003). Therefore, the second article of the amendment states that "the right to the use of land may be transferred according to law."

5.1.2 Second Amendment to the Current Constitution of China

Four years later, the second amendment was adopted by the 8th NPC in Beijing. Nine articles were amended.

In 1992, Deng Xiaoping started his South China tour and gave speeches to the public. He urged a series of government reforms and a focus by the state on economic development.[4] These suggestions were well taken by the Communist Party. The following February, the Central Committee of the CPC submitted its suggestion for a constitutional amendment. This suggestion became a proposal and was submitted to the 8th NPC and adopted on 29 March 1993.

The second amendment to the Constitution consisted of nine articles. It mainly focused on the first two parts of the Constitution; two articles related to the preamble, and five were modified in the section on general principles. One article in the section on citizens' fundamental rights and duties was revised. Another article related to the term of the local-level People's Congress was amended.

The first article in the second amendment declared that "China is at the primary stage of socialism", while it brought the idea of "socialism with Chinese characteristics" to the public. China started to develop a socialist system with its own features.[5]

---

[3] Article One, Amendment to Constitution of People's Republic of China, 1988. Chinese version. Retrieved June 24, 2021, from http://www.npc.gov.cn/wxzl/wxzl/2000-12/05/content_4498.htm.

[4] Foreign Languages Press (April, 2011). Deng Xiaoping's South China Tour (Jan. 1992). Retrieved June 24, 2021, from http://www.china.org.cn/china/CPC_90_anniversary/2011-04/19/content_22392494.htm.

[5] For instance, in this amendment, it also promulgated that "The state practices socialist Market economy".

The second article related to the party system. There were nine political parties in the PRC, including the ruling party, the CPC. The other eight parties in mainland China and the ruling party made up the United Front and exercised their powers via the Chinese People's Political Consultative Conference. This article ensured that the "multiparty cooperation and political consultation system" would exist and continue to develop in China for a long time.

The third article revised the term "state economy" to "state-owned economy". This implied that the ownership of the socialist economy still belonged to the entire population. However, the state would not run the state-owned enterprises directly for the same reason, and the sixth and eighth articles in the amendment modified the term "state enterprises" to "state-owned enterprises".

As noted previously, at the end of the 1980s, the household responsibility system became the main trend in the rural economy instead of the "rural people's communes, agricultural producers' cooperatives" system. After several years of practice, the household responsibility system greatly liberated the productive forces in rural areas. Therefore, the second amendment removed the provision on rural People's Communes and enshrined the household responsibility system.

The establishment of socialism with Chinese characteristics in the constitution not only meant the government would develop its own political system but also indicated the direction of economic reform. The planned economy was considered the best economic system for the socialist state; in contrast, the market economy was the best option for capitalist states. However, the amendment put forward the creative idea of a "socialist market economy", and the state would "strengthen economic legislation, improve macroregulation and control" to better practice a socialist market economy.

Collective economic organization is an important part of the state-owned economy, and the amendment deleted the "guidance of the state plan". This gave collective economic organization more space to develop.

The final revision in the amendment extended the term of the county-level People's Congress. Before, its deputies were elected every three years; the amendment extended this term to five years. At this point, except for the term for township-level People's Congress, which was three years, the terms for the all levels of the People's Congress were five years.[6]

5.1.3 Third Amendment to the Current Constitution of China

The last amendment in the twentieth century was adopted in March 1999, and it contained six articles. The amendment process was the same as in 1993. The Standing Committee of the NPC accepted a proposal to amend the Constitution submitted by the Central Committee of the CPC and submitted an official proposal to the Second Session of the Ninth NPC (Xu, 2003).

---

[6] Amendment to Constitution of People's Republic, 1993. Englsih version. Retrieved June 24, 2021, from http://www.npc.gov.cn/englishnpc/Constitution/node_2828.htm.

5.1 Development of the Constitution of China …

The first article modified the seventh paragraph of the preamble, revising two main parts. The previous amendment stated, "China is at the primary stage of socialism", and the 1999 amendment affirmed this primary stage of socialism and noted that it would take a long time to advance. Another major modification added Deng Xiaoping Theory as guidance along with Marxism-Leninism and Mao Zedong Thought.

The second article altered the provision on the rule of law. The establishment of the rule of law in China touched off a 20-year debate beginning in 1979. There were three main positions. The first argued that the rule of law was important, the second asserted that a combination of the rule of law and rule of men was needed, and the third considered the rule of law a capitalist legal concept and argued that China as a socialist state should create a socialist legal system instead. The crucial point in this debate occurred in 1997. The Report of the 15th National Congress of the CPC expounded on the importance of the rule of law, and two years later, the rule of law was enshrined in the Constitution (Li, 2008). This was one of the milestones of the Chinese legal system. Another article in the amendment was also related to the legal system. Article 28 removed the provision on "counterrevolutionary activities", and since the Criminal Law of the PRC was modified in 1997, "crimes of endangering national security" have been outlawed instead of "counterrevolutionary crimes" (Xu, 2003).

The remaining three articles were related to the economy. The provisions on the basic economic and distribution systems were revised. Public ownership was dominant; however, diverse forms of ownership were permitted to develop side by side. The dominant principle allows diverse modes of distribution to coexist according to work. On the rural economy, the revision noted that "the rural collective economic organizations apply the dual operation system characterized by the combination of centralized operation with decentralized operation on the basis of operation by households under a contract".[7] Households under a contract system had basic status; however, because China is a socialist state, collective economic organization was recognized by the Constitution. Another change in the economic system was that the status of the individual and private sectors of the economy increased, and they are now considered "an important component of the socialist market economy".[8]

---

[7] Article 15, Amendment to Constitution of People's Republic of China, 1999. English version. Retrieved June 24, 2021, from https://www.cecc.gov/resources/legal-provisions/1999-amendment-to-the-constitution-of-the-peoples-republic-of-china.

[8] Amendment to Constitution of People's Republic of China, 1999. English version. Retrieved June 24, 2021, from https://www.cecc.gov/resources/legal-provisions/1999-amendment-to-the-constitution-of-the-peoples-republic-of-china.

5.2 Development of the Constitutions of the Visegrad States in the Transformation Period

In the 1980s, although their living standards improved, the Visegrad states experienced an economic crisis because of their planned economies. Many economists and decision-makers believed that only systematic change could save the economies of the Visegrad states. Meanwhile, the new Soviet Union leader Gorbachev believed that changes were needed in socialist states, and a more tolerant atmosphere developed in the Eastern Bloc with the Soviet Union's permission (Asmus et al., 1994).

All these developments led to a series of significant events in socialist states, including the Visegrad states, in 1989, which we now call the Revolutions of 1989. The peaceful transitions in the Visegrad states dramatically changed their state structures, the socialist system ceased to exist in official documents, Czechoslovakia split into two countries, and there were officially four countries in the Visegrad region. The evidence of change could also be found in government documents, especially laws. Here, the author examines the notable changes in the constitutions of each state during the transformation period.

5.2.1 Development of the Constitution of Hungary in the Transformation Period

Hungary managed to peacefully transform itself into a rule-of-law state as declared in a constitutional amendment. The Constitution of 1949 was heavily revised in 1989, the beginning of the transformation period, and it declared that these modifications would be in force until a new constitution was adopted. Initially, no one expected this period to last long; however, the new constitution was not ultimately adopted until 2011. After the 1989 amendment, the Constitution of 1949 was amended several more times; here, the author examines the final version of the 1949 Constitution, which was last amended in 2009.[9]

There were 15 chapters in the constitution. Its basic structure was not changed significantly. It could still be divided into six parts and a short introduction with the purpose of the amendment. It acted as a provisional constitution for "a constitutional state, establishing a multiparty system, parliamentary democracy and a social market economy"[10] until the new Constitution was adopted by the National Assembly.

The first part contained the general provisions, which no longer declared that Hungary was a "socialist state" and that "the State of Hungary is a republic". The state's ultimate principles were covered in this chapter. From the economic system to the political system, from people's fundamental rights to foreign policy, the first

---

[9] Each amendment of 1949 Hungarian Constitution is available. Retrieved June 24, 2021, from http://www.kozlonyok.hu/nkonline/MKPDF/hiteles/MK09150.pdf.

[10] Act of 31,1949 Hungarian Constitution, final version. English version. Retrieved June 24, 2021, from http://www.wipo.int/wipolex/en/text.jsp?file_id=190398.

chapter provided the first glance at the state and the core interests of the Republic of Hungary.

Hungary abandoned the socialist-style political system, which was very centralized, and one-party rule. Article 3 of the amendment stated that "political parties may be established and function freely." Implementing a multiparty system, the amendment's brief introduction stated that "no single party may exercise exclusive control of a government body."

Hungary adopted a market economy system, which had once been attacked by socialist states. The public economy and private economy would be equally protected by law, and freedom of competition would be guaranteed.

The amendment also guaranteed fundamental human rights to citizens of the Republic of Hungary and stated that this was the primary obligation of the state.

On foreign policy, the Republic of Hungary turned to Western Europe, seeking to join and assimilate into the European Union. This became the government's primary diplomatic task.[11]

The Republic of Hungary also made several radical changes to the political system. Parliament was still considered the supreme body of state power; its mandates were carried out in sessions, and there were regular sessions each year. However, the period of each session was extended; the first session started on February 1 and finished on June 15, and the second session lasted from September 1 to December 15. National referenda would be held if there were enough registered voters. Moreover, the checks and balances system was introduced. Parliament's exercise of its duties required the cooperation of the President of the Republic, who would be elected by the parliament and considered the head of state. The amendment introduced four other positions, which were closely related to the parliament. A Constitutional Court would monitor the implementation of the constitution per Act XXXII of 1989, which is explored in detail in the following section. The Republic of Hungary would protect its citizens' civil rights by establishing a special office, the Parliamentary Ombudsman. Two national offices, the State Audit Office and the National Bank of Hungary, were created to ensure the country's financial health.

The provisions on the Hungarian central government were also changed. A prime minister would be elected by the parliament based on the recommendation of the president. In addition to the basic duties of government, the Hungarian government and parliament were tasked with managing the country's integration into the European Union. Moreover, three national institutions were introduced to the public. The Hungarian armed forces and police would protect public security, maintain law and order, and guard the borders of the state. A national financial supervision authority (the State Auditor Office of Hungary) was designated to maintain the economic health of the state. National media and info-communication authorities would be responsible for facilitating the smooth operation of the electronic communication market.[12]

---

[11] Chapter One, final version of 1949 Hungarian Constitution.

[12] From Chapter Two to Chapter Nine, which introduced the political system in Republic of Hungary. final version of 1949 Hungarian Constitution.

The third part related to the judiciary. The highest court in Hungary would be the Supreme Court. The President of the Supreme Court would be selected by the parliament based on the recommendation of the President of the Republic, and other positions on the Supreme Court would be appointed by the National Council of Jurisdiction. Judges on the court could not be members of any political party or engage in political activities to ensure their judgments would be fair and without prejudice.

The office of the Public Prosecutor would undertake the task of protecting individuals, constitutionality, and state security. The Prosecutor in Chief was the highest officer of the prosecutorial system. The election of the Prosecutor in Chief was similar to that of the President of the Supreme Court. Public prosecutors could not be members of political parties or engage in political activities.[13]

Citizens of the Republic of Hungary enjoyed numerous rights according to the constitution, and several duties were required of citizens to protect the smooth rule of the country. In general, citizens were encouraged and guaranteed the right to participate in political and social affairs. It was more difficult to change the provisions on civil rights. To guarantee the stability of their protection, a two-thirds majority vote by parliament members was required. Hungarian citizens were also asked to fulfill several duties, such as protecting the homeland by paying taxes.[14]

The fifth part concerned electoral principles. Representatives at each level and mayors of cities would be elected by direct secret ballot by voting citizens, and each vote would count equally.

The last part adopted a national anthem and removed the socialist symbol from the national flag and coat of arms. In addition, it ensured the fundamental status of the constitution and that laws were obligated to serve Hungarian citizens.

5.2.2 Development of the Constitution of Czechoslovakia in the Transformation Period

Although some crucial changes occurred in the socialist regime in early 1989, Czechoslovakian citizens did not expect the "Velvet Revolution" to take place in their homeland. However, the solid communist regime suddenly collapsed at the end of that year, and Czechoslovakia turned its face to the west (Mcdermott, 2015).

The unexpected successful transformation of Czechoslovakia encouraged people, and drafting of a new constitution was planned by a special constitutional commission. For the same reason, the newly-elected President of Czechoslovakia, Vaclav Havel, and the parliament were to serve two-year terms instead of the regular four-year ones.

---

[13] Chapter Ten and Chapter Eleven regulated the judiciary system in Hungary, final version of 1949 Hungarian Constitution.

[14] Chapter Twelve, final version of 1949 Hungarian Constitution.

As Cutler and Schwartz's article indicates (Cutlert & Schwartz, 1991),[15] a Constitutional Commission was formed in the parliament in September 1990 to prepare a new constitution and submit it to the parliament. A new country was to be born with a new constitution.

The following issues required special attention to ensure a smooth constitution-drafting period.

The first issue was federalism. Czechoslovakia passed an important amendment in 1968, making the country a federal state instead of a unitary one. As a result, the structure of the government, economic policy and jurisdiction in Czechoslovakia were also revised.[16] After the collapse of the communist regime in Czechoslovakia, the federal state appeared weakened. The loose federalism of Czechoslovakia could be traced to the constitutional crisis, which referred to the name of the federal state. On 29 March 1990, the Czechoslovakian Parliament adopted a constitutional amendment since the communist party had lost its ruling position; therefore, a socialist system no longer applied in the state. The new name "Czechoslovak Federal Republic" replaced the old name "Czechoslovak Socialist Republic".[17] However, Slovaks were not satisfied with the new name, and several demonstrations occurred in the Slovakia region. Luckily, the crisis did not last long, and in April, after less than one month, a new constitutional amendment was adopted, naming the country the Czech and Slovak Federative Republic.[18] The unofficial name Czechoslovakia, which was accepted by the world for more than 70 years, was changed slightly to "Czecho-Slovakia" (Rychlik, 2016). This implied that Czechoslovakia as a whole was receiving decreasing support in Czechoslovakia, especially in the Slovakia region.

The second issue was civil rights. The most notable constitutional amendment on human rights and freedom was adopted on 9 January 1991 by the parliament. In contrast to early bills of rights in other countries, the structure of Czechoslovakia's Charter of Fundamental Rights and Freedoms[19] (hereafter the Charter) was more like a small constitution. It included a preamble, general provisions and detailed articles (Cutlert & Schwartz, 1991).

The preamble to the Charter addressed the democratic and self-governing traditions of Czechoslovakia, which were suppressed during the communist period. The chapter was included at the request of the Czech National Council and Slovak National Council to protect human rights and freedom in Czechoslovakia and "join in dignity the ranks of countries cherishing these values", i.e., join the European Union.

---

[15] This article was the result of the request of President Vaclav Havel, and sponsored by 77-New York Foundation and the Salzburg Seminar.

[16] Constitution of Czechoslovak Federation, 1968. English version. Retrieved June 24, 2021, from http://czecon.law.muni.cz/content/en/ustavy/1968/.

[17] Act No. 81 of 1990, Constitutional act. Slovakian version. Retrieved June 24, 2021, from http://www.noveaspi.sk/products/lawText/1/38417/1/2.

[18] Act No. 101 of 1990. Constitutional act. Slovakian version. Retrieved June 24, 2021, from http://www.noveaspi.sk/products/lawText/1/38417/1/2.

[19] Act No. 23 of 1991. Constitutional act. Czechia version. Retrieved June 24, 2021, from https://www.usoud.cz/fileadmin/user_upload/ustavni_soud_www/Pravni_uprava/23-1991.pdf.

The second part of the Charter contained the general provisions. It consisted of four articles ensuring that people's fundamental rights and freedoms would be equal for all and could not be taken away by any person or institution without a legal trial. Fundamental duties could only be imposed by law if fundamental rights and freedoms were respected.

The detailed provisions in the Charter were divided into four sections. The first section concerned human rights and fundamental freedoms. It consisted of two parts: fundamental human rights and freedoms and political rights. In general, such rights could be found in other countries' bills of rights. Since such rights were considered universal, they would be enjoyed by everyone, regardless of nation, sex and age. The section on fundamental human rights, for instance, stated that people would enjoy the right to life; freedom of movement, residence and thought; and protection from forced work and slavery, regardless of whether they had Czechoslovakian citizenship. The section on political rights encouraged citizens to participate in political movements and enjoy the freedom to express their own opinions.

The second section covered the rights of national and ethnic minorities. Germans in the Czech region and Hungarians and Roma in the Slovakia region constituted the major minorities in Czechoslovakia. This section ensured that the languages and cultures of minorities would be protected by the state.

The third section concerned economic, social, and cultural rights. On paper, citizens of Czechoslovakia enjoyed more rights than their Western neighbors. They had a combination of rights from socialist states and capitalist states. For example, they were entitled to free education at elementary and secondary schools and even universities.

The fourth section dealt with the right to judicial and other legal protection. Provisions in this part were more inclined to the European tradition. Article 37, in particular, stated that "everybody has the right to refuse to make a statement if he or she would thereby incriminate himself or herself or a close person."

The last part of the Charter contained the joint provisions. They included some technical provisions so that it could be implemented more smoothly.[20]

The third issue, which particularly concerned the Governors, was the independence of the judiciary. As mentioned in the constitution, the judiciary, especially the courts, could be divided into two parts: the Constitutional Court and the general court system. The constitutional provision on the Constitutional Court was amended in 1968; however, because this provision never entered into force, the constitution made some modifications to the Constitutional Court. Since constitutionality review in the Visegrad states and China is compared in the final part of this chapter, here, the author only briefly references these modifications to the general court system. As indicated above, revisions to the constitution in this part were focused on the independence of the general court system. The most significant change was adopted in July 1991. That constitutional amendment required judges to perform their duties bound by law only.[21] In addition, a previous amendment mandated that newly-elected

---

[20] This part was based on the Act No. 23 of 1991 and Lloyd Cutlert and Herman Schwartz's article.
[21] Act No. 326 of 1991. Retrieved June 24, 2021, from https://www.zakonyprolidi.cz/cs/1991-326.

judges take an oath affirming that they would only be bound by the constitution and other laws and make their judgments independently and impartially.[22]

Nevertheless, the expected new constitution was never adopted by the parliament since Czechoslovakia peacefully split into the Czech Republic and Slovakia at the end of 1992. The transformation period in Czechoslovakia was quite short. It started in 1989 and ended in 1992 when the Czech Republic and Slovak Republic adopted their new constitutions. In addition to the constitutional amendments mentioned above, the following amendment was notable. Act No. 135 of 1989 made two very significant revisions. The first deleted the leadership of the Communist Party of Czechoslovakia in the National Front. The second stated the cultural policy, specifically that the development of education would be guided by the "spirit of scientific knowledge and in accordance with the principles of patriotism, humanity and democracy" instead of "directed in the spirit of the scientific world outlook, Marxism, Leninism."[23] Another amendment adopted in 1990 changed the national symbols of Czechoslovakia.[24]

5.2.3 Development of the Constitution of Poland in the Transformation Period

During the 1980s, the Polish People's Republic was famous for its trade union movement, Solidarity, which began in August 1980. In 1989, Solidarity reached its climax and played a crucial role during the transformation period in Poland (Balaban, 1993; Bartkowski, 2009; Gorski, 2014).[25]

As in Poland's neighbors in the Visegrad region, after the collapse of the Communist Party in Poland, Poland's constitution saw several important revisions. Among these amendments, three were widely considered the most significant. Thus, the author focuses on these three. The first amendment was adopted in April 1989, and the second in December of the same year. The last amendment was the so-called Small Constitution, which was adopted in 1992. These amendments significantly changed the 1952 Polish Constitution, and then the current Constitution was adopted in 1997.

The transformation period in Poland started in 1989, and a constitutional amendment was adopted in April of the same year (Banaszak et al., 2012).

During the transformation period, so-called Round Table Talks were first initiated in Poland between the government and protesters, most of whom came from Solidarity, in 1989, followed by Hungary and Czechoslovakia (Kennedy, 2002). The outcome of the Round Table Talks was a constitutional amendment that was adopted on 7 April 1989. The amendment made two major changes.

---

[22] Act No. 376 of 1990. Retrieved June 24, 2021, from https://www.zakonyprolidi.cz/cs/1990-376.
[23] Act No. 135 of 1989. Retrieved June 24, 2021, from https://www.zakonyprolidi.cz/cs/1989-135.
[24] Act No. 102 of 1990. Retrieved June 24, 2021, from https://www.zakonyprolidi.cz/cs/1990-102.
[25] Especially when Solidarity won the Parliamentary election in both Houses in June of 1989.

The first change was new parliamentary election procedures. Elections for the senate would now be totally free, and in elections of Sejm deputies, 35% of the members would be freely elected, with the remaining positions reserved for the United Polish Workers' Party.

The amendment also introduced new constitutional institutions. As noted above, the two-house system was restored. In addition, the Sejm and Senate constituted one part of the country's parliamentary system. The second institution, which was restored in Poland, was the head of state, the President of the Polish People's Republic, who was granted broad powers. A new institution was introduced to the public, the National Judiciary Council, to strengthen the function of Poland's judicial branch, and the new judicial body would appoint the judges of the court (Banaszak et al., 2012).

After the April amendment entered into force, an election was held in June, and Solidarity won. The same year, another important constitutional amendment was adopted on 29 December 1989. It radically changed Poland's political system, and the Communist Party lost its ruling position.

The 1989 amendment made two major changes. The first was introducing freedom of the political system, and a multiparty system was established in Poland. The most significant change was restoring the traditional name of the state. The Republic of Poland replaced the Polish People's Republic, which had been adopted in the 1952 Constitution. Moreover, the amendment removed political control of Poland from the Communist Party, which lost its dominating position, and political parties and politicians were allowed to register freely if they followed the laws and constitution (Balaban, 1993). Since the socialist system was completely abandoned in Poland, the socialist ideology also lost its dominant position. The amendment removed the socialist-style preamble in the 1952 Constitution, and the first two articles of the new constitution announced that "a democratic state of law realizing the rules of social justice" and "the highest authority belongs to the nation" (Gorski, 2014). The new state was no longer based on the socialist ideology, and the democratic system was elaborated in the constitutional amendment.

The second revision in the amendment introduced a free economic system. The sixth and seventh articles in the Constitution removed the socialist economic system. Public and state ownership lost the dominant position, with the amendment stating that "the Republic of Poland guarantees freedom of economic activity regardless of the form of ownership." In addition, the socialist-economic-style "national socioeconomic plan" was eliminated in the amendment (Banaszak et al., 2012).[26]

Solidarity continued its victories in political elections, with its leader, Lech Walesa, winning the presidential election in December of 1990 (Gorski, 2014). With the development of Solidarity in Poland, the Polish constitution also improved. The most important amendment during the transformation period was adopted on 17 October 1992 and was famous for its unofficial name, the Small Constitution, since

---

[26] Amendment to 1952 Polish Constitution, 29 December 1989. Retrieved June 24, 2021, from http://prawo.sejm.gov.pl/isap.nsf/download.xsp/WDU19890750444/T/D19890444L.pdf.

it included a preamble, general principles, and detailed chapters on Poland's political system.[27]

The preamble to the Small Constitution stated the purpose of the amendment: "improving the activity of the supreme authorities of the State, pending the passing of a new Constitution of the Republic of Poland."[28]

The general principles section contained two articles. The first divided state power into three parts. Legislative power would be shared by the Sejm and the Senate. Executive power would be shared by the President of the Republic of Poland and the Council of Ministers. Judicial power would belong to independent courts. The second article required central-level officers to perform their duties under the law and to report their financial situations at the beginning and end of their terms of office.

Four chapters contained detailed provisions on Poland's political system. The first part regulated the legislative power. As noted above, the Republic of Poland restored the two-house system with a constitutional amendment in April 1989. The Sejm consisted of 460 deputies who were elected via secret ballot in general, equal, direct, and proportional elections. The Senate consisted of 100 senators chosen by administrative regions for the term of the House of Representatives, by secret ballot, in free, general, and direct elections. The amendment contained several provisions guaranteeing the ability of Sejm deputies to perform their duties independently. For instance, after election, a Sejm deputy could not be subject to recall simply for not following instructions from his or her constituents. During and after the Sejm session, deputies' performance could not be prosecuted unless their activities violated human rights. The Sejm and Senate would cooperate in their exercise of legislative power, and any statute adopted by the Sejm would be submitted by the Marshal of the Sejm to the Senate, which might or might not adopt it. If the Senate accepted the bill, then the Marshal of the Sejm would submit it to the President of the Republic of Poland. If the Senate did not accept the bill, it would return to the Sejm; however, if the Sejm passed the statute with an absolute majority vote, then the Sejm could overrule the Senate's rejection. Additionally, in the law-making process, the president would have powers similar to those of the Senate. The principle of checks and balances was embodied in this amendment.

The second part addressed executive power, which was shared by the President of the Republic of Poland and the Council of Ministers. Chapter three of the Small Constitution listed the president's powers. The president would be directly elected by secret ballot with a five-year term. Considered the head of state, the president would play an important role in relationships with other states, as the observer of the Polish constitution, and would be the supreme commander of Poland's armed forces. The president would also appoint the prime minister of the government, and as noted above, had an important role in law-making.

---

[27] Small Constitution in Poland, 1992. Polish version. Retrieved June 24, 2021, from http://prawo.sejm.gov.pl/isap.nsf/download.xsp/WDU19920840426/T/D19920426L.pdf. English version is available. Retrieved June 24, 2021, from http://www.servat.unibe.ch/icl/pl02000_html.

[28] Small Constitution in Poland, 1992.

Chapter four of the Small Constitution focused on the other executive entity, the Council of Ministers, or the so-called government. The Council of Ministers consisted of a prime minister, deputy prime minister, ministers, and other officers. The prime minister was the chief officer in the government and shared executive power with the President of the Republic of Poland. The Council of Ministers was considered the most important executive entity in the state, implementing statutes, supervising local governmental activities, safeguarding the security of the homeland, and issuing regulations to fulfill these duties.

Regulations on local self-government were promulgated in chapter five. The Small Constitution gave broad power to local government to act in the interests of local residents. It enjoyed great freedom in governing, limited only by laws. Officers in the local self-government would be directly elected by local residents.

The last chapter of the Small Constitution contained transitional and final provisions. The first article in this chapter provided a reason for the deputy or senator who appointed the officers mentioned in Article 8. The provisions in the Small Constitution would replace those in the 1952 Polish Constitution. The Small Constitution would enter into force 14 days after its promulgation.

From 1989 until the 1997 Constitution was promulgated, one amendment was adopted, in 1994. After the collapse of the communist regime, although the 1952 Constitution had introduced significant changes, adopting a new democratic constitution became the desire of the masses. The most significant change in this amendment was that a draft constitution could be submitted in Poland if over 500,000 citizens signed the petition (Garlicki & Garlicka, 2010).[29]

5.3 Comparative Analysis of the Development of Constitutions in China and Visegrad States in the Transformation Period

The Revolutions of 1989 dramatically changed the political environment in the Visegrad states and affected the ruling policies in the PRC. In the last section, the author examined the critical constitutional amendments in the Visegrad states during the transformation period. Additionally, some modest revisions of the Chinese constitution created a better political and economic environment for the development of the Chinese economy, which has seen miraculous growth in the past thirty years. In this part, the author assesses the similarities and differences in constitutional development in China and the Visegrad states during the transformation period.

---

[29] Amendment to 1952 Polish Constitutional, 1994. Polish version. Retrieved June 24, 2021, from http://prawo.sejm.gov.pl/isap.nsf/download.xsp/WDU19940610251/T/D19940251L.pdf.

5.3.1 Similarities

The PRC and the Visegrad states witnessed a pivotal moment at the end of the 1980s. However, after the Revolutions of 1989, the Visegrad states abandoned the socialist system and officially announced this in their constitutional amendments. In China, several important constitutional amendments were adopted by the NPC, although the state declared that it would continue to be socialist but with so-called Chinese characteristics.

The first similarity in the constitutional development in the PRC and the Visegrad states was that each country made its own serious decisions on its own future. There was no longer any Soviet influence. The roads to development in the PRC and the Visegrad states seemed to lead to opposite directions, and this was reflected in the states' constitutional amendments.

The Chinese constitutional amendments adopted during the transformation period retained the socialist system, but the creative minds in the CPC added Chinese characteristics. In addition, the amendments divided socialism into stages, and China in the transformation period would be in the primary stage for a long time to come.[30] The above revisions showed the creativity of the Communist Party and led China to build its own path of socialist construction.

The Visegrad states chose another road to develop their countries. The socialist system and the ruling position of the communist party in their constitutions were abandoned immediately after the Revolutions of 1989. For example, the Hungarian constitutional amendment was the outcome of the Round Table Talks, which were inspired by the Polish model. The preamble to Act 31 of 1989 in Hungary, which was also a constitutional amendment, stated that Hungary would be a "multiparty system, parliamentary democracy", which would lead to a "peaceful transition to a Constitutional state" (Tokes, 2002).[31] Many constitutional traditions before the Second World War were restored in the new constitutional documents. Poland reestablished the two- house system, and the position of president was reinstated in the Polish and Hungarian constitutions.

Another notable similarity concerned the economic doctrine of socialism, i.e., the planned economy was jettisoned in each state, including China.

It is easy to understand why the Visegrad states abandoned planned economies in their constitutions, since they were giving up the socialist system and restoring their

---

[30] In 1993 Amendment to Constitution of the People's Republic of China, it modified the Preamble part, and firstly introduced so called socialism with Chinese characteristics theory, in order to build Chinese socialist system. In the same Article, it stated that "China is at the primary stage of socialism." Later, in the next Constitutional amendment which adopted in1999, it predicted that the primary stage of socialism in China shall last a long time to come. Amendment to Constitution of the People's Republic of China, 1993. Retrieved June 24, 2021, from http://www.npc.gov.cn/wxzl/wxzl/2000-12/05/content_4585.htm. Amendment to Constitution of the People's Republic of China, 1999. Chinese version. Retrieved June 24, 2021, from http://www.npc.gov.cn/wxzl/wxzl/2000-12/10/content_7075.htm.

[31] Act 31 of 1989, Amendment to the Hungarian 1949 Constitution, 1989.

constitutional traditions. Therefore, during the transformation period, the market economy in each state was reestablished and regulated in the constitution.

The Chinese constitution also abandoned the planned economy and was amended in 1993. Article Fifteen was changed to, "the state has put into practice a socialist market economy", which meant that in Chinese socialist theory, the market economy was not unique to capitalism, and it was possible to have a market economy in a socialist state. The so-called socialist market economy was the most important part of Deng Xiaoping's economic theory (Li, 1999). Deng made a very famous analogy regarding China's choice between a market economy and a planned economy: "It does not matter whether the cat is black or white, so long as it catches mice."[32] The same consideration was reflected in the Chinese economic system; whether a market or planned economy, the Chinese economy simply needed a good system. However, in a socialist state with Chinese characteristics, China's market economy also gained an adjective, "socialist".

During the transformation period, crucial amendments on political and economic issues were adopted in China and the Visegrad states, and some of the modifications were even quite similar; however, the extended changes in the Visegrad states were much deeper than those in China.

5.3.2 Differences

Compared with differences between the communist regimes in China and the Visegrad states in the establishment and reform periods, the differences in constitutional development in the transformation period were starker. States in the Visegrad region deserted the socialist system and tried to integrate with their Western neighbors. Meanwhile, the PRC kept the socialist system, but some changes were made and reflected in constitutional amendments. In this part, the author does not compare how the provisions of the constitutional documents were changed in each state, since this information is obvious and easily obtained on the Internet. Rather, the main focus is on the reasons for the different choices in the constitutional development in China and the Visegrad states. Although each country in the Visegrad region had its own social conditions, the main trends of constitutional development were similar, the socialist system collapsed, and the states dramatically revised their constitutions in the transformation period; later, new capitalist constitutions were adopted. Therefore, in the following analysis, the Visegrad states are treated as a single entity, and the comparative analysis is conducted in two parts: legal tradition and political practices.

---

[32] In quotes: Deng Xiaoping (August 20, 2014). China Daily. Retrieved June 24, 2021, from http://www.chinadaily.com.cn/china/2014-08/20/content_18453523.htm.

5.3.2.1 Legal Tradition

After the Second World War, the PRC and Visegrad states adopted socialist systems and constitutions. Socialism functioned in these countries for forty years. However, if we examine the legal traditions in China and the Visegrad states, especially the constitutional culture, huge differences are apparent, and events during the transformation period also show how the different legal traditions in China and the Visegrad states led the two groups to choose different paths and constitutions.

The Chinese legal education system teaches that there are currently four main legal systems in the world: the civil law legal system, the common law legal system, the Islamic legal system and so-called Sharia and the socialist legal system. However, in China's legal history and even that of the entire Far East, the Chinese legal system has dominated for centuries (Zhou, 2002).[33]

The Chinese legal system is believed to have originated in three sovereign and five emperor periods; it first developed in the Qin and Han Dynasties more than two thousand years ago and was finally formalized in the Tang Dynasty with the promulgation of the Tang Code. It was a hybrid of Legalism, Confucianism and Taoism, with Confucianism playing a particularly vital role. Three cardinal guides and five constant virtues,[34] as the major principles of legislation in the Chinese legal system, were assimilated into Chinese daily life. In terms of the relationship between government and the people in ancient China, the masses were considered the subjects of the governor; they were to express loyalty to the governor, and the governor was to take care of them (Korolkov, 2017; Zhang, 2011). This legal thought dominated from ancient times until the late Qing dynasty forced China to adopt the Western legal system (Zhang, 2011).[35] The modern concept of a constitution first appeared in China at the end of the nineteenth century; later, the Qing dynasty collapsed, and its successor, the Republic of China, nominally united China. However, war constantly broke out in China, and the implementation of a constitution became almost impossible (Zhang, 2012). With this consideration, the Founding Father of the Republic of China, Sun Yat-sen, created his political road map in the Outline for Founding the Nationalist Government. Three stages were presented: military politics, tutelage politics and constitutional politics (Zhang, 2012). This led to the third stage when the Constitution of the Republic of China was passed in 1947.

The Visegrad states had different legal traditions regarding constitutions in previous eras. The most notable example is Poland's 1791 Constitution, in which Polish people have always taken pride as the second-earliest constitution in the world. This constitution was adopted by the Sejm on 3 May 1791. It was the result of a compromise among multiple interests after the republican revolution and

---

[33] The Introduction of legal system is one major part in Jurisprudence course in China. However, the study of Chinese legal system should be conducted in the legal history course.

[34] Three cardinal guides: ruler guides subject, father guides son, husband guides wife. The five constant virtues were benevolence, righteousness, propriety, knowledge, and sincerity.

[35] The government in late Qing sent its ministers to other states and examined the legal system, finally the governor decided to adopt Japanese legal system which was considered as a successful follower of western legal system.

numerous negotiations. The king of the Polish-Lithuanian Commonwealth, Stanislaw August, failed to control the whole country, and the 1791 Constitution gave the Sejm more fundamental rights and radically reformed the law on government (Butterwick, 2012). Although some authors claim it never entered into force (Gogut & Kugler, 1991), it shows how completely the legal traditions differed in ancient China and Poland.

As an independent country, Hungary saw its first written constitution in 1949, which, as noted in the previous chapter, was a complete copy of the 1936 Soviet Union Constitution. Before its loss in the First World War, Hungary was one constitutional state in the Austro-Hungarian monarchy. During the compromise period, a new constitution was adopted in December 1867. This document, called the liberal constitution, gave the Reichsrat (Imperial Council) legislative power and more rights to citizens (Okey, 2002; Taylor, 1976).[36] Czechoslovakia was independent from the Austro-Hungarian monarchy from 1918 until the end of the First World War; a liberal constitution was adopted in 1920. Even in the monarchy period, Czechs, along with the other liberals, fought for a legal constitution in the 1860s (Kwan, 2013).

These different legal traditions led China and the Visegrad states to choose different paths. After the Revolutions of 1989, the Visegrad states' legislatures restored their precommunist constitutions, and this was welcomed by the masses. In China, the liberal constitution was never implemented. Most people preferred to be led by a strong central government, much like their ancestors a thousand years earlier.

5.3.2.2 Political Practices

The constitutions of China and the Visegrad states show clear differences on paper. However, examining how they worked in practice shows an even larger gap.

Two examples relating to elections are illustrative. A Massachusetts historical journal describes Americans voting with beans and corn one hundred years ago (January Meeting, 1924). Surprisingly, a similar electoral method was employed in rural areas of China in the 1930s and 1940s. In the Electoral Law of 1953—the early stage of the PRC—secret ballots and show of hands were the legal voting methods. Later, during the Cultural Revolution, applause became the main method (Niu & Mi, 2014).

Voting methods in the Visegrad states were more advanced and liberal than in China. For example, Hungary held its first general election in 1848, and Acts IV and V of 1848 regulated parliamentary elections (Seifert, 2001). Act V detailed the election procedure: Eligible voters would vote personally, and voting would be recorded to make the elections fair.

---

[36] Hungary as a unitary state in Monarchy, entitled much more competences than other latter independent states in Monarchy.

Another difference between elections in China and the Visegrad states during the communist period involved elections of national representatives. In China, inequalities in voting rights between rural and urban areas have existed in practice since 1953, when the PRC's first electoral law was adopted. Deputies to the NPC from rural areas represented eight times more people than those from urban areas. This was later reduced to 4:1. Each voter should have same rights regardless of whether they reside in a rural or urban area, as was recognized by an amendment adopted in 2010 (Tang, 2011). Although this unequal election system did not function constantly, for the 10 years from 1965 to 1975, the NPC did not operate (Xu, 2003).[37]

In conclusion, the differences between China and the Visegrad states in legal traditions and political practices led to the different paths chosen by each state after the Revolutions of 1989. The masses in China, unlike citizens of the Visegrad states, who were strongly influenced by modern democratic theories, preferred a strong leader to lead the state to prosperity. Under the influence of Chinese legal tradition and fewer political practices in the forty years from 1949 to 1989, although the Tiananmen Incident occurred, the Communist Party ultimately quelled the nationwide protests led mainly by university students. Nevertheless, several constitutional amendments were adopted, focused mainly on economic reform.

5.4 Comparative Analysis of the Constitutionality Review Systems in China and the Visegrad States

One of the criticisms of socialist states is that their constitutional provisions only function on paper. In practice, the supreme organ of state power is regarded only as a rubber stamp. How to ensure constitutionality in practice is a challenge that not only socialist but also capitalist states face. An increasing number of states have adopted a so-called constitutionality review system to ensure that provisions in their constitutions are actually implemented.

According to Ginsburg and Versteeg's article, constitutionality review originated in the United States, specifically in the *Marbury v. Madison* case. Later, this system spread worldwide; in 1951, 38% of constitutional states had adopted a constitutionality review system; by 2011, this number had increased to 83% (Ginsburg & Versteeg, 2013).

In this part, the author examines constitutionality review in China and the Visegrad states.

---

[37] On 4th January 1965, the First Plenary Session of the Third National People's Congress closed, the next plenary session held in January of 1975.

5.4.1 Constitutionality Review System in the People's Republic of China

The current Constitution of the PRC states that in 1982, during the transformation period, three amendments were adopted. However, these modifications mainly focused on the economic system, and there is no single amended article related to constitutionality review.

There have been four versions of the Constitution of the PRC. None of the first three sought to establish a constitutionality review system in China. The first version, adopted in 1954, was heavily influenced by the 1936 Soviet Union Constitution. It tasked the NPC with amending the Constitution and supervising its enforcement.[38] Since the NPC gathered only once a year for a couple of days, it had difficulty carrying out such broad duties, and the 1954 Constitution soon became the law only on paper. In practice, it lost the support of the ruling party and the masses.

The second version of the Constitution, adopted at the very end of the Cultural Revolution, contained only 30 articles and went so far as to remove the NPC's supervisory power. This version was doomed by the failure of the Cultural Revolution, and the third version, adopted in 1978, restored the powers of the NPC, the permanent organ, and empowered the NPC's Standing Committee to interpret the Constitution.[39]

The current Constitution was promulgated in 1982 and has since been amended five times. It maintained the powers of the NPC and its Standing Committee and empowered the Standing Committee to supervise the enforcement of the Constitution.[40] This provision makes more sense because the Standing Committee of the NPC is a permanent organ, unlike the NPC, whose deputies gather in Beijing for only a few days (approximately 10–12) each year.

In the transformation period, a system of constitutionality review was not yet established in China. However, a notable experiment with judicialization of the constitution occurred in China at the beginning of the twenty-first century, with several significant cases considered leading cases.

Among these, Qi's case is particularly notable (Zhang, 2012; Zhu, 2010).[41] The case began in 1999, and after a two-year trial, the final judgment was given by the Shandong Higher People's Court. In an official Reply,[42] the Supreme People's Court

---

[38] Article 27, Constitution of People's Republic of China 1954.

[39] Article 25, Constitution of People's Republic of China 1978.

[40] Article 67, Constitution of People's Republic of China 1982.

[41] A brief introduction of Qi case: Plaintiff, Qi Yuling, female, 28 years old (in 2001), lives in Shandong Province. Defendant, Chen Xiaoqi, female, the same age in 2001 and lives in Shandong province. In 1990, Qi passed the entrance examination, Chen did not. However, with the help of Chen's father, Chen got QI's admission letter and had the chance to attend the school and got her further education. 11 years later, Qi was unemployed, Chen got a job in Bank of China. Finally, Qi found that her right of education was infringed by Chen and sued Chen Xiaoqi el al. in 1999, the Final Decision made by Shandong Higher People's Court in 2001.

[42] Official Reply of the Supreme People's Court on Whether the Civil Liabilities Shall Be Borne for the Infringement upon a Citizen's Basic Right of Receiving Education [expired], Retrieved June 24, 2021, from http://www.lawinfochina.com/display.aspx?lib=law&id=1954&CGid.

cited a constitutional provision, which appeared in the final judgment. The former Vice President of the Supreme People's Court, Huang Songyou, commented, "It creates the precedent of judicialization of the constitution" (Huang, 2001).

These cases seemed to suggest the arrival of a new era of constitutionality review in China. However, this experiment with judicialization of the Constitution did not ultimately succeed, and the discussion of constitutionality review through the Supreme People's Court ended without a decision. Nevertheless, some conclusions can be drawn here; that is, an increasing number of legal experts have asserted the importance of constitutionality review and implementation of the Constitution in practice (Fan, 2015). Nevertheless, numerous works were needed.

5.4.2 Constitutionality Review System in Hungary

The Hungarian national Round Table Talks led to several compromises. Among these fruitful outcomes, Hungary created a new constitutional supervisor organ, the Constitutional Court. Detailed provisions on this new organ were presented in Act XXXII of 1989, which was also one of the most critical constitutional amendments promulgated during the transformation period.

The new amendment, adopted on 29 October 1989, had five chapters and 59 articles. It was Hungary's first time establishing its own constitutionality review system. The amendment set out the court's powers, the procedures for elections of the constitutional judges and the court's rules of operation. The original provision stated that 11 Constitutional Judges would be elected by the National Assembly for nine-year terms. This new organ would be responsible for the constitutionality of governance and legislation with specific proceedings.[43]

Before the establishment of the Constitutional Court, the Hungarian government created the Council of Constitutional Law as Hungary's supervisory organ for constitutionality. It was first introduced in the 1983 constitutional amendment.[44] Detailed provisions on the Council of Constitutional Law were later promulgated in Act I of 1984, which was officially replaced by Act XXXII of 1989.[45]

Hungary's National Assembly elected the first five Constitutional Judges in November 1989. The Constitutional Court then commenced its constitutionality review on 1 January 1990.[46] The remaining six Constitutional Judges were elected in June 1990 by the freely and newly elected National Assembly (Kis, 2003).

---

[43] Act XXXII of 1989, Amendment to 1949 Hungarian Constitution.

[44] Act II of 1983, Amendment to 1949 Hungarian Constitution.

[45] "Simultaneously with the entry into force of this statute, Act I. of 1984 on the Council of Constitutional Law is repealed." Paragraph 1, Article 58, Act XXXII of 1989, Amendment to 1949 Hungarian Constitution.

[46] Brief history of the Constitutional Court of Hungary. In the website of the Constitutional Court of Hungary. Retrieved June 24, 2021, from http://hunconcourt.hu/history/.

5.4.3 Constitutionality Review System in Czechoslovakia

Czechoslovakia as a unitary country only lasted two years after the Revolutions of 1989. At the beginning of 1993, Slovakia officially announced its independence. However, the earliest constitutionality review system was established during the period of Czechoslovakia. It is believed that Czechoslovakia established a Constitutional Court even before the communist regime was established.

Czechoslovakia and its neighboring state, Austria, created this specialized judicial organ in 1920.[47] Czechoslovakia's first constitution, adopted in 1920, stipulated in its first provisions that conflicts between laws and the constitution were to be resolved by this special Court. It established a constitutionality review system in Czechoslovakia. Act 162 of 1920, which was later expanded, stipulated that the Constitutional Court would consist of seven judges serving ten-year terms.[48]

However, compared with today's popular constitutionality review systems, several shortcomings of Czechoslovakia's system should be noted. First, Constitutional Judges were nominated by certain bodies instead of elected. Specifically, the President of Czechoslovakia would nominate three judges with the recommendation of the Chamber of Deputies, the Senate, and the Diet of Russinia (Carpathian Ruthenia). Among the three judges, one would be appointed President of the Constitutional Court by the President of Czechoslovakia. Regarding the other four Judges, "two each are taken from the ranks of the judges of the Supreme Court of Justice and the Supreme Administrative Court."[49] Second, the Constitutional Court would decide the constitutionality of the law, and only certain bodies could make such a motion (Constitutional Court in Czechoslovakia, 1922).[50] In such situations, Czechoslovakia's constitutionality review system rather resembled an exclusive club only available to the ruling class. Individual constitutional complaints or petitions that were currently popular were excluded.

Czechoslovakia restored the Constitutional Court in 1968, and the same constitutional amendment established a federal system. The federal-level Constitutional Court would consist of twelve members, eight judges and four alternates who would be elected by the Federal Assembly. In compliance with the equality principle, four

---

[47] Constitutional court of the Czechoslovak republic and its fortunes in years 1920–1948. In the website of the Constitutional Court of Czech Republic (Excerpt from the monograph: Langasek, T. (2011) Ústavní soud Československé republiky a jeho osudy v letech 1920–1948. Vydavatelství a nakladatelství Aleš Čeněk, s. r. o.) Retrieved June 24, 2021, from https://www.usoud.cz/en/constitutional-court-of-the-czechoslovak-republic-and-its-fortunes-in-years-1920-1948/.

[48] Act 162 of 1920, Czechoslovakia. On the Constitutional Court. English version. Retrieved June 24, 2021, from https://ia600209.us.archive.org/32/items/cu31924014118222/cu31924014118222.pdf. The Act is widely considered as one part of the Constitutional Law, adopted on 9 March 1920.

[49] Act 162 of 1920, Czechoslovakia. On the Constitutional Court. English version. Retrieved June 24, 2021, from https://ia600209.us.archive.org/32/items/cu31924014118222/cu31924014118222.pdf.

[50] The following bodies may propose a motion. Supreme Court of Justice or the Supreme Administrative Court, the Electoral Court, the Chamber of Deputies, the Senate or the Diet of Russinia.

judges and two alternates would be elected from the citizens of the Czech Socialist Republic, and the rest would be citizens of the Slovak Socialist Republic. The term for judges on the Constitutional Court was seven years. Individuals could initiate constitutional complaints with certain conditions.[51] However, this advanced constitutionality review system never entered into force during the communist period. Then, in February 1991, the Federal Assembly adopted a Constitutional Act on the Constitutional Court that reestablished the constitutionality review system. The act considered the Constitutional Court a judicial body for protection of constitutionality. The act's detailed provisions were very similar to those of Act 162 of 1920. Namely, 12 Constitutional Judges would be appointed by the President of the Republic, not elected by the Federal Assembly. The Constitutional Court would mainly resolve the unconstitutionality of laws at the governing level. Citizens or organizations would not have the ability to make a constitutional complaint, as was permitted in the 1968 Constitutional Amendment (Pehe, 1991).[52] The Constitutional Court, as the third branch of the state power, was intended to play an important role in the checks and balances in Czechoslovakia's government.

However, Czechoslovakia was separated into two independent states at the end of 1992. Its constitutionality review systems existed mostly on paper.[53]

5.4.4 Constitutionality Review System in Poland

The Polish Constitutional Tribunal was introduced in the constitutional amendment adopted in March 1982 (Czeszejko-Sochacki, 1996), which contained two articles. It gave the general structure of the Constitutional Tribunal, which was the judicial organ that would review the constitutionality of all legal acts (Brzezinski, 1998).[54] Detailed provisions on the Constitutional Tribunal were finally promulgated on 29 April 1985. There were 12 judges in the tribunal: one president, one vice president and ten judges. All the judges would be elected by the Sejm with eight-year terms. Only certain bodies could initiate a motion on the conformity of "a legislative act with the Constitution or another normative act with the Constitution or a legislative act" (Article 2 of the Act of 1985). Inspired by Western constitutionality review systems

---

[51] Act 143 of 1968, Czechoslovakia. Constitutional Act. English version. Retrieved June 24, 2021, from https://www.usoud.cz/fileadmin/user_upload/ustavni_soud_www/History/Constitutional_act_1948.pdf.

[52] Act 91 of 1991, Czechoslovakia. Constitutional Act. English version. Retrieved June 24, 2021, from https://www.usoud.cz/fileadmin/user_upload/ustavni_soud_www/History/Constitutional_act_1991.pdf.

[53] History, the brief introduction of Constitutional Court of Czechoslovakia. In the website of Constitutional Court of Czech Republic. Retrieved June 24, 2021, from https://www.usoud.cz/en/history/.

[54] Amendment to Constitution of Polish People's Republic 1982. Polish version. Retrieved June 24, 2021, from http://prawo.sejm.gov.pl/isap.nsf/download.xsp/WDU19820110083/O/D19820083.pdf.

and Poland's own realities, there were three methods of initiating a constitutional case in Poland. In the first method, mentioned above, certain bodies could raise questions on conflicts between laws and the constitution to the tribunal. The second method concerned constitutional questions that existed in a specific case, and a regular court could submit such a constitutional question to the Tribunal. In the final method, the Constitutional Tribunal could volunteer to begin the proceeding (Brzezinski, 1998). The 12 judges were elected by the Sejm in November 1985, and the Tribunal began operating on 1 January 1986. A constitutional amendment adopted in 1989 expanded the Tribunal's powers, empowering it to adjudicate the unconstitutionality of the aims or activities of a political party.[55] Additionally, several acts enlarged the scope of constitutionality review. First, the Tribunal could review a statute that the President of the Republic delivered to it with a request for a constitutional inquiry. Second, it could give universally binding interpretations of statutes, a power that previously belonged to the Council of State (Brzezinski, 1998). Before the current Constitution was adopted, legal scholars suggested that the Tribunal review the constitutionality of international agreements.[56]

5.4.5 Similarities

It is difficult to perform a detailed comparison of the structures and powers of the organs of constitutionality review in China and the Visegrad states, since a constitutionality review system that meets the Western democratic standard has not yet been fully established in China. In Europe, however, the Visegrad states sought to follow their Western neighbors, and each established such a system.

As socialist states, their communist theorists attacked the separation of powers and checks and balances and their derivative constitutional courts. In classical communist theory, state power belongs to the entire people, and supreme organs of state power must represent the people to exercise state power. Therefore, there is no need to establish a constitutional court as an individual and independent judicial power.

The PRC and the Visegrad states in the communist period followed this rule. However, after the worldwide campaign for democracy in the last century, especially in the 1970s, states in the Visegrad region began to protect constitutionality. In Poland, the Council of State was empowered to protect the constitutionality of laws in the 1976 constitutional amendment. The Presidential Council of the Hungarian People's Republic had similar power. Later, Hungary adopted a new amendment in 1983. A new organ, the Constitutional Council, was created to ensure the constitutionality of laws. Laws on constitutionality issues in Czechoslovakia were different. The heavily amended constitutional document adopted in 1968 restored the Constitutional Court

---

[55] Amendment to Polish Constitution 1989. Polish version. Retrieved June 24, 2021, from http://prawo.sejm.gov.pl/isap.nsf/download.xsp/WDU19890750444/T/D19890444L.pdf.

[56] This suggestion was adopted by National Assembly and regulated in the Constitution of the Republic of Poland.

as the guardian of the Constitution. In China, because of the Cultural Revolution, the current 1982 Constitution empowered the NPC and its Standing Committee to supervise the enforcement of the Constitution. The NPC could amend it, and the Standing Committee would interpret it. Therefore, in most socialist states, at least on paper, the task of constitutionality review was assigned to a nonjudicial body.

The former communist regimes in Visegrad adopted constitutionality review systems like most of their Western neighbors and created constitutional courts or tribunals. However, in China, the role of guardian of the constitutionality of laws still belongs to the NPC and its Standing Committee. The Legislation Law of the PRC was adopted in 2000,[57] empowering the NPC and its Standing Committee to amend or repeal legal documents considered to violate the Constitution. Certain bodies may request a constitutionality examination if they consider legal documents to violate the Constitution. A special committee of the NPC can review the constitutionality of laws and regulations.

5.4.6 Differences

After the Revolutions of 1989, the socialist systems collapsed in the Visegrad states. As many scholars noted, the new democracies adopted constitutional courts in their constitutions and (re)established constitutionality review systems (Robertson, 2010). Since then, relatively similar constitutionality review systems have been established in Europe (Bricker, 2016).

In the Chinese case, the regime is still governed by the CPC. The limited constitutionality review system only applies to the constitutionality of laws and regulations. The power to review the Constitution belongs exclusively to the NPC and its Standing Committee.

The main difference between the constitutionality review systems in China and the Visegrad states is obvious, and fully Western systems were established in the Visegrad states after the collapse of the socialist system (Sadurski, 2005). However, in China, which is still ruled by a communist party, a constitutionality review system has not been fully established.

Given this huge gap between China and the Visegrad states, several differences are clear. First, the role of constitutionality review in the Visegrad states is undertaken by constitutional courts or tribunals. However, in China, reviewing the Constitution is the exclusive power of the NPC and its Standing Committee. Second, individuals play a much more active role in constitutionality review in the Visegrad states than in China.

Comparing the constitutionality review systems of China and the Visegrad states is difficult since China's system has progressed much more slowly. Whether to build a Western-style constitutionality review system in China was still debated in the

---

[57] Legislation Law of People's Republic of China was adopted on 15 March 2000. This Law was modified in 2015.

transformation period. As noted above, the ruling party is much more cautious about political and judicial reform than about economic reform.

5.5 Conclusion

In this chapter, the author introduced the development of constitutions in China and the Visegrad states during the transformation period, which was a crucial point for both regions. The Visegrad states abandoned the socialist system and returned to their Western neighbors. In China, the Tiananmen Incident occurred and caused the ruling party to make some important reforms, especially to the economy, which in hindsight were the main internal reasons for the economic miracle in China.

After the Revolutions of 1989, the Visegrad states' constitutions saw some critical amendments, although new versions of the constitutions would be adopted a few years or even two decades later (in the Hungarian case). As Western-style democratic constitutions were established in the Visegrad states, some important constitutional amendments were also adopted in China during the transformation period. Whatever the specific road chosen by each country for its development, it is most important that they make the best choice for themselves.

In the last part of this chapter, the author introduced the constitutionality review system in each state and performed a comparative analysis. This was easy since it is obvious that there is no space for constitutional courts in the Chinese constitution. Therefore, while constitutionality review systems have existed in the Visegrad states since the 1980s, it is still being debated whether China should create such a Western-style system. However, China should study and learn lessons from the experiences of the systems in the former socialist states in the Visegrad region.

References

Asmus, R. D., Brown, J. F., & Crane, K. (1994). *Soviet foreign policy and the revolutions of 1989 in Eastern Europe*. Rand Corp.
Balaban, A. (1993). Developing a new constitution for Poland. *Cleveland State Law Review, 41*, 503–509.
Banaszak, B., et al. (2012). *Constitutional law in Poland* (1st ed.). Wolters Kluwer.
Bartkowski, M. (2009). *Poland's solidarity movement (1980–1989)*. International Center on Nonviolent Conflict. Working paper. Retrieved June 24, 2021, from https://www.nonviolent-conflict.org/wp-content/uploads/2016/02/Poland-Solidarity-Movement.pdf
Bricker, B. (2016). *Visions of judicial review: A comparative examination of courts and policy in democracies* (1st ed.). ECPR Press.
Brzezinski, M. (1998). *The struggle for constitutionalism in Poland* (1st ed.). St. Martin's Press.
Butterwick, R. (2012). *The polish revolution and the Catholic church, 1788–1792: A political history* (1st ed.). Oxford University Press.
Constitutional Court in Czechoslovakia: Empowered to Pass on Validity of Legislative Acts but Only on Motion of Certain Bodies. (1922). *American Bar Association Journal, 8*(8), 464.

References

Retrieved June 24, 2021, from http://heinonline.org/HOL/Page?public=false&handle=hein.journals/abaj8&page=464&collection=journals

Cutlert, L., & Schwartz, H. (1991). Constitutional reform in Czechoslovakia: E Duobus Unum? *The University of Chicago Law Review, 58*(2), 511–553.

Czeszejko-Sochacki, Z. (1996). The Origins of constitutional review in Poland. *St. Louis-Warsaw Transatlantic Law Journal, 1996*, 15–32.

Deng, X. (1993). 邓小平文选 (第三卷) *[Selected works of Deng Xiaoping, Vol. 3]*. People's Press.

Fan, J. (2015). Constitutional transplant in the People's Republic of China: The influence of the soviet model and challenges in the globalization era. *BRICS Law Journal, 2*(1), 50–99.

Garlicki, L., & Garlicka, Z. A. (2010). Constitution making, peace building and national reconciliation: The experience of Poland. In L. Miller & Aucoin (Eds.), *Framing the state in times of transition: Case studies in constitution making* (pp. 391–416). U.S. Institute of Peace Press.

Ginsburg, T., & Versteeg, M. (2013). Why do countries adopt constitutional review? *The Journal of Law, Economics, & Organization, 30*(3), 587–622.

Gogut, A., & Kugler, J. (Eds.) (1991). *The polish road to democracy: The constitution of May 3, 1791* (1st ed.). The Sejm Publishing House.

Gorski, G. (2014). Constitutional changes in Poland between 1989 and 1997. *Law and Administration in Post-Soviet Europe, 1*(1), 5–15.

Huang, S. (2001, August 13). 宪法司法化及其意义--从最高人民法院今天的一个《批复》谈起 [Judicialization of constitution and its meaning: Discussion on today's "reply" of Supreme People's Court] People's Court Daily, B1. Retrieved June 24, 2021, from http://www.gongfa.com/huangsyxianfasifahua.htm

Kennedy, M. D. (2002). Negotiating revolution in Poland: Conversation and opportunity in 1989. Project essay of University of Michigan. Retrieved June 24, 2021, from https://www.ucis.pitt.edu/nceeer/2002-815-10g-Kennedy.pdf

Kis, J. (2003). *Constitutional democracy* (1st ed., Translation by Z. Miklosi). CEU Press.

Korolkov, M. (2017). Legal process unearthed: A new source of legal history of early imperial China. *Journal of the American Oriental Society, 137*(2), 383–391.

Kwan, J. (2013). *Liberalism and the Habsburg monarchy, 1861–1895* (1st ed.). Palgrave Macmillan.

Li, B. (2008). 依法治国历史进程的回顾与展望 [The historical process of governing the country by law: Reviewing and looking ahead]. *Legal Forum, 23*(4), 5–12.

Li, T. (1999). Former leadership of Communist Party of China, 社会主义市场经济理论的形成和重大突破-纪念中国共产党第十一届三中全会20周年 [The formation and significant breakthrough of socialism market economic theory. In Memorial of the 30th anniversary of the third plenary session of the eleventh central committee of CPC]. *Economic Research Journal, 3*, 3–15.

Mcdermott, K. (2015). *Communist Czechoslovakia, 1945–89: A political and social history* (1st ed.), Palgrave.

January Meeting. (1924). Gifts to the society; voting with beans and corn. (1923). *Proceedings of the Massachusetts Historical Society, 57*, 229–240. Retrieved June 24, 2021, from http://www.jstor.org/stable/25080155

Niu, M., & Mi, Y. (2014). 豆选 *[Bean voting]*. China Renmin University Press.

Okey, R. (2002). *The Habsburg monarchy, 1765–1918: From enlightenment to eclipse* (1st ed.). Palgrave Macmillan.

Pehe, J. (1991). *Constitutional court to be establishment*. RFE/RL. Report on Eastern Europe (Prague, March 15, 1991). Retrieved June 24, 2021, from http://www.pehe.cz/clanky/1991/1991-15March1991RFERL.pdf

Robertson, D. (2010). *The judges as political theorist: Contemporary constitutional review* (1st ed.). Princeton University Press.

Rychlik, J. (2016). The "Velvet Split" of Czechoslovakia (1989–1992). In M. M. Stolarik (Ed.), *The czech and Slovak Republics: Twenty years of independence, 1993–2013* (1st ed., Chap. 1). CEU Press.

Sadurski, W. (2005). *Rights before court: A study of constitutional courts in post-communist states of central and Eastern Europe* (1st ed.). Springer.

Seifert, T. (2001). General elections 1848–1998. In M. Ormos & B. K. Kiraly (Eds. Translation by N. Arato), *Hungary: Governments and politics 1848–2000* (1st ed.). Atlantic Research and Publications, Inc.

Tang, Y. (2011, November 21). An equal chance: Amendments to the electoral law guarantee equality. *Beijing Review*. Retrieved June 24, 2021, from http://www.bjreview.com/print/txt/2011-11/21/content_406841.htm

Taylor, A. J. P. (1976). *The Habsburg monarchy 1809–1919: A history of the Austrian Empire and Austria-Hungary*. University of Chicago Press.

Tokes, R. L. (2002). Institution building in Hungary: Analytical issues and constitutional models, 1989–1990. In A. Bozoki (Ed.), *The roundtable talks of 1989: The genesis of hungarian democracy: Analysis and documents* (1st ed.). Central European University Press.

Wu, J., & Zhang, Y. (2008). 家庭联产承包责任制研究30年回顾 [Looking back 30 years: Research on system of household contract responsibility]. *Economic Theory and Business Management, 11*, 43–47.

Xu, C. (2003). 中华人民共和国宪法史 *[Constitution history of People's Republic of China]* (1st ed.), Fujian People's Publishing House.

Zhang, Q. (2012). *The constitution of China: A contextual analysis* (1st ed.). Hart Publishing.

Zhang, S. (2014). 社会主义初级阶段论及其时代意义 [The theory of primary stage of socialism and its significance]. *CPC History Studies, 1*, 47–56.

Zhang, Z. (2011). 中华法系道德文化精神及对未来大中国法的意义 [The spirit of ethical culture of Chinese legal system and its meaning for greater China law in the future]. *Law Science, 5*, 45–50.

Zhou, W. (2002). *法理学[Jurisprudence]* (1st ed.). People's Court Press.

Zhu, G. (2010). Constitutional review in China: An unaccomplished project or a mirage? *Suffolk University Law Review, 43*(3), 625–653.

Chapter 6
Development of the Constitutions in China and the Visegrad States After the Transformation Period

Abstract In this chapter, the author will follow the constitutional development in each country and make a comparative analysis on the constitutional change and constitutionality review after the transformation period. The first part of this chapter will provide the development of the Chinese constitution after the transformation period. The second part will present how the Visegrad States develop their constitutions after the transformation period. The third part will focus on the constitutionality review in China and the Visegrad States.

In the previous chapters, the author paid attention to the constitutional development in China and the Visegrad states before the Revolutions of 1989, more specifically, comparing the countries' socialist constitutions. After the collapse of the Eastern Bloc, the Visegrad states abolished the socialist system and followed their Western neighbors, namely, adopting democratic political systems and reestablishing capitalism. However, the constitutions in the Visegrad region were not changed immediately, especially in Hungary, whose current Constitution was not adopted until 2011. China, in contrast, continued as a socialist regime, although its 1982 Constitution has been amended five times.

In this chapter, the author follows the constitutional development in each country and compares constitutional changes and constitutionality review after the transformation period. The first part of this chapter discusses the development of the Chinese constitution after the transformation period. The second part addresses how the Visegrad states developed their constitutions. The third part focuses on constitutionality review in China and the Visegrad states. The previous chapter also compared constitutionality review in these regions. The author continues this comparative study for two reasons: First, constitutionality review operates in different social systems; in the previous chapter, all the countries were considered socialist states, but after the Revolutions of the 1989, the Visegrad states abandoned socialism and remade their constitutions with democratic doctrines. Second, as the countries develop their practice of constitutionality review, they develop more guiding doctrines and principles. For example, in China, the very first decision of unconstitutionality was made in 2020, when the Central State Power ruled that regulations on teaching in minority languages in schools in ethnic autonomous regions were unconstitutional. Therefore,

© The Author(s), under exclusive license to Springer Nature Singapore Pte Ltd. 2021
L. Da, *Development of the Constitutions in China and the Visegrad States*,
https://doi.org/10.1007/978-981-16-5636-1_6

the comparative study of constitutionality review in China and the Visegrad states must be continued here. The last part of the chapter makes general conclusions on constitutional development in China and the Visegrad states.

6.1 Development of the Constitution of China After the Transformation Period

The current Chinese constitution was adopted in 1982 with 5 amendments. The first three amendments were introduced in the previous chapter, the fourth was adopted in 2004, and the last amendment was adopted in 2018.

6.1.1 Fourth Amendment to the Current Constitution of China

The fourth amendment was adopted by the Second Session of the 10th NPC in 2004. The amendment consisted of 14 articles and introduced principles and policies that the 16th National Congress of the CPC[1] decided to include in the Constitution.

The first two articles in the fourth amendment focused on the preamble to the Constitution. Article 18 improved the narrative in the 7th paragraph of the preamble. The important thought of Three Represents, the guiding social-political theory in China credited to former Chinese leader Jiang Zemin, was introduced in the preamble, following "the Marxism-Leninism, Mao Zedong Thought, Deng Xiaoping Theory". The second change in this paragraph was the deletion of the word "building" in the sentence "along the road of *building* socialism with the Chinese characteristics" so that it read "along the road of socialism with the Chinese characteristics". The third change was the addition of the phrase "promote the coordinated development of the material, political and spiritual civilizations" in this paragraph.

The second article in the fourth amendment added the phrase "all builders of socialism" in the 10th paragraph of the preamble, which enlarged the circle of the united front of the PRC.

Twelve additional articles addressed social developments in China. They covered the basic rights of citizens; the powers of the People's Congress, the President of the PRC and the State Council; the state of emergency and the national anthem.

On the topic of protecting citizens' basic rights, the following changes were made: (1) The provisions on expropriation and requisition of land were revised. The new parts are as follows: First, in accordance with the provisions of law; second, the state shall make compensation. (2) The provisions in the economic section were revised, with Article 11, paragraph 2 changed to read: "The state protects the lawful

---

[1] In this meeting, Hu Jintao was elected as the general secretary of the CPC, he promoted the fourth Amendment to the Chinese Constitution.

rights and interests of the nonpublic sectors of the economy, such as the individual and private sectors of the economy. The state encourages, supports and guides the development of the nonpublic sectors of the economy and, in accordance with law, exercises supervision and control over the nonpublic sectors of the economy." (3) The provisions on the private property of citizens were revised. The amendment stated that "citizens' lawful private property is inviolable" and that the state "protects the rights of citizens to private property", and it also addressed compensation for private property in the case of expropriation or requisition. (4) "A sound social security system" was established. (5) The Constitution stated a commitment to "respecting and preserving human rights".

On the topic of the powers of the People's Congress, the President of the PRC and the State Council, the following parts of the Constitution were revised: (1) The number of deputies in the NPC. Since the sovereignty of Hong Kong and Macau was transferred to China, special administrative regions (i.e., Hong Kong and Macau) would also have their own deputies to the NPC. (2) The Standing Committee of the NPC had the power to declare a state of emergency instead of imposing martial law. (3) The President of the PRC could proclaim a state of emergency instead of proclaiming martial law. (4) In addition to the power to receive foreign diplomatic representatives, the President of the PRC could engage in activities involving state affairs according to the fourth amendment. (5) Following the previous changes regarding states of emergency, the State Council could declare a state of emergency in parts of provinces, autonomous regions, and municipalities instead of imposing martial law there. (6) The term of the local People's Congress would be five years, changed from three years in the previous version.

The last article in the fourth amendment introduced the national anthem of the PRC: the March of the Volunteers.

Compared to the previous amendments, the fourth amendment is notable for its protection of the basic rights of citizens, legislation of states of emergency and constitutionalization of the social-political theory of the leadership. These revisions deeply influenced the social order and research in China. The following revisions are examples: (1) Respecting and preserving human rights was stipulated in the Constitution. Since then, research on human rights has become popular in China, with some universities establishing research bases in human rights and Chinese researchers arguing that the rights to subsistence and development are primary human rights. This has also justified the campaign of poverty reduction in China. (2) The fourth amendment also changed references to martial law to a state of emergency, such as the COVID-19 outbreak in China. Criteria to declare a nationwide state of emergency or a state of emergency in parts of the provinces needed to be discussed (Li, 2021).[2] (3) It is an unspoken rule to constitutionalize the leadership's social-political theory in China. The important thought of Three Represents is promoted by Jiang Zemin,

---

[2] China didn't announce a nationwide state of emergency in accordance with its Constitution. In general, the governments from different levels preformed their duties in accordance with the Prevention and Treatment of Infectious Diseases Law of the PRC, and the Emergency Response Law of the PRC.

the former President of the PRC. His successor Hu Jintao was elected president in 2003, and he promoted the fourth amendment. One of the goals of this amendment was to constitutionalize the important thought of Three Represents.

6.1.2 Fifth Amendment to the Current Constitution of China

The latest amendment was adopted in 2018; it included 21 articles covering important topics. It has drawn international attention. However, most reporters have focused on to the lifting of term limits for the President of the PRC and ignored other important revisions, such as its (1) imposition of the supervisory system; (2) reorganization of the NPC's Law Committee and renaming it the Constitution and Law Committee, empowered to review the constitutionality of laws and regulations; and (3) emphasis of CPC leadership.

The fifth amendment revised the preamble to the Constitution of the PRC more significantly than previous amendments had. There were four articles related to the preamble. The first revised several parts of the 7th paragraph: (1) the leaders' thoughts were introduced into the Constitution, namely, the Scientific Outlook on Development (from former President Hu Jintao) and the Xi Jinping Thought on Socialism with Chinese Characteristics for a New Era (from current President Xi Jinping); (2) the words "legal system" were replaced with "rule of law"[3]; (3) following the revision of rule of law, it also emphasized the new era by adding "implement the new development concept" to the same paragraph; (4) with economic development, the importance of environmental protection was also reflected in the Constitution by referring to "ecological civilizations". The second article revised the 10th paragraph of the preamble: (1) it changed "in the long years of revolution and construction" to "in the long years of revolution, construction and reform"; (2) it enlarged the circle of the united front of China, and "all patriots devoted to the rejuvenation of the Chinese nation" was added. The third article of the fifth amendment revised the description of the relationships among the nationalities in China and emphasized that there is not only "equality, unity, mutual assistance" but also "harmony". The fourth article dealt with international relations. It declared that China's path of development is peaceful with a reciprocal opening-up strategy and promoted the building of a community with a shared future for humankind.

One of the most important aspects of the fifth amendment was its revision to Article 1, paragraph 2 by adding the sentence "the leadership of the Communist Party of China is the defining feature of socialism with Chinese characteristics." Most of the articles in the fifth amendment were related to the establishment of the supervisory system. In addition, the amendment (1) described the relationships among the

---

[3] Legal system in Chinese as "法制" and pronounced as "fa zhi", coincidentally, the rule of law in Chinese as "法治" also pronounced as "fa zhi". It suggested that the legal system with socialism characteristics in China has been established in China, as Wu Bangguo, the former chief legislator of the PRC announced it in a National People's Congress meeting in 2011. After the announcement, the term of "rule of law" is more popular in China.

Chinese nationalities as harmonious (Article 4, paragraph 1); (2) advocated socialist core values (Article 24, paragraph 2); (3) added a new paragraph to Article 27 stating that "all state functionaries shall take a public oath to the Constitution when taking office;" (4) revised Article 70, paragraph 1, changing the special NPC "Law Committee" to the "Constitution and Law Committee"; (5) removed the term limits for the President of the PRC (Article 79, paragraph 3); (6) gave the State Council the new power "to direct and administer… ecological civilization construction" (Article 89, paragraph 6); and (7) empowered the People's Congresses and standing committees of cities to divide areas into districts to "draft… regulations" (Article 100, paragraph 2).

Although the latest amendment received wide criticism abroad for its abolition of term limits for the president and the constitutionalization of the CPC leadership, several other significant revisions merit study (Lin, 2019). The first revision established the supervisory system; the second renamed the NPC's Constitution and Law Committee. China realized rapid economic development and tried to address international concerns. It declared that the path of Chinese development is peaceful. China is trying to promote the building of a community with a shared future for humankind.

6.1.3 Conclusion

After the transformation period, two constitutional amendments were adopted under Hu's and Xi's leadership. Both amendments had as their main task introducing the major theoretical ideas and policies of the National Congress of the CPC into the Constitution. One of the characteristics of the constitutional amendments in China is the constitutionalization of the leadership's thoughts. The fourth amendment introduced Jiang's important thought of Three Represents into the Constitution under Hu's leadership. The fifth amendment endorsed Hu's "Scientific Outlook on Development" and Xi's "Xi Jinping Thought on Socialism with Chinese Characteristics for a New Era". In general, both amendments reflected socioeconomic developments in China, although some of their changes generated widespread disagreement. The fifth amendment deserves more attention to and discussion of its reconstituted organ for constitutionality review, anti-corruption supervisory system, and attitude toward international relations, not just the abolition of term limits for the president. The revisions of the Constitution not only were decided by the ruling party but also reflected demands from the bottom (Zhang & Ginsburg, 2019). In this chapter, the author explores the changes to the reconstituted special Constitution and Law Committee of the NPC. The later decision by the Standing Committee of the NPC empowered the Constitution and Law Committee to review the constitutionality of laws and regulations. How did constitutionality review function in China? Is a constitutionality review system necessary in a socialist regime? With consideration of these questions, a comparative analysis of constitutionality review in China and the Visegrad states is conducted in the third part of this chapter.

6.2 Development of the Constitutions in the Visegrad States After the Transformation Period

After the Revolutions of 1989, the Visegrad states turned to their Western neighbors and abandoned their socialist constitutions. The first significant change occurred in Czechoslovakia. Havel, the former political dissident, was elected president in a landslide after the Velvet Revolution. However, his popularity could not dispel the tension between the two nations. The dissolution of Czechoslovakia occurred in 1992; the next year, Havel was elected the first President of the Czech Republic. At the same time, the newly independent countries Czech and Slovakia adopted their constitutions in 1992. The other two Visegrad states reconstituted their constitutions relatively late; the Polish constitution was adopted in 1997 and Hungary's new constitution in 2011.

In this part, the author discusses how the constitutions developed in the Visegrad states after the Revolutions of 1989. Given that constitutional development in the transformation period was touched upon in the previous chapter, only the newly adopted constitutions and amendments are discussed here.

6.2.1 Development of the Constitution of Hungary After the Transformation Period

Hungary was ruled by the nominal Constitution of 1949, which was comprehensively amended in 1989, with the sense of rule of law until 2011. The current Constitution was adopted on 18 April 2011 with 262 to 44 votes. Due to an overwhelming victory in the 2010 parliamentary election, Fidesz gained 263 seats and reached the required two-thirds majority for constitution-making (Facsar, 2010). Fidesz, the ruling party, promoted the process of constitution-making and became the only party voting in favor in 2011 (Dempsey, 2011). However, the one-party Constitution aroused international attention because of its lack of checks and balances (Breitenbach & Levitz, 2011; Fleck et al, 2011).

The current Constitution (Fundamental Law) of Hungary has been amended 9 times, with the latest amendment adopted in 2020 (Walker, 2020).[4] It contains six chapters: the National Avowal (preamble); Foundation; Freedom and Responsibility; The State; Special Legal Order; and Closing and Miscellaneous Provisions.

The National Avowal emphasizes the importance of Christian values in the Hungarian nation; it also recognizes the historic constitution of Hungary. In contrast, the Constitution of 1949 is considered an outcome of foreign occupations and is not recognized by the current government. The question arises whether the decisions made by the Constitutional Court based on the Constitution of 1949 (amended in 1989) are still valid. The National Avowal answers this question, considering 2 May

---

[4] The latest constitutional amendment targeted on the LGBT group with the reason of defending the Christian values. Shaum Walker 'Hungarian government mounts new assault on LGBT rights Constitutional amendment proposed to enshrine defence of so-called 'Christian values".

1990 to be the beginning of the country's new democracy and constitutional order. Therefore, the decisions by the Constitutional Court are recognized, and the principle of the stability of law (Constitution) is to be applied. Therefore, in some senses, the 1989 amendment of the 1949 Constitution is treated as a "new Constitution".[5]

The National Avowal is followed by the chapter on the foundation. This part establishes certain important principles of Hungary, such as the country's name, form of government, capital, official language, coat of arms, national flag, national anthem, national holidays and official currency. One article aroused international attention. Article D reads, "Hungary shall bear responsibility for the fate of Hungarians living beyond its borders… shall support their efforts to preserve their identity… the establishment of their community self-governments… and shall promote their cooperation with each other and with Hungary." After the two wars, Hungary lost a significant amount of territory and population; therefore, many people who speak Hungarian were considered Hungarian people who live in neighboring countries. This article caused tensions between Hungary and its neighbors. However, according to a report by the Venice Commission, this provision means supporting and assisting Hungarians abroad and is not a basis for extraterritorial decision-making. It was formally confirmed by the Hungarian authorities.[6]

The next chapter, Freedom and Responsibility, covers people's basic rights. It contains 31 articles and was influenced by the EU Charter of Fundamental Rights and Freedoms. It states that "human dignity shall be inviolable" and guarantees economic rights; freedom of religion, thought, assembly, and expression; and the right to education. This chapter also covers the rights of national minorities to practice their own national identities and languages; however, national minorities are groups who lived in Hungary for a certain length of time, and the details are provided in the cardinal act. In addition to rights, Hungarians have several duties, such as contributing for the common needs and defending the country.

The next chapter covers the organization of the state and the powers, duties and organization of the National Assembly, the President of the Republic, the government, the Constitutional Court and other courts, the prosecution services, the Commissioner for Fundamental Rights, local governments, public security, and the military. The country's name was changed from "the Republic of Hungary" to "Hungary", which shows that Hungarians cherish their country's history. The parliamentary system and form of government were retained. This chapter also addresses national referenda.

---

[5] The discussion of the invalidity of the Constitution of 1949 is considered as a political narrative by the Venice Commission, and it pointed out this statement is rather than an expression to draw a clear line between the democratic system and the former communist regime. CDL-AD (2011). Opinion on the New Constitution of Hungary Adopted by the Venice Commission at Its 87th Plenary Session. Retrieved June 24, 2021, from https://www.venice.coe.int/webforms/documents/CDL-AD(2011)016-E.aspx.

[6] CDL-AD (2011). Opinion on the New Constitution of Hungary Adopted by the Venice Commission at Its 87th Plenary Session. Retrieved June 24, 2021, from https://www.venice.coe.int/webforms/documents/CDL-AD(2011)016-E.aspx.

However, there were several issues on which it is forbidden to hold a national referendum, including amending the Fundamental Law (Constitution). The details of the Constitutional Court will be discussed later in the section on constitutionality review.

The chapter on special legal order mainly addresses national crises and states of emergency. It endows the National Assembly with the power to declare a state of emergency in several cases where lawful order, life and property may be endangered. Based on Article 48 (1) b), the National Assembly declared and extended a state of emergency due to the COVID-19 pandemic.[7]

The last chapter is closing and miscellaneous provisions, and it decreed that the Constitution of Hungary would enter into force on 1 January 2012. The adoption of transitional provisions was also required in the last chapter. Transitional provisions were first adopted on 31 December 2011, and the Constitutional Court later found them unconstitutional. To resolve this issue, the first two amendments reaffirmed that the transitional provisions were considered a part of the Constitution. However, these two amendments were also invalidated by the Constitutional Court (Trocsanyi & Sulyok, 2015).

Hungary was the last country in the region to adopt a Western-style constitution. This delay may have resulted from several factors. First, the comprehensively revised amendment of 1989 may have functioned as a new constitution; it eliminated all the socialist features from the 1949 Constitution and amended it to meet the standard of rule of law. Therefore, there was no need to rush to adopt a new constitution. Second, it was difficult to obtain the two-thirds vote by the members of the National Assembly required to adopt a new constitution. Before the adoption of the Constitution in 2011, which was promoted by the ruling party, Fidesz, the left-liberal government met this requirement; however, the government coalition then dissolved, and the left-liberal government failed to adopt a new constitution (Trocsanyi & Sulyok, 2015).

6.2.2 Development of the Constitution of the Czech Republic After the Transformation Period

After of the dissolution of Czechoslovakia, the National Council of the Czech Republic adopted the country's new Constitution on 16 December 1992. Based on Czechoslovakia's 1920 Constitution (Glos, 1994), it consisted of 113 articles and a preamble and eight chapters. Beginning with the first amendment in 1997 and most recently in 2013, the Constitution has been amended eight times. Compared to those of other countries in the region, the Constitution of the Czech Republic is the shortest and most abstract.

The preamble to the Constitution addressed the three parts of the Czech Republic: Bohemia, Moravia and Silesia. As the Czech Republic was a newly independent country that was abandoning its socialist features in the Constitution, the preamble

---

[7] State of emergency now in place, About Hungary (Budapest, 11 November 2020) Retrieved June 24, 2021, from http://abouthungary.hu/news-in-brief/state-of-emergency-now-in-place/.

emphasized the value of democracy and rule of law. The end of the preamble implied that the Constitution was adopted by the representatives in the National Council.

The first chapter is Fundamental Provisions, which contains the principles of the rule of law. The fundamental rights and freedoms of Czech citizens are considered one part of the Constitution and are promulgated separately. This chapter designates the capital and state symbols, such as the state emblem, state colors, state flag and national anthem.

Following the principle of separation of the powers, the next three chapters cover legislative, executive, and judicial power.[8] Chapter two addresses legislative power. Following the tradition, the legislative power, i.e., the parliament, in the Czech Republic consists of two chambers, the Assembly of Deputies and the Senate. The Assembly of Deputies has 200 members, and the Senate has 81. Elections to both chambers follow the American method, i.e., by proportional representation in the Assembly of Deputies and by majority rule in the Senate; every second year, one-third of the senators must be reelected. The Senate enjoys significantly fewer powers than the Assembly of Deputies. For example, the Senate may not adopt legislative measures concerning the Constitution, the state budget, the final state accounting, electoral laws, or treaties with an international organization or institution. In fact, at the establishment of the Czech Republic, the Senate's duties were performed by the Assembly of Deputies according to the Transitional and Final Provisions of the Constitution and later by the Provisional Senate. It seems that without the presence of the Senate, no problems arise (Glos, 1994). This chapter discusses the requirements for adoption of a constitutional act and assent to the ratification of international treaties.

The next chapter concerns executive power, including the President of the Czech Republic and the government. It regulates the mode of election and powers of the president. The president is elected via secret ballot based on general, equal and direct voting.[9] Individuals must be at least forty years old to run for president. The president cannot be elected more than twice in succession, and one term is five years. The government shares executive power with the president and regards the president as the highest body of executive power. The government consists of the prime minister, the deputy prime minister, and ministers. The prime minister is appointed by the president, and the Assembly of Deputies must affirm the appointment with a vote of confidence. If the vote of confidence is lost, the president may appoint the prime

---

[8] As mentioned above, the Constitution of 1992 of Czech Republic was heavily influenced by the Constitution of Czechoslovakia in 1920. In the Constitution of 1920, it arranged the structure of the Constitution with the principle of separation of the powers, namely the Legislative Powers, Constitution and Competency of Parliament and of Both its Chambers, Governmental and Executive Power and Judicial Power. However, unlike the Constitution of 1920, the Constitution of 1992 of Czech Republic didn't regulate the fundamental rights of citizens in the Constitution, rather to publish Charter of Fundamental Rights and Freedoms as "a part of the constitutional order of the Czech Republic" (Article 3 of the Constitution of Czech Republic). The Constitution of Czechoslovakia of 1920. Retrieved June 24, 2021, from https://archive.org/details/cu31924014118222/page/n41/mode/2up.

[9] The Constitution of Czech Republic has been amended in 2012, according to the amendment, the presidential election shall be directly. No. 71/2012 Sb.

minister again. If the second-round appointment fails to generate a vote of confidence, then the president may appoint another candidate for prime minister based on the proposal of the Chairperson of the Assembly of Deputies.[10]

The next chapter addresses judicial power, which has two components: the Constitutional Court and the other courts. This chapter emphasizes the independence of the courts and judges. The Constitutional Court is designated to protect constitutionality. It contains 15 justices serving 10-year terms. To be appointed by the president with the consent of the Senate, a justice must be a Czech citizen who is at least forty years old with a university law degree who has practiced law for at least 10 years. The Constitutional Court reviews the constitutionality of legal provisions, such as statutes and regulations. It may also decide the constitutionality of activities of political parties and even dissolve political parties. The other courts consist of the Supreme Court; the Supreme Administrative Court; and superior, regional, and district courts. Judges are appointed by the president with unlimited terms.

The next two chapters address the Supreme Auditing Office and the Czech National Bank. The President and Vice President of the Supreme Auditing Office are appointed by the President of the Republic after nomination by the Assembly of Deputies.

Chapter seven concerns territorial self-government. It states that municipalities are the basic and regions the higher territorial self-governing units. The first amendment of the Constitution revised this chapter and annulled Article 103, which gave higher territorial self-government the power to decide the title (region or land).[11] Article 99 has been revised to read "the Czech Republic is subdivided into municipalities, which are the basic territorial self-governing units, and into regions, which are the higher territorial self-governing units." (Glos, 1994).[12]

The last chapter contains transitional and final provisions, given that several organs that are regulated in the Constitution were not established at the time of adoption. Therefore, the powers of these organs were performed by existing bodies. For example, the duties of the Senate were carried out by the Assembly of Deputies and later by the Provisional Senate. The duties of the State Attorney's Office were performed by the Office of the Procuracy of the Czech Republic. The chapter stated that the Constitution would enter into force on 1 January 1993.

---

[10] The case of incumbent PM Andrej Babis is a good example, Mr. Babis was appointed by the President and he lost in the vote of confidence. Therefore, he was appointed again by the President and this time he won the vote of confidence. Reuters Staff (2018, April 16). Czech PM Babis wants deal on ministries this week in renewed govt talks. Reuters. Retrieved June 24, 2021, from https://www.reuters.com/article/us-czech-politics/czech-pm-babis-wants-deal-on-ministries-this-week-in-renewed-govt-talks-idUSKBN1HM0QP.

[11] OECD paper (1999, September 1). Public Management Profiles of Central and Eastern European Countries: Czech Republic. Sigma Public Management Profiles. Retrieved June 24, 2021, from https://www.oecd-ilibrary.org/governance/czech-republic_5kmk1828j4q0-en.

[12] In the Constitutional-making of Czech Republic, the title of the higher territorial self-government was heated debated, traditionally, Czech was formed into two parts: the Czech land and the Moravian-Silesian land. In the communist period, the region system was introduced.

The Charter of Fundamental Rights and Freedoms (introduced in the previous chapter) is also considered a part of the Constitution. In general, the Charter covers the basic rights of citizens. Since it was adopted before the dissolution of Czechoslovakia (in 1991), its preamble declared that it was proposed by the Czech National Council and the Slovak National Council. After the independence of the Czech Republic, the Charter was recognized by the Presidium of the Czech National Council in 1993. In 1998, Article 8(3) was revised to "a person who is detained shall be immediately informed of the grounds for the detention, questioned, and within 48 h at the latest, either released or turned over to a court." The original number "24" was replaced by "48". As the Charter included proposals of the Slovak National Council and was adopted by the Federal Assembly of Czechoslovakia, should the Charter unconditionally apply to Slovakian citizens after dissolution? In any case, the Czech Republic and Slovakia joined the EU in 2004, and citizens of both countries are universally protected by the EU Charter of Fundamental Rights.

Unlike Hungary and Poland, Czechoslovakia elected the Federal Assembly in 1990. The Federal Assembly was considered not only a constituent assembly but also a working parliament (Fitzmaurice, 1998). However, it failed to constitute a Constitution, and the voice of Slovakian independence was heard by the Federal Republic. The turning point came with the parliamentary election in Czechoslovakia; on the Czech side, the right-of-center Civic Democratic Party won; and in Slovakia, the left-of-center Movement for a Democratic Slovakia was considered the winner. On the Slovakian side, a loose federal structure was the acceptable choice. However, the Czech Republic and the federal government favored tightening the federal system (Cottey, 1995). After a bitter debate, the leaders of the Czech Republic and Slovakia decided to split. The dissolution of Czechoslovakia provided a chance for each country to adopt a new constitution. Apart from the independence of the two nations, Czechoslovakia's constitutional tradition also contributed substantially to constitution-making in the Czech Republic and Slovakia. The 1920 Constitution of Czechoslovakia is widely considered democratic. As a result, the constitutions of the Czech Republic and the Slovak Republic both followed its structure and restored several institutions, such as the bicameral legislature in the Czech Republic and the constitutional courts in the Czech Republic and Slovak Republic.

6.2.3 Development of the Constitution of the Slovak Republic After the Transformation Period

The Slovak Republic or Slovakia was becoming independent again (Gabris & Letkova, 2018)[13] if we count its time as a satellite state of Nazi Germany in World War II as a time of independence (Goldman, 1999). The Slovaks decided to leave the Federal Republic and establish a new republic in the Visegrad states. The Constitution of Slovakia was adopted in September 1992, less than two months after the Slovak

---

[13] The constitutional history of Slovakia may see Tomas Gabris and Alexandra Letkova's article.

Republic's declaration of sovereignty (Bealey, 1995; Berdisova, 2013). It consists of a preamble and 9 chapters. Nineteen direct constitutional amendments have been adopted to date (Drugda, 2019; Lalik, 2017),[14] most recently in December 2020 on reform of the judiciary.[15]

The preamble indicated the dissolution of Czechoslovakia ("recognizing the natural right of nations to self-determination") and its Christian traditions by stating the "spiritual heritage of Cyril and Methodius". It declared that Slovakia has a democratic form of government and that the Constitution was adopted by representatives of Slovakian citizens.

The first chapter is divided into three parts. The first contains the basic provisions. It asserts that Slovakia is a democratic country, state power originates from citizens, and natural resources are the property of Slovakia. Notably, transporting water from Slovakia to outside the country via vehicles or pipelines is prohibited except for personal use and for humanitarian reasons. This part also addresses conditions for acquisition and loss of Slovakian citizenship, the official language of the Slovak Republic, requirements to enter a state union (under the circumstances of recession of the EU in 2004), ratification of international treaties and support for Slovaks (without Slovakian citizenship) living abroad. The next part addresses state symbols. It specifies the state emblem, national flag, state seal and national anthem. The last part of chapter one establishes Bratislava as the capital of Slovakia.

The second chapter is on basic rights and freedoms. It consists of 8 parts. Unlike the current Constitution of the Czech Republic, the Slovak Republic did not create a single charter for basic rights and freedoms, and its Constitution includes the basic rights and freedoms of the citizens of Slovakia. The first part is the general provisions. It states that basic rights are inviolable and guaranteed to everyone. Duties are only imposed by laws, international treaties and government ordinances. Additionally, it states that human life, even before birth, is protected. Article 11 was repealed in 2001; the original provision stated that international treaties on human rights were more important than domestic laws. The second part covers basic human rights and freedoms, and all the important and fundamental rights and freedoms are adopted in this part. However, several provisions are notable. First, capital punishment is prohibited in the Slovak Republic. The privacy of letters and secrecy of messages via "other ways" or "other similar means" (such as digital methods) is guaranteed by the Constitution. The right to have or not have a religious creed is guaranteed, and churches and religious communities are free to govern themselves. These rights are guaranteed only if they do not endanger the public order, public health, morals, or the rights and freedoms of others. Slovakian citizens are exempted from military service

---

[14] According to Drugda, there are 18 direct constitutional amendments and 19 indirect constitutional amendments, however, in December 2020, a new constitutional amendment on the matter of judiciary reform has been adopted by the Parliament. Several important constitutional amendments from 2008 to 2016 had been analyzed by Lalik.

[15] Consultative Council of European Judges (CCJE): Opinion of the CCJE Bureau Following a Request by the CCJE Member in Respect of Slovakia as Regards the Reform of the Judiciary in Slovakia, Council of Europe (9 December 2020). Retrieved June 25, 2021, from https://rm.coe.int/opinion-slovakia-2020-/1680a0a961.

only if conscription is against their conscience or religious creed (Brett et al., 2021).[16] The next part concerns political rights. Slovakian citizens have freedom of speech, assembly, and association and the rights to petition and participate in public affairs via free elections. The fourth part addresses the rights of national minorities and ethnic groups. Minorities have the rights to develop their own culture, use their own language, associate in national minority associations and establish educational and cultural institutions, in addition to basic rights and freedoms. However, the practice of minority rights is limited. It may not disrupt Slovakia's sovereignty or territorial integrity or cause discrimination against other citizens in minority regions. The fifth part covers economic, social, and cultural rights. It guarantees citizens' social welfare and defines marriage in Slovakia exclusively as a union between a man and a woman. The rights to the protection of the environment and cultural heritage and to judicial and other legal protection are addressed in the following two parts. The last part contains the common provisions for the first two chapters. Citizens are referred to in the first two chapters as citizens of the Slovak Republic. Foreign nationals enjoy basic rights and freedoms unless they are only granted to citizens in the Constitution.

The third chapter has two parts: one on the economy and the other on the Supreme Audit Office of the Slovak Republic. The first part declares that Slovakia is a socially and ecologically oriented market economy. The second part designates the Supreme Audit Office to manage budgetary resources, property, property rights, funds, obligations and claims in Slovakia. The office is headed by a Chairman who is elected by the National Council of the Slovak Republic.

The next chapter is on territorial self-administration. As in the Czech Republic, the basic unit of territorial self-administration is the municipality. The Constitution provides more details on territorial self-administration, including its form and powers.

Chapter five regulates the legislative power. The first part stipulates the form, powers, and duties of the National Council of the Slovak Republic. Unlike the Czech Republic, the Slovak Republic chose a unicameral system, having only one entity. The National Council is the sole constitutional and legislative body of the Slovak Republic, and it consists of 150 MPs for terms of 4 years via general, equal, and direct elections. MPs cannot be prosecuted for performing their duties. The National Council enjoys great powers in legislation and other important issues. Adopting a constitutional amendment or constitutional law, approving an international treaty, impeaching the president, and declaring a war require the consent of a three-fifths majority of MPs, namely, over 90 votes. The role of Speaker of the National Council is also regulated in this part; the Speaker is elected by the MPs via secret ballot. The second part addresses referenda. It was revised in 2001 prior to accession to the EU. Article 93(1) reads, "A referendum is used to confirm a constitutional law on

---

[16] The conscription is suspended in Slovakia. However, the provision didn't abolish, and in the case of emergency, the conscription may apply to the Slovakia citizens. Also, the refusal of conscription of Jehovah's witness based on the conscientious objection caused the discussion not only in Slovakia, but in the rest of the Europe.

entering into a union with other states, or on withdrawing from that union." (Mazak, 2001).

The next chapter focuses on executive power and contains two parts: the president and the government of the Slovak Republic. After a 1999 constitutional amendment, the President of Slovakia is elected directly instead of in the National Council via secret ballot. Candidates for president must be citizens and at least 40 years old, and they must be nominated by more than 15 MPs or over 15,000 citizens. The president is empowered to govern Slovakia with other state organs, such as representing Slovakia in international activities, appointing and recalling some important officials and making other significant decisions. The president can be prosecuted only for violating the Constitution or high treason. The second part is the government of Slovakia, which is regarded as the supreme body of executive power. The government is led by the prime minister, who is appointed by the president. The government makes decisions on draft laws, legal documents, appointing and recalling state officials, and other critical issues.

Chapter seven addresses judicial power. The first part covers the Constitutional Court of Slovakia and the second the other courts. The Constitutional Court is responsible for reviewing the constitutionality of laws and activities. It consists of 13 judges who are appointed by the president based on proposals of the National Council for 12-year terms. The Constitutional Court may decide the constitutionality of laws, government ordinances, legal regulations, and petitions. It cannot decide on the constitutionality of draft legal regulations, namely, *ex ante* review is not applied in Slovakia's constitutionality review system. The constitutional act no. 90/2001 Coll. amended the Constitution heavily to strengthen the general judiciary and increase public confidence in the judiciary,[17] creating the Judicial Council of the Slovak Republic. The new organ is designated to supervise the judicial system. It consists of 18 members, 9 of whom are elected by the judges of Slovakia and the other 9 by the National Council, president, and government. The term of membership on the Judicial Council is 5 years and may be renewed once. General provisions on the other courts of Slovakia are also presented in this section. The courts rule on civil and criminal matters. The court system consists of the Supreme Court and other courts. To be appointed as a judge by the President of Slovakia after proposal by the Judicial Council, a citizen must be at least 30 years old and have a university education in law. The term of office for a judge is unlimited.

The next chapter establishes Slovakia's prosecutor system. The Prosecutor's Office is headed by the Prosecutor General for the protection of the interests of natural and legal persons and the state. Several constitutional amendments were adopted to establish an ombudsman institution in Slovakia. The constitutional act

---

[17] For a long time, the low-level trust of citizens in the independence and transparency of the judiciary is considered as a problem in Slovakia. The establishment of the Judicial Council is expected to improve the independence and transparency of the judges of Slovakia. European Rule of Law Mechanism: Input from Slovakia for the 2020 Rule of Law Report, point 10. Retrieved June 25, 2021, from https://ec.europa.eu/info/sites/info/files/2020_rule_of_law_report_-_input_from_m ember_states_-_slovak_republic.pdf.

no. 90/2001 Coll. introduced the Public Protector of Rights (Kanzelsberger, 2018).[18] The ombudsman must be a Slovakian citizen who is at least 35 years old and is elected by the National Council based on proposal by at least 15 MPs. The term of office is 5 years.

The last chapter mainly contains transitional provisions. As noted above, Slovakia adopted its Constitution hastily before the dissolution of Czechoslovakia. Therefore, several provisions dealt with the rules, institutions and officials established in the Czechoslovak Federation. For example, legal documents from Czechoslovakia shall remain in force unless they conflict with the current Constitution. Judges elected under the previous legislation shall remain in office.

Slovakia, as the earliest country in the Visegrad states to adopt a Constitution, reflected the idea of parliamentary sovereignty. At its founding, how the Slovaks would develop their country greatly concerned people at home and abroad. Then-Prime Minister Vladimir Meciar was portrayed as an authoritarian figure (Bealey, 1995). However, with the implementation of the Constitution, Slovakia may continue its democratic trend and move toward the rule of law. Unlike its counterpart, the Czech Republic, Slovakia took a mild and pragmatic position on the legislation of the previous regime. It recognized the validity of previous legislation in the Federal Republic unless it conflicted with the current Constitution. Additionally, the significant number of constitutional amendments in Slovakia reflect not only the debates within Slovakian society but also the relative ease of amendment (only a three-fifths majority of MPs is needed, in contrast to the Czech Republic, which requires a three-fifths majority in both chambers).

6.2.4 Development of the Constitution of the Republic of Poland After the Transformation Period

The current Constitution of the Republic of Poland was adopted in 1997 after lengthy preparation for constitution-making. Poland is considered the first country in the region to have democratized with the Solidarity movement. Constitution-making started in Poland after the first free elections for the two assemblies (the Senate with a direct election and the Sejm with a partially free election) were held. General Jaruzelski, the leader of the communist party, was elected president by the two assemblies, and Mazowiecki, backed by the Solidarity movement, was elected by the Sejm. Therefore, a "Your President, our Prime Minister" structure was created in Poland (Gorski, 2014).

The previous structure did not last long as another presidential election was held in 1990, only one year later. Walesa, the leader of Solidarity, was elected president.

---

[18] The origin name of this institution is "verejného ochrancu práv", and it usually translated as "The Public Protector of Rights" or "The Public Defender of Rights". Both of them are used in the official documents from Slovakia government.

Although Walesa had overwhelming support from Poles (with approximately three-fourths of the votes in his favor), Solidarity became less united and split into factions. This was reflected in the following year's Sejm elections, in which the strongest party took only 62 MPs (Gorski, 2014). The newly formed Sejm and the Senate finally prepared and adopted the so-called Small Constitution.

The Small Constitution did not last long, especially after the 1995 presidential election, and Kwasniewski became the president. For this reason, he had to resign from his position of chairperson of the drafting committee for constitution-making. A total of seven proposals were made: one from then-President Walesa, one from the Senate, and others from different parties. The Church also played an important role in constitution-drafting, ensuring that Christian values would be represented in the new document. A draft Constitution was finally prepared and sent to the Sejm on 2 April 1997, and it was approved by a national referendum with 52.8% in favor (Fitzmaurice, 1998).

The current Constitution of the Republic of Poland consists of a preamble and 13 chapters. A chapter amending the Constitution has been added. Compared to those in other countries, the Polish requirements to amend the Constitution are stringent. Adoption of an amendment requires at least two-thirds of the votes with at least half of the Sejm present and an absolute majority of votes with at least half of the Senate present. Some provisions must be approved by referendum. Therefore, only two amendments have been adopted in Poland. The first is directly related to Polish accession to the EU. Poland's Constitutional Tribunal ruled that a provision of the Code of Criminal Procedure was incompatible with the Polish Constitution. To follow the EU decision on the European Arrest Warrant, the Constitution had to be revised (Nussberger, 2008). The next constitutional amendment was adopted three years later under the same party's (PiS) governance. Article 99 added a new provision on election of the Sejm and the Senate: "No person sentenced to imprisonment by a final judgment for an intentional indictable offence may be elected to the Sejm or the Senate". This revision was made when some popular politicians were facing trials to eliminate the possibility of criminals being elected in the Sejm or Senate. The amendment was adopted on 2 May 2009 by the Sejm with a vote of 404–0 and only three abstentions (Matthes, 2016).

The preamble is notable for two features. The first is the cited Christian values. The preamble reads, "God as the source of truth, justice, good and beauty" and "for our culture rooted in the Christian heritage of the Nation and in universal human values." This indicates the reality of a large percentage of Poles, with Roman Catholics making up 92.8% of the population.[19] As noted above, the Church played an important role in the drafting of the Constitution, and Pope John Paul II originally came from Poland. He also played an active role in democratization in Poland (Fitzmaurice, 1998).[20] The

---

[19] Infographic—Religiousness of Polish inhabitants. Retrieved June 25, 2021, from https://stat.gov.pl/en/infographics-and-widgets/infographics/infographic-religiousness-of-polish-inhabitiants,4,1.html.

[20] The referendum of the Constitution was held on 25 May 1997, just before the visit of Pope. Given the fact that Pope John Paul II is rather popular in Poland at that moment, and the Constitutional Drafting Committee was worried about Pope will cause uncertainty in the constitution-making.

second feature shows the Poles' national pride. In the preamble, the words "heritage" and "tradition" appear three times. The preamble demonstrates that Poland was not only influenced by the Church but also took its form of government from its history; the current government is the Third Polish Republic (Raabe, 2008).[21]

The first chapter is on the Polish Republic and addresses basic issues, such as the form of government, state structure, religion, relation between the Republic and international law, rule of law, basic freedom, marriage (a man and woman) and family, official language, and capital.

The next chapter mainly addresses the freedoms, rights, and obligations of persons and citizens. It covers personal, political, and economic, social and cultural freedoms and rights, as well as the defense of these freedoms, rights and obligations. In general, the current Constitution guarantees basic rights and freedoms to people who do not hold Polish citizenship. It even asserts that the public authorities will combat epidemics to protect public health. The provisions regarding people's freedoms and rights are believed to account for more than 25% of the Constitution (Biernat & Kawczynska, 2019).

The next chapter discusses the sources of law, limiting them to the Constitution, statutes, ratified international agreements, and regulations.

Based on the separation of powers, the following five chapters address legislative, executive, and judicial power. Chapter four focuses on the legislative power. Poland's parliament has a bicameral structure, with the Senate the upper house and the Sejm the lower house, both with four-year terms of office. The Sejm is composed of 460 deputies chosen via direct and proportional elections, and the 100 senators are elected by direct elections. To be elected to the Sejm, a person must be a Polish citizen and at least 21 years old; to be a senator, one must be at least 30. Because parliamentarism overwhelmed presidentialism in the drafting of the Constitution, the Polish Constitution gives the Sejm expansive powers (Brzezinski, 1998). For example, in addition to introducing legislation, it can declare a state of war. Referenda, also introduced in the Constitution, are to be held on matters of particular state importance. The Sejm or president with the consent of the Senate can decide to hold a referendum.

The President of Poland is elected directly by Poles. The president has a 5-year term and may be reelected only once. A candidate who receives half of the valid votes shall be the president. This means that there may occasionally be a runoff election in cases where no candidate wins half of the valid votes in the first round. According to the Constitution, the president is the supreme representative and the supreme commander of Poland's armed forces. The president appoints the prime minister, judges, the President of the Supreme Court, the Constitutional Tribunal, and the Supreme Administrative Court.

The central government in Poland is the Council of Ministers, and it is led by the President of the Council of Ministers (prime minister). In addition to the prime

---

[21] According to the Constitution, the current government of Poland is the Third Polish Republic, even though the ruling Party PiS trying to establish a so-called Fourth Polish Republic by arguing the Third Republic is a heritage of the communist regime.

minister, the Council of Ministers consists of deputy prime ministers and ministers. After being appointed, the prime minister submits a program of activity of the Council of Ministers to the Sejm, and the prime minister survives if he or she receives an absolute majority in a vote of confidence in the Sejm. The Voivode (a local governor) is the representative of the Council of Ministers in a voivodeship and is appointed and dismissed by the Council of Ministers.

The basic unit of local self-government in Poland is the Commune (Gmina). In general, local government enjoys great power in its communities. However, the actions of the local government are subject to review by the prime minister, Voivodes and regional audit chambers. If any local government entity flagrantly violates the constitution or a statute, it will be dissolved by the Sejm.

Poland's judiciary consists of courts and tribunals. The court system includes the Supreme Court, common courts, administrative courts, and military courts. Judges are appointed by the president and exercise their power independently. The National Council of the Judiciary ensures the independence of the courts and judges via submitting an application to the Constitutional Tribunal. This chapter also states that the Constitutional Tribunal will safeguard the constitutionality of several important state matters. The Tribunal of State is an independent judicial organ that decides the constitutional responsibilities of some important public officials, such as the President of the Republic, the prime minister and other ministers.

Several organs are introduced in the Constitution to audit the state and safeguard freedoms and rights. The Supreme Chamber of Control audits the activities of government entities, and it is led by the President of the Supreme Chamber of Control, who is appointed by the Sejm. The Commissioner for Citizens' Rights safeguards citizens' basic rights and freedoms. To protect freedom of speech, the National Council of Radio Broadcasting and Television is introduced in the Constitution.

The chapter on public finance sets the principles for management of public financial resources. The following chapter addresses extraordinary measures to control situations of particular danger, such as martial law, states of emergency and states of natural disaster. It also addresses the process to amend the Constitution. The submission of bills of amendment is allowed by the deputies (at least one-fifth of the members of the Sejm), the Senate, and the President of the Republic. The process for adopting amendments was described *supra*. Compared to the procedures for constitutional amendment in other Visegrad countries, the Polish procedures are stringent.

The last chapter contains final and transitional provisions. Because the current Constitution replaced the Small Constitution and could potentially create difficulties in state governance, provisions were added to resolve these issues.

Although the preparation of the Constitution was a lengthy process, its adoption could be described as a narrow victory. The Sejm approved it on 2 April 1997 with support from the left wing before the visit of the Pope and Poland's 1997 parliamentary elections. The referendum was held one month later, with 52.7% votes in favor and only 42.86% eligible voters taking part. The validity of the referendum result was debated. The act on referenda requires the participation of at least 50% of voters for validity. The interpreters of this act ruled that the act only applies to ordinary bills; therefore, the referendum on the Constitution did not require at least 50% of voters. Obviously, this interpretation did not persuade the masses, but they had to accept the result. There have only been two amendments to date, and several proposed amendments have failed to be adopted (Matthes, 2016).[22] A new development occurred in 2020, when the ruling party proposed a new amendment to extend the term of office to seven years. The current provision of the Constitution sets the term of office of the President of the Republic at five years (Plucinska & Ptak, 2020).

6.2.5 Comparative Analysis of the Development of Constitutions in China and the Visegrad States After the Transformation Period

It is difficult to compare China's Constitution and those of the Visegrad states. However, comparative constitutional law emerged as an academic discipline after the end of the Second World War due to the East/West divide (Rosenfeld & Sajo, 2012). Here, the author does not wish to make this comparison with a heavy ideological bent, as was often the case during the Cold War (Rosenfeld & Sajo, 2012). The contextual analysis instead focuses on the arrangement of state power. New developments in constitutionality review in China and the Visegrad states are presented *infra*.

6.2.5.1 Arrangement of State Power in China and the Visegrad States After the Transformation Period

People's Congress system versus separation of powers.

According to the current Constitution, China maintains the People's Congress system. Article 2, paragraphs 1 and 2 read:

All power in the People's Republic of China belongs to the people.

The National People's Congress and the local people's congresses at various levels are the organs through which the people exercise state power.

The Constitution itself regards the People's Congress system as the basis of the PRC and an important means to ensure that people have a say in matters of the country (Xu & Niu, 2019). Unlike the accepted principle of separation of powers in the Visegrad region, China insists on the People's Congress system. Namely, the NPC is to empower other state organs and rule the entire country in the name of Chinese people.

Chapter three of the Chinese Constitution regulates the structure of the state. The NPC is the highest organ of state power. Given that it only holds one annual

---

[22] Several unsuccessful amendments have been presented by Matthes, in her article, the protection of unborn life (2007), reorganizing the tasks and competencies of the President (2010), and the Introduction of the Euro and Poland's relation to international institutions (2011).

meeting for 10–12 days, it has a permanent body, the Standing Committee of the NPC (Article 57). Under the NPC and its Standing Committee, there are the following organs: the State Council for executive affairs, the Supreme People's Court, the Supreme People's Procuratorate for judicial affairs, the Supervisory Commission for supervisory affairs, and the Central Military Commission for military affairs. The president of the PRC is elected by the NPC. The constitutional amendment of 2004 empowered the president "to be involved in State affairs". It changed the president from a titular head of state to a more active entity. However, compared to the relations between the NPC and the other five organs, the President of the PRC is relatively detached from the NPC.

In the Visegrad states, based on the principle of separation of powers, the constitutions distribute state power as follows: legislative, executive, and judicial. Two of the four countries have introduced bicameralism, namely, legislative power composed of two chambers.[23] Executive power usually has two components: the government and the president. The constitutions of these countries, except for Hungary, provide that the president of the republic is elected by universal, equal, and direct secret ballot; therefore, the presidents in these three countries are not titular heads of state and are actively involved in governing. In Hungary, the president is elected by the members of the National Assembly. In contrast to the other three Visegrad states, presidential elections in Hungary occur via indirect secret ballot. This is also reflected in the powers of the president; in Hungary, the prime minister is elected by the National Assembly on the proposal of the president. In the other three countries, the president appoints and removes the prime minister, although after appointment, the prime minister must win a vote of confidence in the Sejm. In general, judicial power in the Visegrad states has two components: the constitutional court (tribunal) and the (normal) courts. The constitutional court (tribunal) is considered a special judicial organ for defending the constitution. However, according to the Chinese constitutional amendment of 2018 and decisions by the Standing Committee of the NPC, the Constitution and Law Committee shall ensure the constitutionality of normative documents.

The previous paragraphs analyzed how the Chinese and Visegrad states organize state power. China has the People's Congress system, and the 2018 amendment argues that this system has been chosen by the Chinese people throughout Chinese history in wartime. The amendment emphasizes the importance of the NPC, which empowers other state organs, all of which are accountable to the NPC. State power in China is not checked or balanced. According to the Constitution, the state organs are empowered by and accountable to the NPC. The power of the NPC comes from the people, and the NPC is accountable to the people. In the Visegrad states, the arrangement of state power follows the classic theory of checks and balances; it is divided into three parts, and for each part, one or more state organs exercises this state power. To protect the separation of powers, the constitutions in these countries

---

[23] In Czech Republic, the Parliament consists of Senate and Chamber of Deputies. In Poland, the Parliament consists of Senate and Sejm. The rest of two countries, Hungary and Slovakia only have one chamber.

emphasize the independence of state organs; for example, independent courts are always required in a democratic constitution.

To carry out the tasks of governing, similar state organs have been established in China and the Visegrad states, such as the president of the republic, the courts, the government, and legislative organs (although the names of the latter two may differ by country). The president of the republic in each country is the head of the state and is considered the representative of the country in foreign affairs and to receive letters of credence from other countries. The president may sign legislation and publish it in the official law journal. The courts handle civil and criminal cases according to the law. However, some special courts may be established, such as maritime, military, financial, and IP courts in China. Such courts may specialize in initial trials involving maritime, military, financial, and IP issues. The central government in each country is headed by the prime minister and composed of vice prime ministers and ministers. The powers of the government cover different areas, such as the economy, education, and foreign affairs.

Conducting this comparison, two different theories of distribution of state power appear to have caused the differences between China and the Visegrad states. China declares, "all power belongs to the people, the representatives of the people, the people's congress at all levels, shall exercise State power." Therefore, China adopted the People's Congress system, in which all other state organs are elected by and accountable to the People's Congress. In the Visegrad states, after the Revolutions of 1989, following a classic constitutional doctrine of checks and balances, countries introduced the principle of separation of powers in their constitutions (Banaszak et al, 2012).[24] Legislative, executive, and judicial power are distributed to different state organs to ensure that no single organ has absolute control over others and that each state organ is independent and has the power to limit the powers of others. The author does not wish to judge the pros and cons of these two systems because both in fact have their weaknesses. In general, China's system has fulfilled its main task of rapidly developing China's economy. In the Visegrad states, balancing all interests with the rule of law is highly valued; therefore, these countries adopted Western constitutions and embraced the EU criteria in them.

6.3 Comparative Analysis of the Constitutionality Review Systems in China and the Visegrad States After the Transformation Period

In the late people's republics in the Visegrad states, constitutional courts or tribunals were introduced into the constitutions. Czechoslovakia restored its Constitutional Court in the Constitution of 1968. However, this Court did not operate until an

---

[24] Even though, in the book of Constitutional Law in Poland, the authors described the system of form of government as division of powers and gave Montesquieu credit for the idea of division of powers.

amendment was adopted in 1991 (Cutlert & Schwartz, 1991). Poland adopted a constitutional act to create the Constitutional Tribunal in 1982, and the first constitutional case was heard in 1986 (Lukaszuk & Lukaszuk, 2011). After the Revolutions of 1989, the Visegrad states introduced their own constitutionality review systems. Constitutionality review emerged in China in 2017. A report of the 19th National Congress of the CPC declared an intent "to advance the constitutionality review". In this part, the author discusses the development of constitutionality review in each country. First, an introduction presents two constitutional cases from China and Poland and explains why constitutionality review should be compared among the different countries. Each country's system of constitutionality review is examined *infra*.

6.3.1 Introduction: Abortion Ban and Custody-and-Education Abolition

In October 2020, the Polish Constitutional Tribunal ruled that abortion laws in Poland were inconsistent with the Constitution of the Republic of Poland.[25] This meant that almost all kinds of abortions are banned in Poland. This judgment triggered nationwide protest, although Poland was facing the second wave of the COVID-19 pandemic (Easton, 2020). The protests occurring in Poland were supported by people from neighboring countries (Erdo-Bonyar, 2020; Zahradnicek-Haas, 2020).[26] Dunja Mijatovic, the Commissioner for Human Rights at the Council of Europe, tweeted that it was "a sad day for women's rights".

In December 2019, the Standing Committee of the NPC of the PRC handed down a decision abolishing China's custody-and-education system.[27] Four months later, in April 2020, Li Keqiang, the Prime Minister of the State Council of the PRC, signed the Decree, and it abolished the Measures for the Custody-and-Education of Persons Engaging in Prostitution and Whoring (2011 Revision, hereafter the Measures).[28] The custody-and-education system was developed to educate and rescue people engaging in prostitution and other forms of sex work and to prevent the spread

---

[25] [2020] Ref. No. K 1/20 (PL). Retrieved June 25, 2021, from https://trybunal.gov.pl/en/hearings/judgments/art/11300-planowanie-rodziny-ochrona-plodu-ludzkiego-i-warunki-dopuszczalnosci-przerywania-ciazy.

[26] Hungarians held a peaceful demonstration in front of the Polish Embassy to Hungary in Budapest, Czechs also showed their supporting in Prague.

[27] Xinhua (2019, December 30). Custody and Education' Penalty for Prostitution Abolished by Lawmakers. *China Daily*. Retrieved June 25, 2021, from https://www.chinadaily.com.cn/a/201912/30/WS5e09549fa310cf3e355815e0.html.

[28] China Amends, Abolishes Administrative Regulations (2020, April 2). Xinhua News. Retrieved June 25, 2021, from http://www.xinhuanet.com/english/2020-04/02/c_138942052.htm.

of sexually transmitted diseases.[29] Recently, this system has been strongly criticized at home and abroad (He, 2016).[30] According to the Filing and Reviewing Working Report of the Commission of Legislative Affairs of the Standing Committee of the NPC, CPPCC members advised on the constitutionality of the custody-and-education system and asserted that legislation on this system was inconsistent with the Constitution (Regulations Filing & Review Department of Legislative Affairs Commission of the Standing Committee of the NPC, 2020).

Poland's abortion ban violated women's right to make decisions about their bodies in the name of protecting unborn children's dignity.[31] In China, the right to terminate a pregnancy is easily accepted and respected (Tatlow, 2012).[32] However, some in the Visegrad states feel differently. The same month that the Polish Constitutional Tribunal declared the unconstitutionality of the abortion laws, conservatives in Slovakia promoted legislation tightening the abortion rules that had been voted on in the parliament. The draft bill failed to restrict abortion in Slovakia, with a result of 59–58.[33] Late that same month, Hungary, the Republic of Poland, and 31 other countries signed the so-called Geneva Consensus Declaration to protect women's health and strengthen families against abortion (Borger, 2020).[34]

Similarly, in formulating the Decision of the Standing' Committee of the NPC on the Strict Prohibition against Prostitution and Whoring (hereafter the Decision), the government justified the custody-and-education system as protecting women's health and defending the values of society (He, 2016).[35] However, as the system

---

[29] Article 1, Measures for the Custody-and-Education of Persons Engaging in Prostitution and Whoring (2011 Revision). Retrieved June 25, 2021, from http://www.gov.cn/gongbao/content/2011/content_1860773.htm.

[30] Asia Catalyst (2013). "Custody and Education": Arbitrary Detention for Female Sex Workers in China. Asia Catalyst report. Retrieved June 25, 2021, from https://asiacatalyst.org/wp-content/uploads/2014/09/AsiaCatalyst_CustodyEducation2013-12-EN.pdf.

[31] [2020] Ref. No. K 1/20 (PL). Retrieved June 25, 2021, from https://trybunal.gov.pl/en/hearings/judgments/art/11300-planowanie-rodziny-ochrona-plodu-ludzkiego-i-warunki-dopuszczalnosci-przerywania-ciazy.

[32] The Article 35 of the Population and Family Planning Law of PRC (revised in 2015) only prohibited one situation of Sex-selective pregnancy termination for non-medical purposes, and the Article 51(1) of the Protection of Women's Rights and Interests Law of PRC (revised in 2005) read that "Women have the right to child-bearing in accordance with relevant regulations of the state as well as the freedom not to bear any child." And the article 37 of the Constitution of PRC (revised in 2018) provided that "Freedom of the person of citizens of the People's Republic of China is inviolable." Actually, China is the one of the largest countries with the abortion cases.

[33] Reuters Staff (2020, October 21). Slovak parliament narrowly rejects tightening of abortion rules. *Reuters*. Retrieved June 25, 2021, from https://www.reuters.com/article/uk-slovakia-abortions/slovak-parliament-narrowly-rejects-tightening-of-abortion-rules-idUKKBN2752M1.

[34] "better health for woman" and "strengthening of family as the foundational unit of society" are two pillars that the Declaration tries to achieve. Geneva Consensus Declaration is available. English version. Retrieved June 25, 2021, from https://www.hhs.gov/about/agencies/oga/global-health-diplomacy/protecting-life-global-health-policy/geneva-declaration.html.

[35] Prior to the adoption of the Decision, some areas set up a place for prostitutes who have Sexually transmitted infections. In these places, the government will treat these prostitutes and give them vocational training. In the Explanation on the Decision of the Strict Prohibition against Prostitution

operated, criticism grew', and CPPCC members even brought it to constitutionality review. The custody-and-education system was abolished in 2019.

These cases have some interesting similarities. First, both involved women's rights. In the abortion case, Poland's Constitutional Tribunal ruled that the Family Planning Act of 1993 was inconsistent with the Constitution. Therefore, Poland has become one of the strictest countries with regard to abortion in Europe. From the view of the Constitutional Tribunal, a woman's right to choose is less important than the dignity of unborn children. In the Chinese case, it is believed that the State Council initiated the custody-and-education system to protect women's rights, since sex work and prostitution were generally considered destructive to families and women's rights at the time that the measures were passed. Second, the representatives of the legislature promote the review of laws. In the abortion case, a group of deputies of the Sejm submitted an application to the Polish Constitutional Tribunal, and it initiated a constitutionality review of the Polish Abortion Act (Rakowska-Trela, 2020). In the case of the custody-and-education system, 30 NPC deputies brought a bill to abolish the system to the session of the NPC. Prior to the deputies' bill, CPPCC members submitted a bill requesting constitutionality review of the custody-and-education system (Regulations Filing & Review Department of Legislative Affairs Commission of the Standing Committee of the NPC, 2020).

Although these cases have similarities, there are differences in the constitutionality review in Poland and China. First, its subjects differ. Poland, along with the other Visegrad states, follows an Austro-German model, with a constitutional court (tribunal) charged with constitutionality review. However, in China, according to the constitutional laws, the NPC's Constitution and Law Committee and the Legislative Affairs Commission of the NPC Standing Committee play the main roles in constitutionality review. Second, the powers of the organs of constitutionality review in Poland and China differ. In Poland, the Tribunal has the right to decide whether a bill conforms to the Constitution upon the request of the President of the Republic (Article 122, paragraph 3), namely, it can conduct *ex ante* review. It also has the power to review constitutional complaints or constitutional applications, namely, to conduct *ex post* review. In China, whether the organ of the constitutionality review has the power to conduct *ex ante* review is open to question. A so-called Recording and Review system is expected to perform this function. Third, the organization of the organs of constitutionality review differs. In Poland, 15 Constitutional Judges, including one President and one Vice President of the Constitutional Tribunal, are elected by the Sejm, and the judges' term is 9 years. In China, the NPC Constitution and Law Committee has 18 members, including one Chairman and seven Vice Chairmen. There are no term limits for members, and one term is 5 years. The author will stop enumerating the differences between constitutionality review in Poland

---

and Whoring, it mentioned that the prostituting and whoring severely degraded the social conduct. The custody-and-education system is one of the measures to prevent the prostituting and whoring and defend the social conduct and value. The explanation of draft bill is available at NPC's website. Retrieved June 25, 2021 from http://www.npc.gov.cn/wxzl/gongbao/2000-12/28/content_5002615.htm.

and China here, since there are obviously many comparisons to be made, and the comparative analysis continues below.

The main purpose of the examples of the Polish abortion ban and custody-and-education abolition in China is to present three basic ideas: First, constitutionality review exists in Poland (the Visegrad states) and China. Second, the Polish (the Visegrad states') model of constitutionality review is very typical of Kelsenian-type constitutional courts, but the Chinese one is difficult to define (some may describe it as constitutional review with Chinese characteristics). Third, and most important, although there are many differences between the Polish and Chinese constitutionality review systems, some rules are universally applied, and the author considers them as constitutional consensus.

6.3.2 Constitutionality Review in China After the Transformation Period

In China, most provisions on constitutionality review are stipulated in the Constitution. The current Constitution of the PRC was promulgated in 1982. The latest amendment, adopted in 2018, contains the provision related to constitutionality review.[36]

In contrast to its bold legislation on economic issues, China's ruling party is more cautious in political and judicial reforms. In 2017, the Report of the 19th National Congress of the CPC emphasized the goal "to advance the constitutionality review".[37] The fifth amendment renamed the Law Committee of the NPC the Constitution and Law Committee of the NPC, and according to a Decision by the Standing Committee of the NPC, one of the committee's duties is "to advance the constitutionality review". Hence, the task of constitutionality review is carried out by the NPC's Constitution and Law Committee.[38]

As noted above, there were two waves of constitutionality review in China. The first took place at the turn of the century, and several significant cases were considered leading cases. Details on the first wave were presented in the previous chapter on constitutional development in the transformation period.

---

[36] In 2017, the 19th National Congress of the CPC declared "to advance the constitutionality review".

[37] According to a news report, the concept of the "constitutionality review" for the first time mentioned in the official documents was happened in 1998, a work report of the Standing Committee of the NPC that mentioned the concept of "constitutionality review". Xinhua News (2017, October 20). Constitutionality review to strengthen rule of law. Retrieved June 25, 2021, from http://www.xinhuanet.com/english/2017-10/20/c_136694449.htm.

[38] Xinhua News, (2018, June 22). Duties of NPC constitution and law committee approved. Retrieved June 25, 2021, from http://www.xinhuanet.com/english/2018-06/22/c_137274151.htm.

The second wave of constitutionality review, triggered by the 19th National Congress of the CPC in 2017, emphasized the aim "to advance the constitutionality review".[39] In March 2018, the fifth constitutional amendment was adopted by the NPC. It renamed the Legal Committee of the NPC the Constitution and Legal Committee of the NPC. According to the amendment, the Standing Committee of the NPC made the following Decision: "Besides continuing the duties of reviewing draft laws, the Constitutionality and Law Committee of the NPC shall carry out the duties of promoting the constitutional implementation, operating constitutional interpretation, advancing constitutionality review, strengthening constitutional supervision and coordinating with the constitutional publicity."[40] Hence, the Constitution and Law Committee of the NPC has the duty to review the constitutionality of laws and regulations.[41] However, the structure and organization of constitutionality review in China are still not established, and there is no single constitutionality review case decided by the Constitution and Law Committee of the NPC.

Nevertheless, some progress in constitutionality review has been achieved. For example, since 2017, an annual report on the work of recording and reviewing has been released by the Legislative Affairs Commission of the Standing Committee of the NPC. In the 3 released reports (from 2017 to 2019), constitutionality review was mentioned 6 times in total (each report mentioning it twice), and the case mentioned in the first part was discussed in the 2018 and 2019 reports.

The very first case of constitutionality review in China was released in the report of the filing and review in 2020. The report states that in the case, the regulation on compulsory teaching of the languages of ethnic minorities in ethnic minority schools was ruled incompatible with the Constitution. According to Article 19, paragraph 5 of the Constitution, "the State promotes the nationwide use of Putonghua (or Mandarin, common speech based on Beijing pronunciation)" (Shen, 2021). However, the report did not provide more information on this case at the moment of writing.

6.3.3 *Constitutionality Review in Hungary After the Transformation Period*

Hungary's Constitutional Court was established in 1989. Creating a Constitutional Court was not one of the original goals of the Round Table. It planned to leave the

---

[39] The Report of the 19th National Congress of the CPC. Retrieved June 25, 2021, from http://www.chinadaily.com.cn/interface/flipboard/1142846/2017-11-06/cd_34188086.html.

[40] 全国人民代表大会常务委员会关于全国人民代表大会宪法和法律委员会职责问题的决定 [Decisions on the Duties of the Constitution and Law Committee of the NPC], NPC of the People's Republic of China official website. Retrieved June 25, 2021, from http://www.npc.gov.cn/npc/c30834/201806/e5d0e4ba9f6d4ba8b8400d347d299a7f.shtml.

[41] In general, the highest state power in China, the National People's Congress has the power to supervise the constitutional. However, considering that the NPC only operate once a year, the major tasks are carried out by its Standing Committee and its special committees, especially the Constitution and Law Committee of the NPC.

6.3 Comparative Analysis of the Constitutionality …

creation of this Court to the Parliament, which was expected to be freely elected in 1990 (Csink & Schanda, 2015). However, the unexpectedly successful discussion on the Constitutional Court accelerated the court's establishment. Act XXXII of 1989 declared the purpose of creating the Constitutional Court, "to establish rule of law, to protect constitutional order and the fundamental rights and to foster the division of powers and their equilibrium."[42]

Following the European model of centralization, Hungary's Constitutional Court is considered an independent organ to protect the constitution (Dezso, 2010). The constitution provides that it consists of 15 justices who serve 12-year terms and may not be reelected. The court is headed by the president, who is selected by the parliament.

The history of the Constitutional Court the be divided into two stages: The first began with the formation of the court and ended with the adoption of the current Constitution (1989–2010), and the second is from 2011 to the present (Albi, 2019; Csink & Schanda, 2015).[43] Scholars describe the first stage as "activist" (Csink & Schanda, 2015; Halmai, 2002), and constitutionality review in this stage was considered "strong" (Zhao, 2020).

In the first stage, the court was first led by Laszlo Solyom (from 1990 to 1998) and consisted of 11 justices. According to the act, the President of the Constitutional Court is elected by the justices themselves for a term of three years (Schwartz, 2000). The Solyom Court was widely considered an activist Court (Csink & Schanda, 2015; Halmai, 2002); Justice Solyom, who later became the President of Hungary, presided protecting the fundamental rights of citizens based on the rule of law, democracy, and equality before the law. Under his leadership, the court ruled in cases on capital punishment, the regulation of abortion, and the legal equality of same-sex partnerships (Solyom & Brunner, 2000).[44] However, the court's activism was not welcomed by everyone. For example, Bela Pokol (currently serving as a Justice of the Constitutional Court), the constitutional law professor, criticized the court's decisions as based only on "superabstract" legal principles (Halmai, 2002). Although the Solyom Court gained international prestige because of its bold decisions, the court has since had to turn in a different direction.

The turning point for the court occurred in 2010 (Drinoczi & Bien-Kacala, 2021).[45] That year, the parliamentary election demonstrated Hungarians' desire for change. The current nationalist ruling party gained two-thirds of the MPs, and with

---

[42] In current Constitution of Hungary, the Article 24 regulated that the Constitutional Court is expected as the supreme body for the protection of the Fundamental Law.

[43] Such kind of divisions of the Constitutional Court in Hungary may refer to Anneli Albi's article..

[44] The Constitutional Court ruled the capital punishment was unconstitutional and abolished it. Decision No. 23/1990. The Constitutional Court left an open door to the Parliament to decide whether the fetus is or is not a person, according to the Constitutional Court, if the fetus was considered as a person, then the fetus deserved the absolute protection of life, if the fetus was not considered as a person, then only relative protection shall be applied to. Decision 64/1991. The Constitutional Court also recognized the same sex partnership in the Decision 14/1995.

[45] The Constitutional development in Hungary and Poland for an illiberal turning started from 2010 and 2015 respectively.

this majority, a new Constitution was adopted in 2011. Following Hungary's legislative process, in a sense, the will of the nationalist Fidesz could be considered de facto legislation; this phenomenon sparked a discussion of populist constitutionalism in Hungary (Gardos-Orosz, 2021). In addition, prior to the adoption of the Constitution, significant legislation on the Constitutional Court was passed. The new laws raised the number of justices on the court to 15 from 11. The term of office became 12 years with no possibility of reelection. The most important change involved the election of the President of the Constitutional Court, which was previously done by the constitutional justices. Although the vice president continues to be elected by the constitutional justices, the revised act provided that the president would be selected by the parliament. As Fidesz continues to maintain its ruling position in Hungary, all of the current constitutional justices were elected by the Fidesz-ruled parliament.[46] The Constitutional Court in its second stage has been widely criticized in the EU and beyond (mainly in the US) for its illiberal turn (Chronowski et al, 2019). Within Hungary, experts have also decried the country's current constitutional culture as "government without checks, weakening of the protection of fundamental rights, and political preferences in the Fundamental Law." (Halmai, 2019)[47] One of the features of the current constitutional culture is the significance of Christianity. The current Constitution reads, "[Christianity] made our country a part of Christian Europe" and "we recognize the role of Christianity in preserving nationhood". The Constitution also overruled Decision 14/1995 of the Constitutional Court on same-sex partnership, in which "the regulation of partners in a domestic partnership and relatives was arbitrary, violating the right to human dignity in 70/A." Because of the Decision, the Civil Code was revised, changing the provision on domestic partnership from between "men and women" to "persons" (Solyom & Brunner, 2000). However, the current Constitution states "Hungary shall protect the institution of marriage as the union of a man and a woman." Additionally, *ex ante* review has been introduced to the Constitutional Court.

At present, Hungary's system of constitutionality review faces wide criticism for its illiberal turn. Fidesz, the ruling party, is generally held accountable for the decline of constitutionalism (Scheppele, 2015). Due to the lack of checks and balances, a dispute over the former President of the National Judicial Office (NJO) caused a constitutional crisis. The former NJO President was accused of breaking the law regarding recruitment and promotion of judges. However, the Fidesz-controlled parliament decided to keep her in office in 2019[48] and elected her a constitutional justice in late 2019. Given the close relations between the Constitutional Court and the parliament (all the current constitutional justices were elected by the Fidesz-ruled parliament), the court is considered a close ally of Fidesz. For this reason, attention

---

[46] Up to April 2021, the Constitutional Court of Hungary consists of 14 Judges: one President and 13 Judges. Please see the official website of the Constitutional Court of Hungary. Retrieved June 25, 2021, from https://hunconcourt.hu/current-members.

[47] In Prof. Halmai's article, he argued there are 6 flaws in the constitutionalism in Hungary.

[48] Hungarian Helsinki Committee (2019, July 9). *A Constitutional Crisis in the Hungarian Judiciary*. Retrieved June 25, 2021, from https://helsinki.hu/wp-content/uploads/A-Constitutional-Crisis-in-the-Hungarian-Judiciary-09072019.pdf.

should continue to be paid to how the Constitutional Court keeps its independence in constitutionality review and how the principle of checks and balances applies to the parliament and government.

6.3.4 Constitutionality Review in the Czech Republic After the Transformation Period

Czechoslovakia was one of the first countries to introduce the Constitutional Court model into its Constitution in 1920.[49] However, from 1920 to 1948, the court left no significant mark on the history of constitutional development.[50] The Constitutional Court was restored in 1968 in the Federal Constitution only on paper and did not operate until 1991, when a constitutional act (91/1991 Coll.) was adopted.

After the dissolution of Czechoslovakia, the Constitution of the Czech Republic was adopted in December 1992. Article 62 empowered the President of the Republic to appoint justices, the President, and the Vice President of the Constitutional Court with the consent of the Senate (however, the Senate did not operate until 1996). In June 1993, almost one month before the Constitutional Court began operating, the Constitutional Court Act (182/1993 Sb.) was adopted. The act detailed the court's structure, powers and procedures, stating that the court would be seated in Brno and have 15 members serving 10-year terms. Following the justices' term of office, the Constitutional Court can be analyzed in 10-year phases. The Court's first 10 years (1993–2003) may be summarized as marked by conflicts between it and the ordinary courts. In the second 10 years (2003–2013), with the development of the jurisprudence of constitutionality review, the Constitution and constitutional reasoning were taken more seriously (Kuhn, 2017). The third stage started in 2013 and will end in 2023. Pavel Rychetsky is the President of the court, reappointed for the second time in 2013. Given the increased populism in the Czech Republic, the court has become less activist and is now the most self-restrained Court since the Revolutions of 1989 (Kuhn, 2021). Havel, the former President of the Czech Republic, appointed the court's first 12 justices (including the president) on 15 July 1993, and the last 3 justices were appointed in 1993 and 1994. This marked the official operation of the Constitutional Court in the Czech Republic.

---

[49] Czechoslovakia and Austria are the first two countries established a specialized constitutional court after the First World War. Prior to the independence of the Czechoslovakia, Austro-Hungary covers Czech and Slovakia's land, especially for the urban area of Czechia, many German-speaking Austrians lived in Prague. For example, the designer of the Constitution of First Austrian Republic, Hans Kelsen was born in Prague.

[50] Constitutional court of the Czechoslovak republic and its fortunes in years 1920–1948. In the website of the Constitutional Court of Czech Republic (Excerpt from the monograph: Langasek, T. (2011) Ústavní soud Československé republiky a jeho osudy v letech 1920–1948. Vydavatelství a nakladatelství Aleš Čeněk, s. r. o.) Retrieved June 24, 2021, from https://www.usoud.cz/en/constitutional-court-of-the-czechoslovak-republic-and-its-fortunes-in-years-1920-1948/.

The Constitutional Court is designed as a negative legislator (Kuhn, 2011). To protect constitutionality, it may form a plenum or panel to review the constitutionality of normative documents or decisions by other courts (Kuhn, 2011).[51] Compared to the constitutional organs in the other Visegrad states and China, the Czech Constitutional Court enjoys broader powers to guarantee constitutionality (Prochazka, 2002). For example, the court may decide disputes between state bodies and bodies of self-governing regions. It also adjudges constitutional petitions not only by the work of rapporteurs and panels but in some cases also through oral hearings and/or evidence. If the decisions of an international tribunal are binding on the Czech Republic pursuant to international treaties, the Constitutional Court will guarantee the implementation of such decisions. In particular, these decisions are related to human rights or fundamental freedoms (Fitzmaurice, 1998). With the activism of the Constitutional Court and following the constitutional provision that "enforceable decisions of the Constitutional Court are binding on all authorities and persons." (Article 89 (2)), the discussion of "who has the last word in the legal order" has been widely debated in the Czech Republic. The legislature tried to ignore a decision by the Constitutional Court (in a notable case involving statutes on salaries of the judiciary). Therefore, conflicts between the Constitutional Court and the parliament (Chamber of Deputies) have increased (Priban, 2002).

As noted above, the Constitutional Court reviews not only the constitutionality of normative documents but also decisions by ordinary courts (Kuhn, 2011). From the court's latest statistics, among the 4200 petitions before it in 2019, 4172 were constitutional complaints and others. Plenums have been held 28 times.[52] In its daily practice of constitutionality review, the court has been heavily influenced by the German Constitutional Court and has followed some important doctrines of German constitutional law, such as the radiation effect of fundamental law (Kuhn, 2011), which ensures the highest position of constitutional law in cases in ordinary courts. In addition to the German influence, the Czech Constitutional Court used to take an EU-friendly approach in its exercise of constitutionality review. According to the current Constitution, to ratify an international treaty, *ex ante* review of constitutionality is needed (Fruhstorfer & Moormann-Kimakova, 2016). Therefore, before the Treaty of Lisbon could be ratified, the Constitutional Court assessed its constitutionality, although the Treaty was ultimately not approved by the then-Euroskeptic President of the Czech Republic and senators (Brink, 2010).[53] However, this EU-friendly trend in the court is beginning to reverse. The most notable and frequently-discussed example of this is its decision in the Slovak Pensions case (PL. US 5/12). This decision challenged the EU framework, or, more specifically, the judgment of the Court of Justice of the European Union (CJEU), arguing that the CJEU had exceeded the

---

[51] Not like the Austrian (Kelsenian) model of Constitutional Court, the Czechia Constitutional Court shall not only review the constitutionality of norms, but also the criminal or civil cases which judged in the ordinary courts.

[52] Year Book of the Constitutional Court of Czech Republic. Retrieved June 25, 2021, from https://www.usoud.cz/fileadmin/user_upload/ustavni_soud_www/Rocenky/Rocenka_US_2019_EN.pdf.

[53] The Decisions 2009/11/03 Pl. US 29/09: Treaty of Lisbon II. Retrieved June 25, 2021, from https://www.usoud.cz/en/decisions/2009-11-03-pl-us-29-09-treaty-of-lisbon-ii.

powers that the Czech Republic transferred to the EU and that it was therefore *ultravires* (Bobek, 2014; Komarek, 2012; Kuhn, 2019; Pitrova, 2013).[54]

6.3.5 Constitutionality Review in Slovakia After the Transformation Period

As one of the component parts of Czechoslovakia, the Slovak Republic established its own constitutionality review system in the 1990s. Although this was the first time Slovakia established a constitutionality review system as a newly independent country, Slovaks did not question the establishment of the Constitutional Court in the Constitution of the Slovak Republic because the experiences of the former Federation endorsed the legitimacy of constitutionality review (Malova, 2002).[55] Therefore, the creation of a Constitutional Court in the hastily-adopted Constitution was taken for granted.

The current Constitution contains detailed provisions on the structure and powers of the Constitutional Court. However, several modifications have been made to the constitutional justices. The first is the term of office. Previously, this was seven years, shorter than the 10-year term for justices in the Constitutional Court of the Czechoslovakia Federation. The then-ruling Party Movement for Democratic Slovakia argued that a seven-year term was necessary for "testing" the court's independence (Malova, 2002). The constitutional amendment of 2001 lengthened the term from seven to twelve years. Another revision regarding the term of office concerned reappointment. The Constitutional Court Act of 1993 offered the option for a second appointment; however, it was revised by a 2018 constitutional amendment. Article 134 (3) of the new version of the Constitution reads, "The same person cannot be reappointed as a

---

[54] After the release of the Decision of the PL.US 5/12. Retrieved June 25, 2021, from https://www.soud.z/fileadmin/user_upload/ustavni_soud_www/Decisions/pdf/Pl%20US%205-12.pdf. A handful of articles discussed the narrative of the "ultra vires" of the judgment of the C-399/09 of the Court of Justice of the European Union. Retrieved June 25, 2021, from https://eur-lex.europa.eu/legal-content/EN/TXT/PDF/?uri=CELEX:62009CJ0399&from=EN. Some of the articles defended the Decision of the Constitutional Court, and asked should Czech "to eat humble pie". Also, some of the articles described the "ultra vires" of the C-399/09 of the CJEU as the Constitutional Court protecting the "judicial egos" of the respective national constitutional justices. One thing should be mentioned here is the Slovak Pensions saga involved the long-term conflict between Supreme Administrative Court and Constitutional Court. Some articles may help readers to understand the Landtova and Holubec cases and the conflict between Supreme Administrative Court and Constitutional Court.

[55] Prior to the dissolution of the Czechoslovakia, Constitutional Court had been established for twice, from 1921 to 1939, the Constitutional Court of Czechoslovakia performed the role of protection of constitutional implementation via abstract judicial review and constitutionality control of the laws. In the period of Second World War, the Slovak side was shortly "independent" as a satellite Sate of Nazi Germany, but the tradition of constitutional review couldn't keep in this period. The second wave of constitutional review building started in 1968, however such efforts of re-establishment of Constitutional Court didn't finalize until 1992. The Constitutional Court of Czechoslovak Federation only operated for one year since the split of the Czechoslovakia.

judge of the Constitutional Court again." The second change is related to the number of justices. In January 1993, at the establishment of the Constitutional Court, the President of Slovakia selected ten justices from twenty candidates nominated by the parliament. The revision to the Constitution increased the number of justices, and thirteen serve on the current Court.

The Constitution enumerated the court's powers through amendments. Generally, the court's main task is to protect constitutionality. In addition to *ex post* review of constitutionality, *ex ante* review was also implemented through a constitutional amendment. Namely, Article 125a (1) empowers the court to assess the constitutional conformity of negotiated international treaties. A treaty that is ruled inconsistent with the Constitution will not be ratified.

Based on the Kelsenian model of constitutionality review, Slovakia's Constitutional Court resolves conflicts between regulations and the Constitution, constitutional acts, or (and) promulgated international treaties, and provisions ruled unconstitutional will lose their effect. However, bodies that have issued unconstitutional regulations have six months to revise these regulations to harmonize them with the Constitution, constitutional laws, and promulgated international treaties. In addition, the court judges the conformity of referenda with the Constitution.

Constitutional complaints are also permitted in Slovakia's constitutionality review system. Natural or legal persons may submit such complaints to the Constitutional Court in cases of infringement of fundamental rights or freedoms. To protect their ability to self-govern, territorial self-government entities can also submit constitutional complaints to the court.

In addition to these normal powers, the Slovakian Constitution gives the court the following powers: (1) to interpret the Constitution; (2) to verify or reject verification of the mandate of an MP; (3) to decide elections of some important offices from the central to the local levels; (4) to decide the results of referenda and plebiscites on the recall of the President of the Slovak Republic; (5) to decide on the dissolution or suspension of a political party or movement; (6) to decide prosecutions against the President of the Slovak Republic on infringement of the Constitution or treason; (7) to decide the constitutionality of declarations of an exceptional state or emergency state. Decisions by the Constitutional Court are universally binding in the country.

Berdisova's textbook on the Slovakian Constitution concludes that the following doctrines have been accepted in the court's daily practices: subsidiarity, minimization of interference with the powers of other bodies, interpretation in conformity with Constitution, substantive rule of law, and proportionality (Berdisova, 2013).

Generally, compared to other constitutional courts in the Visegrad states, Slovakia's Court is relatively self-restrained. However, a constitutional decision made in January 2019 drew international attention to its jurisprudence. In this "Slovakian Marbury" case, the court ruled that a constitutional amendment was unconstitutional due to violating the substantive core of the Constitution (Lalik,). The Court "created" a new power for itself: to review the constitutionality of constitutional amendments. However, this ruling did not receive sufficient attention at home because at that time, Slovakians were about to elect their first female president (Drugda, 2019). The constitutional amendment adjudicated unconstitutional was introduced in 2014. The main issue in the amendment was a requirement for judges (including constitutional justices) to submit to a security clearance by the National Security Authority (intelligence agency). By proposing this amendment, the then-ruling party, Smer, sought to win the confidence of Slovaks, given that trust in Slovak courts was at a historical low at that time. The amendment was supported by Smer and other parties, with 102 MPs voting in favor (Domin, 2019; Moormann-Kimakova, 2016).

The 2019 decision by the Constitutional Court showed activism on the court and endorsed the theory of the substantive core of the Constitution, namely, in Article 1 (1), "The Slovak Republic is a sovereign, democratic state governed by the rule of law". It not only broadened the court's powers but also enriched the jurisprudence of constitutionality review in Slovakia. Therefore, a hierarchy of constitutional norms has been established, including substantive core and other constitutional norms (Lalik,). However, the Slovakian Constitutional Court soon reached a turning point. As only 90 MPs are needed to amend the Constitution in Slovakia, after the 2019 presidential election and the 2020 parliamentary election were resolved, the National Council (parliament) adopted a new constitutional amendment with 91 votes in favor versus 40 votes against in December 2020 (TASR, 2020). Among the amendment's provisions, revised Article 125 (4) stated that the Constitutional Court cannot decide on the constitutional conformity of constitutional amendments (Drugda, 2020). This amendment was criticized by legal scholars as "on its way to illiberal democracy" (Lalik,). Now the ball is in the Constitutional Court's court. Will it rule the latest amendment unconstitutional? Will a constitutional crisis erupt between the court and parliament? These questions should be followed now and in the near future.

6.3.6 Constitutionality Review in Poland After the Transformation Period

In the previous chapter, the author provided some information on constitutionality review in Poland in the transformation period. In short, the Constitutional Tribunal was introduced in Poland through different acts even before the Revolutions of 1989. The Polish Constitutional Tribunal was introduced in a constitutional amendment that was adopted in March 1982, and detailed provisions on it were finally promulgated on 29 April 1985.

The current Polish Constitution was adopted in 1997 and approved by a national referendum the same year. However, only 43% of eligible voters participated in the referendum, resulting in a bare majority (52.7%) of supporting votes. Due to the low support, opponents challenged the legitimacy of the newly adopted Constitution. However, this effort failed. The Polish Supreme Court supported the legitimacy of the 1997 Polish Constitution, and it was finally signed by the President of the Republic of Poland and entered into force on 17 October 1997 (Cole, 1998).

The current Polish Constitution created the system of constitutionality review (Constitutional Tribunal), which first appeared in the Polish People's Republic based on the Kelsenian model (Granat, 2018).

According to the 1997 Constitution, individuals may access the Constitutional Tribunal,[56] as was previously advocated by legal scholars (Brzezinski, 1993). The current Constitution expanded the groups that can access the Tribunal, as well as the scope of the Tribunal's constitutionality review. It can review statutes, international agreements, legal provisions, political parties and constitutional complaints (Brzezinski, 1993).[57] Its number of judges also increased. The current Tribunal has 15 members with nine-year terms, while the previous Tribunal had 12 members with eight-year terms.[58] However, examining the exercise of constitutionality review in Poland, it seems that the system does not always function independently (Easton, 2020).[59] Occasionally, political and religious factors affect judgments in constitutionality review. Discussion of a possible constitutional crisis in Poland has never ended (Bunikowski, 2018; Matczak, 2020; Tomczak, 2020).[60] A notable constitutional crisis occurred in 2015, when the newly-elected president refused to confirm a list of the 5 constitutional judges elected by the last Sejm (Bunikowski, 2018). This political dispute marked Poland's turn in a conservative-nationalistic direction rather than a pro-EU direction.

In addition to Poland's constitutional crisis, with the development of the jurisprudence of constitutionality review, the so-called constitutional values gained an important place in the daily practice of the Constitutional Tribunal. Namely, the vague concepts of human dignity, common good and justice have been employed by the Tribunal in its reasoning (Granat, 2018).[61]

The question of how to set up a constitutionality review system in a postsocialist state is interesting. Poland's system was established in the Polish People's Republic, and this trend continued after the Revolutions of 1989. The 1997 Polish

---

[56] Article 79, The Constitution of the Republic of Poland of 1997.

[57] Article 188, The Constitution of the Republic of Poland of 1997.

[58] Article 194, The Constitution of the Republic of Poland of 1997. In Prof. Brzezinski's article, it introduced the organization and structure of the Constitutional Tribunal and its judges.

[59] In Poland, it is very interesting to see how the politics and religion affect the Constitutional Tribunal at the same time. Such as the case of teaching religion in public schools in 1990 and the case of abortion in 1993. Mark Brzezinski, The Struggle for Constitutionalism in Poland (1st edn, Macmillan Press Ltd., 1998). Also, the abortion case in 2020 caused an international attention. [2020] Ref. No. K 1/20 (PL). Retrieved June 25, 2021, from https://trybunal.gov.pl/en/hearings/judgments/art/11300-planowanie-rodziny-ochrona-plodu-ludzkiego-i-warunki-dopuszczalnosci-przerywania-ciazy.

[60] The constitutional crisis in Poland started at the appointment of the Constitutional Justices in 2015. Also, the decision on abortion in 2020 also caused the constitutional crisis in Poland.

[61] For example, in the tax-free amount case, the Tribunal tried to connect the tax-free amount with human dignity. Also, in the abortion case in Poland in 2020, the Judgment try to make the connection between human dignity of the unborn children and the abortion. See Constitutional Tribunal of Republic of Poland (Warsaw 22 October 2020). Retrieved June 26, 2021, from https://trybunal.gov.pl/en/hearings/judgments/art/11300-planowanie-rodziny-ochrona-plodu-ludzkiego-i-warunki-dopuszczalnosci-przerywania-ciazy.

Constitution expanded the scope of review and access to the Constitutional Tribunal. However, recent developments in constitutionality review in Poland have attracted widespread criticism. A constitutional crisis occurred in 2015, created by the nationalist ruling party PiS. Like its neighbor, Hungary, the overwhelming populism at home has enveloped the Tribunal's jurisprudence (Brzozowski, 2021; Sadurski, 2019).[62] People have warned that Poland is displaying an illiberal trend (Havlik & Hlousek, 2021)[63] and that politics are affecting the constitutionality review system.

6.3.7 From Activism to Self-restraint in Constitutionality Review: A Comparative Perspective

In this part, the author compared the development of constitutionality review in China and the Visegrad states after the transformation period. In the Visegrad states, constitutionality review systems were established in the 1980s and 1990s. The Polish Constitutional Tribunal was the only one created (1985) prior to the Revolutions of 1989. During nearly thirty years of constitutionality review practice, constitutional cases have enriched the jurisprudence of the constitutional courts/tribunals in these countries. These courts/tribunals, according to the constitutions, are empowered to conduct constitutionality review. In their early operations, some significant rulings were issued to protect fundamental rights and freedoms and establish principles in the *Rechtsstaat* (Solyom & Brunner, 2000).[64] However, with the recent development of populism in the Visegrad states, dealing with nationalist political ruling parties in each country has become a critical issue facing the constitutional courts/tribunals.[65]

In China, debate over whether to establish a special organ to supervise the implementation of the Constitution was heated in the early 1980s, prior to the adoption of the current Constitution in 1982 (Zhang, Qin & Zhang, 2018).[66] However, this organ was not created until the adoption of the 2018 constitutional amendment. It introduced a "new" special committee of the NPC, with the Constitution and Law Committee replacing the Law Committee. It, along with the Legislative Affairs Commission

---

[62] In Brzozowski's article, he argued the populism in Polish constitutional practice didn't create any new theory of constitutionalism.

[63] Not only Poland, but the rest of Visegrad States are facing the same criticism of being illiberal.

[64] For instance, a series of selected cases of Hungarian Constitutional Court from 1990 to 1997 had been offered in Solyom and Brunner's book.

[65] Notably, the Fidesz in Hungary, PiS in Poland, ANO in Czechia, and Smer in Slovakia. All of these political parties may be considered as a populist party and gained a remarkable support at home.

[66] In Zhang, Qin and Zhang's dialogue. Zhang Chunsheng, former Deputy Director of the Legislative Affairs Commission of the NPC Standing Committee, shared the discussion of set-up a special constitutional organ to review the constitutionality, following solutions were provided: 1. To set up a German model of Constitutional Court; 2. To set up an American model of judicial review system; 3. To Set up a Constitutional Council which is at same level of the Standing Committee of the NPC; 4. To empower the Standing Committee of the NPC as a constitutionality review organ.

of the Standing Committee of the NPC, reviews the constitutionality of normative documents.

Comparing the constitutionality review in China and the Visegrad states, the author argued that it is inclining toward a position of self-restraint in both regions. However, the two regions have different reasons for this tendency. The author first analyzes how China has come to this position in its constitutionality review and then does the same with regard to the Visegrad states.

In China, activist constitutionality review may be examined through the notable Chinese Marbury case, the "Qi case", from the turn of the century. This case was part of the first wave of constitutionality review in China, when so-called constitutional judicialization emerged (Sprick, 2019), and the Supreme People's Court took an activist position. It tried to establish a de facto judicial review system in China (Hunang, 2001).[67] This activist constitutional judicialization did not last long, however. Legal scholars criticized it as unconstitutional and proposed a constitutional solution, that is, to review constitutionality via the supreme state power (the NPC and its committees) (Tong, 2009). Constitutional judicialization failed when the Supreme People's Court reversed the ruling in the Reply in Qi's case.[68]

The second wave of constitutionality review in China emerged in 2017 with the Report of the 19th National Congress of the CPC. It emphasized the importance of the Constitution in the rule of law and declared an aim "to advance the constitutionality review".[69] How to address constitutionality review within the People's Congress system has been debated in recent times. First, some options were excluded from the Chinese constitutionality review system; that is, the constitutionality review organ was fully independent from the NPC and played an aggressive role in constitutionality review. Unlike most countries with a constitutional court, China established its power sharing within the framework of the People's Congress system. Namely, all power belongs to the people. People exercise their power via the People's Congress at different levels. Other state organs stem from and are responsible to the People's Congress. Therefore, the daily tasks of constitutionality review are performed mainly by the NPC's Constitution and Law Committee and the Legislative Affairs Commission of the NPC's Standing Committee. The Chinese model of constitutionality review is rather like a negotiable discourse; the constitutionality review organ reviews normative documents with self-restraint, with only those that are explicitly against the Constitution considered unconstitutional. As Gardbaum notes in his article, "the

---

[67] In Huang's article, the then President of the First Civil Court of the Supreme People's Court, advocated the constitutional judicialization for following reasons: 1. It is the requirement for realizing the *Rechtsstaat*; 2. It is the necessity for strengthening the validity of the Constitution; 3. It is the requirement for adjudicating case of the courts.

[68] Official Reply of the Supreme People's Court on Whether the Civil Liabilities Shall Be Borne for the Infringement upon a Citizen's Basic Right of Receiving Education [expired]. Retrieved June, 26, 2021, from http://www.lawinfochina.com/display.aspx?lib=law&id=1954&CGid=.

[69] In Chinese political practice, the party's will usually will be proposed before the National People's Congress or its Standing Committee and adopted as statutes or constitutional amendments. The goal of "to advance the constitutionality review" was carried out by a series of legislation (including constitutional amendment and Decision made by Standing Committee of the NPC).

6.3 Comparative Analysis of the Constitutionality ...

legislature's power to have the last word in response to a court decision" (Gardbaum, 2001). Therefore, it is possible to establish weak constitutionality review in China with self-restraint borne in mind (Da, 2021).

In contrast to the Chinese structure of state power, the Visegrad states are based on the separation of powers and checks and balances. Namely, legislative, executive and judicial power are independent of each other. The constitutional courts/tribunals, as special judicial organs, enjoy great independence, and in their early stages, they took an activist role in the *Rechtsstaat* (Sadurski, 2002; Solyom, 2003).[70]

However, such activism in constitutionality review has faded, in favor of a more self-restrained position. All of these changes began with the recent emergence of populism in the Visegrad states. Populist political parties gradually took over the ruling positions in the parliaments. Fidesz has ruled the Hungarian Parliament for over 20 years; Poland has been ruled by PiS since 2015; the largest party in the Chamber of Deputies (lower parliament) of the Czech Republic is the populist party, ANO, founded by the millionaire PM Babis. In Slovakia, the only change has been that the populist party Smer was replaced by another populist party, OL'aNO (Ordinary People and Independent Personalities) in the 2020 parliamentary election. As Zoltan Szente states in his article, one of the features of populism is anti-elitism (Szente, 2021), and the name of Slovakia's ruling party shows the popularity of this narrative there and beyond.

The constitutional court/tribunal in each Visegrad country faces the challenge of overwhelming populism at home and abroad. According to the constitutions in each country, their parliaments are heavily involved in the election or appointment of constitutional justices. Therefore, it is natural for the ruling populist party to choose legal professionals with a similar outlook (Szente, 2016). In these circumstances, the constitutional courts/tribunals in the Visegrad states are inclined to take a position of self-restraint in constitutionality review, especially in cases where the parliament is involved (Kuhn, 2021).[71] Of course, depending on their individual situations, this trend of self-restraint may vary among the countries. The Slovakian Constitutional Court, for instance, ruled a constitutional amendment unconstitutional in January 2019. The parliament did not fight back initially, since the presidential and parliamentary elections drew more attention. However, when the new parliament was elected, a constitutional amendment was adopted in December 2020, and the amendment forbade the Constitutional Court to review its constitutionality (Lalik, 2020a, 2020b).

In this part, after the comparative analysis, the author holds that constitutionality review in China and the Visegrad states is inclining toward a position of self-restraint, although the causes may differ by country. Here, the author regards self-restraint in

---

[70] In Hungary, the discussion of the activism in the Consitutional Court may refer to Solyom's article. Similar analysis of Czechia, Slovakia, Poland, and Hungary as well have been presented in one book.

[71] For instance, the Abortion case in Polish Constitutional Tribunal was initiated by the MPs, and the Constitutional Tribunal supported this claim. Also, as Zdenek Kuhn noted the self-restraint trend in Czech Constitutional Court, the Court is trying to avoid the direct conflict with other State powers (legislative and/or executive power).

constitutionality review organs as a strategy (Lancos, 2019). When legislative and/or executive power is strong, it is a natural choice to step back and develop constitutional jurisprudence slowly but surely (Lachmayer, 2021; Nowlin, 2002).[72]

6.4 Conclusion

In this chapter, the author first examined the development of constitutions in these countries. After the Revolutions of 1989, the Visegrad states abandoned their socialist constitutions and established so-called democratic ones, which featured the rule of law and separation of powers. The constitutional development in the Visegrad states after the transition was also a way to embrace the EU. These states adopted constitutional amendments before their accession to the EU, and they all needed to address EU legal mechanisms (Albi & Bardutzky, 2019).[73] Recently, populism has challenged constitutionalism in the Visegrad states, and, ruled by populist parties, they are facing criticism for turning to illiberal constitutionalism. In China, constitutional development continued after the adoption of the current Constitution in 1982. China's Constitution has long been more open-minded regarding economic changes. Many bold, even "unconstitutional" experiments were conducted in the economic arena, and these successful experiments eventually prompted amendments to the Constitution (Hao, 1996).[74] Aside from these amendments with economic reforms, the most notable change is the implementation of constitutionality review. The very first case has been decided. However, constitutionality review has not yet been fully institutionalized in China. An act on the procedure for constitutionality review, for example, remains to be adopted.

In this chapter, constitutionality review in China and the Visegrad states is also analyzed. Compared to constitutionality review in the transformation period, the more recent constitutional cases in each state have enriched the jurisprudence of constitutionalism. As noted above, the constitutionality review organs in China and the Visegrad states take a position of self-restraint in constitutionality review. The overwhelming populism in the Visegrad states caused this change. In China, the People's Congress system is the fundamental political system, and the power of all other state organs at different levels stems from the People's Congress. Therefore, the review organ prefers to take a mild, deliberate approach to deciding the constitutionality of normative documents.

---

[72] When met with the populist challenge, to stand in a self-restraint position is not unique, rather a common solution. See Nowlin's article and Lachmayer' book chapter.

[73] For instance, how to deal with the European Arrest Warrant and ESM Treaty in the Visegrad States had been discussed and legislatures in each country are trying to harmonize these EU policies within the country's hierarchy of norms.

[74] In China, there was a debate of benign unconstitutionality in 1990s, it first mentioned by Hao Tiechuan, in Hao's article, he discussed some economic reforms which he considered as unconstitutionality, he justified these "unconstitutionality" reforms with their benignity.

References

Albi, A. (2019). Introductory editorial note to Hungarian report: The Pre-2010 rule of law achievements and the post-2010 illiberal turn. In A. Albi & S. Bardutzky (Eds.), *National constitutions in European and global governance: Democracy, rights, the rule of law* (1st ed., 1435–1437). Springer.

Albi, A., & Bardutzky, S. (Eds.). (2019). *National constitutions in European and global governance: Democracy, rights, the rule of law* (1st ed.). Springer.

Banaszak, B. et al (2012). *Constitutional law in Poland* (1st ed.). Wolters Kluwer.

Bealey, F. (1995). The Slovak constitution. *Democratization, 2*(2), 179–197.

Berdisova, L. (2013). *Constitutional law*. Trnavska univerzita v Trnave.

Biernat, S., & Kawczynska, M. (2019). The role of the Polish Constitution (Pre-2016): Development of a liberal democracy in the European and international context. In A. Albi & B. Bardutzky (Eds.), *National constitutions in European and global governance: Democracy, rights, the rule of law: National reports* (1st ed., pp. 745–793). Springer.

Bobek, M. (2014). Landtova, Holubec, and the problem of an uncooperative court: Implications for the preliminary rulings procedure. *European Constitutional Law Review, 10*(1), 54–89.

Borger, J. (2020, October 22). US signs anti-abortion declaration with group of largely authoritarian governments. *The Guardian*. Retrieved June 25, 2021, from https://www.theguardian.com/world/2020/oct/22/us-trump-administration-signs-anti-abortion-declaration

Breitenbach, D., & Levitz, D. (2011, April 18). Hungary's parliament passes controversial new constitution. *Deutsche Welle*. Retrieved June 24, 2021, from https://www.dw.com/en/hungarys-parliament-passes-controversial-new-constitution/a-14998392

Brett, D., et al. (2021, February 15). *Annual report: Conscientious objection to military service in Europe 2020*. European Bureau for Conscientious Objection. Retrieved June 25, 2021, from https://ebco-beoc.org/sites/ebco-beoc.org/files/attachments/2021-02-15-EBCO_Annual_Report_2020.pdf

Brink, A. D. (2010). The Czech Constitutional Court and the treaty of Lisbon. *Tijdschrift Voor Constitutioneel Recht, 3*, 315–321.

Brzezinski, M. (1993). The emergence of judicial review in Eastern Europe: The case of Poland. *The American Journal of Comparative Law, 41*(2), 153–200.

Brzezinski, M. (1998). *The struggle for constitutionalism in Poland*. Macmillan Press Ltd.

Brzozowski, W. (2021). Whatever works: Constitutional interpretation in Poland in times of populism. In F. Gardos-Orosz & Z. Szente (Eds.), *Populist challenges to constitutional interpretation in Europe and beyond* (1st ed., pp. 174–193). Routledge Taylor & Francis Group.

Bunikowski, D. (2018). The constitutional crisis in Poland, Schmittian questions and Kaczynski's political and legal philosophy. *Journal of Contemporary European Studies, 26*(3), 285–307.

Chronowski, N., et al. (2019). Hungary: Constitutional (r)evolution or regression? In A. Albi & S. Bardutzky (Eds.), *National constitutions in European and global governance: Democracy, rights, the rule of law* (1st ed., pp. 1439–1488). Springer.

Cole, D. H. (1998). *Poland's 1997 constitution in its historical context*. Articles by Maurer Faculty. No. 589, 1-43.

Cottey, A. (1995). *East-Central Europe after the Cold War: Poland, the Czech Republic, Slovakia and Hungary in search of security*. Palgrave Macmillan Press.

Csink, L., & Schanda, B. (2015). The constitutional court. In A. Z. Varga, A. Patyi, & B. Schanda (Eds.), *The basic (fundamental) law of Hungary: A commentary of the New Hungarian Constitution* (revised ed., pp. 185–196). Clarus Press.

Cutlert, L., & Schwartz, H. (1991). Constitutional reform in Czechoslovakia: E Duobus Unum? *The University of Chicago Law Review, 58*(2), 511–553.

Da, L. (2021). 合宪性审查中"弱"事前审查的制度构建——基于法律文本的探讨[The institutional construction of the "weak" ex ante constitutionality review: A textual analysis]. *Journal of East China University of Political Science and Law, 24*(3), 160–170.

Dempsey, J. (2011, April 18). Hungarian Parliament approves new constitution. *The New York Times*. Retrieved June 24, 2021, from https://www.nytimes.com/2011/04/19/world/europe/19iht-hungary19.html

Dezso, M. (2010). *Constitutional law in Hungary* (1st ed.). Wolters Kluwer.

Domin, M. (2019, February 8). A part of the constitution is unconstitutional, the Slovak Constitutional Court has ruled. *VerfBlog*. Retrieved June 25, 2021, from https://verfassungsblog.de/a-part-of-the-constitution-is-unconstitutional-the-slovak-constitutional-court-has-ruled/

Drinoczi, T., Bien-Kacala, A. (2021). *Illiberal constitutionalism in Poland and Hungary: The deterioration of democracy, misuse of human rights and abuse of the rule of law* (1st ed., online version). Routledge Taylor & Francis Group.

Drugda, S. (2019, April 25). Slovak Constitutional Court strikes down a constitutional amendment—But the amendment remains valid. *Blog of the International Journal of Constitutional Law*. Retrieved June 25, 2021, from http://www.iconnectblog.com/2019/04/slovak-constitutional-court-strikes-down-a-constitutional-amendment-but-the-amendment-remains-valid/

Drugda, S. (2020, December 3). On collision course with the material core of the Slovak Constitution: Disabling judicial review of constitutional amendment. *VerfBolog*. Retrieved June 25, 2021, from https://verfassungsblog.de/on-collision-course-with-the-material-core-of-the-slovak-constitution/

Easton, A. (2020, October 23). Poland abortion: Top court bans almost all terminations. *BBC News*. Retrieved June 25, 2021, from

Erdo-Bonyar, K. (2020, October 30). Protest against new Polish law on abortion held in Budapest. *Daily News Hungary*. Retrieved June 25, 2021, from https://dailynewshungary.com/protest-against-new-polish-law-on-abortion-held-in-budapest/

Facsar, F. (2010, April 26). Center-right Fidesz Party sweeps to victory in Hungary. *CNN*. Retrieved June 24, 2021, from https://www.cnn.com/2010/WORLD/europe/04/26/hungary.election.results/index.html

Fitzmaurice, J. (1998). *Politics and government in the Visegrad countries: Poland, Hungary, the Czech Republic and Slovakia*. Palgrave Macmillan Press.

Fleck, Z., et al. (2011). *Opinion on the fundamental law of Hungary*. Retrieved June 24, 2021, from https://lapa.princeton.edu/hosteddocs/amicus-to-vc-english-final.pdf

Fruhstorfer, A., & Moormann-Kimakova, B. (2016). Czech Republic. In A. Fruhstorfer & M. Hein (Eds.), *Constitutional politics in Central and Eastern Europe: From post-socialist transition to the reform of political systems* (1st ed., pp. 39–64). Springer.

Gabris, T., & Letkova, A. (2018). Constitutional history 2000–2015: Slovak Republic. *Krakowskie Studia z Historii Państwa i Prawa, 11*(1), 1–22.

Gardbaum, S. (2001). The new commonwealth model of constitutionalism. *American Journal of Comparative Law, 49*(4), 707–760.

Gardos-Orosz, F. (2021). Constitutional interpretation under the new fundamental law of Hungary. In F. Gardos-Orosz & Z. Szente (Eds.), *Populist challenges to constitutional interpretation in Europe and beyond* (1st ed., pp. 143–159). Routledge.

Glos, G. E. (1994). The constitution of the Czech Republic of 1992. *Hastings Constitutional Law Quarterly, 21*(4), 1049–1069.

Goldman, M. F. (1999). *Slovakia since independence: A struggle for democracy*. Praeger Publishers.

Gorski, G. (2014). Constitutional changes in Poland between 1989 and 1997. *Law and Administration in Post-Soviet Europe, 1*(1), 5–15.

Granat, M. (2018). Constitutional judiciary in crisis: The case of Poland. In Z. Szente & F. Gardos-Orosz (Eds.), *New challenges to constitutional adjudication in Europe: A comparative perspective* (1st ed., pp. 132–143). Routledge Taylor & Francis Group.

Halmai, G. (2002). The Hungarian approach to constitutional review: The end of activism? The first decade of the Hungarian Constitutional Court. In W. Sadurski (Ed.), *Constitutional justice, east and west: Democratic legitimacy and constitutional courts in post-communist Europe in a comparative perspective* (1st ed., pp. 189–212) Kluwer International.

References

Halmai, G. (2019). The making of "illiberal constitutionalism" with or without a new constitution: The case of Hungary and Poland. In D. Landau & H. Lerne (Eds.), *Comparative constitutional making* (1st ed., pp. 302–323). Edward Elgar Publishing.

Hao, T. (1996). 论良性违宪 [On Benign unconstitutionality]. *Chinese Journal of Law, 18*(4), 89–91.

Havlik, V., & Hlousek, V. (2021). Differential illiberalism: Classifying illiberal trends in Central European party politics. In A. Lorenz & L. H. Anders (Eds.), Illiberal trends and anti-EU Politics in East Central Europe (1st ed., pp. 111–136). Palgrave Macmillan.

He, H. (2016). Why the custody and education system should be abolished? *Peking University Law Journal, 4*(1), 1–44. https://www.bbc.com/news/world-europe-54642108

Hunang, S. (2001, August 13). 宪法司法化及其意义--从最高人民法院今天的一个《批复》谈起 [Judicialization of Constitution and its meaning: Discussion on Today's "Reply" of Supreme People's Court] *People's Court Daily*, B1. Retrieved June 26, 2021, from http://www.gongfa.com/huangsyxianfasifahua.htm

Kanzelsberger, J. (2018, April 8). The Ombudsman in the constitutional system of the Slovak Republic. *Projustice*. Retrieved June 25, 2021, from https://www.projustice.sk/ustavne-pravo/The-ombudsman-in-he-constitutional-system-of-the-Slovak-Republic

Komarek, J. (2012, February 22). Playing with matches: The Czech Constitutional Court's ultra vires revolution. *VerfBlog*. Retrieved June 25, 2021, from https://verfassungsblog.de/playing-matches-czech-constitutional-courts-ultra-vires-revolution/

Kuhn Z. (2021). The Czech Constitutional Court in times of populism: From judicial activism to judicial self-restraint. In F. Gardos-Orosz & Z. Szente (Eds.), *Populist challenges to constitutional interpretation in Europe and beyond* (1st ed., pp. 95–108). Routledge.

Kuhn, Z. (2011). Czech Republic: Czech Constitutional Court as positive legislator? In A. R. Brewer-Carias (Ed.), *Constitutional courts as positive legislators: A comparative law study* (1st ed., pp. 445–470). Cambridge University Press

Kuhn, Z. (2017). The constitutional court of the Czech Republic. In A. Jakab, A. Dyevre, & G. Itzcovich (Eds.), *Comparative constitutional reasoning* (1st ed., pp. 199–236), Cambridge University Press.

Kuhn, Z. (2019). The Czech Republic: From a Euro-friendly approach of the constitutional court to proclaiming a court of justice judgment ultra vires. In A. Albi & S. Bardutzky (Eds.), *National constitutions in European and global governance: Democracy, rights, the rule of law* (1st ed., pp. 795–833). Springer.

Lachmayer, K. (2021). Formalism and judicial self-restraint as tools against populism? Considerations regarding recent developments of the Austrian Constitutional Court. In F. Gardos-Orosz & F. Szente, Z. (Eds.), *Populist challenges to constitutional interpretation in Europe and beyond* (1st ed., pp. 75–94). Routledge.

Lalik, T. (2017). Tracing constitutional changes in Slovakia between 2008–2016. *Hungarian Journal of Legal Studies, 52*(2), 117–138.

Lalik, T. (2020). The Slovak Constitutional Court on unconstitutional constitutional amendment (PL. US 21/2014). *European Constitutional Law Review, 16*(2), 328–343.

Lalik, T. (2020, December 18). Slovakia on its way to illiberal democracy: Nullifying the power of the constitutional court to review constitutional amendments. *Blog of the International Journal of Constitutional Law*. Retrieved June 25, 2021, from http://www.iconnectblog.com/2020/12/slovakia-on-its-way-to-illiberal-democracy-nullifying-the-power-of-the-constitutional-court-to-review-constitutional-amendments/

Lancos, P. L. (2019). Passivist strategies available to the Hungarian Constitutional Court. *Heidelberg Journal of International Law, 79*, 971–994.

Li, H. (2021). 紧急状态的宪法实施机制与完善路径[A study on the implementation mechanism and improvement path on the state of emergency based on China]. *Legal Forum, 36*(1), 103–112.

Lin, F. (2019). The 2018 constitutional amendments: Significance and impact on the theories of party-state relationship in China. *China Perspectives, 1*, 11–21.

Lukaszuk, L., & Lukaszuk, M. J. (2011). The constitutional court in Poland at the beginning of its activity. *Revista Europea De Historia De Las Ideas Politicas y De Las Instituciones Publicas, 1*, 1–23.

Malova, D. (2002). The role and experience of the Slovakian Constitutional Court. In W. Sadurski (Ed.), *Constitutional justice, east and west: Democratic legitimacy and constitutional courts in post-communist Europe in a comparative perspective* (1st ed., pp. s349–372). Kluwer Law International.

Matczak, M. (2020). The clash of powers in Poland's rule of law crisis: Tools of attack and self-defense. *Hague Journal on the Rule of Law, 12*, 421–450.

Matthes, C-Y. (2016). Poland. In Fruhstorfer, A., Hein, M. (Eds.), *Constitutional politics in Central and Eastern Europe: From post-socialist transition to the reform of political systems* (1st ed., 11–37). Springer.

Mazak, J. (2001, October 11). *Republic of Slovakia: Further constitutional developments (amendments to the constitution of the Republic of Slovakia from 2001).* Venice Commission. Retrieved June 25, 2021, from https://www.venice.coe.int/webforms/documents/?pdf=CDL(2001)109-e

Moormann-Kimakova, B. (2016). Slovakia. In A. Fruhstorfer & M. Hein (Eds.), *Constitutional politics in Central and Eastern Europe: From post-socialist transition to the reform of political systems* (1st ed., 65–99). Springer.

Nowlin, J. W. (2002). The judicial restraint amendment: Populist constitutional reform in the spirit of the bill of rights. *Notre Dame Law Review, 78*(1), 171–280.

Nussberger, A. (2008). Poland: The constitutional tribunal on the implementation of the European arrest warrant. *International Journal of Constitutional Law, 6*(1), 162–170.

Pitrova, L. (2013). The judgment of the Czech Constitutional Court in the "Slovak Pensions" case and its possible consequences (In light of the fortiter in re suaviter in modo Principle). *The Lawyer Quarterly, 3*(2), 86–101.

Plucinska, J., & Ptak, A. (2020, April 16). Poland's PiS seeks constitutional change to extend president's term. *Reuters.* Retrieved June 25, 2021, from https://www.reuters.com/article/us-health-coronavirus-poland-constitutio-idUSKCN21X3CJ

Priban, J. (2002). Judicial power vs. democratic representation: The culture of constitutionalism and human rights in the Czech legal system. In W. Sadurski (Ed.), *Constitutional justice, east and west: Democratic legitimacy and constitutional courts in post-communist Europe in a comparative perspective* (1st ed., 373–394). Kluwer Law International.

Prochazka, R. (2002). *Mission accomplished: On founding constitutional adjudication in Central Europe* (1st ed.). CEU Pre.

Raabe, S. (2008, August 15). Potential stability—Poland after the end of the 4th Republic. *Konrad Adenauer Stiftung.* Retrieved June 25, 2021, from https://www.jstor.org/stable/resrep10000

Rakowska-Trela, A. (2020, October 24). A Dubious Judgment by a Dubious Court: The abortion judgment by the Polish Constitutional Tribunal. *VerfBlog.* Retrieved June 25, 2021, from https://verfassungsblog.de/a-dubious-judgment-by-a-dubious-court/

Regulations Filing and Review Department of Legislative Affairs Commission of the Standing Committee of the NPC (Ed.). (2020). *Filing and review of the regulatory documents: Selected Cases.* China Democracy and Legal System Publishing House.

Rosenfeld, M., & Sajo, A. (2012). Introduction. In M. Rosenfeld & A. Sajo (Eds.), *The Oxford handbook of comparative constitutional law* (1st ed., introduction part). Oxford University Press.

Sadurski, W. (2019). *Poland's constitutional breakdown* (1st ed.). Oxford University Press

Sadurski, W. (Ed.) (2002). *Constitutional justice, east and west: Democratic legitimacy and constitutional courts in post-communist Europe in a comparative perspective* (1st ed.). Kluwer Law International

Scheppele, K. L. (2015). Understanding Hungary's constitutional revolution. In A. V. Bogdandy & P. Sonnevend (Eds.), *Constitutional crisis in the European constitutional area: Theory, law and politics in Hungary and Romania* (1st ed., 111–124). Hart Publishing.

Schwartz, H. (2000). *The struggle for constitutional justice in post-communist Europe* (1st ed.). the University of Chicago Press.

References

Shen, C. (2021). 全国人民代表大会常务委员会法制工作委员会关于2020年备案审查工作情况的报告 [Report on filing and review of 2020 of the Legislative Affairs Commission of the Standing Committee of the NPC]. *Gazette of the Standing Committee of the National People's Congress of the People's Republic of China, 2*, 350–356.

Solyom, L. (2003). The role of constitutional courts in the transition to democracy: With special reference to Hungary. *International Sociology, 18*(1), 133–161.

Solyom, L., Brunner, G. (2000). *Constitutional judiciary in a new democracy: The Hungarian Constitutional Court* (1st ed.). The University of Michigan Press.

Sprick, D. (2019). Judicialization of the Chinese constitution revisited. *China Review, 19*(2), 41–68.

Szente, Z. (2016). The political orientation of the members of the Hungarian Constitutional Court between 2010 and 2014. *Constitutional Studies, 1*(1), 123–149.

Szente, Z. (2021). Populism and populist constitutionalism. In F. Gardos-Orosz & Z. Szente (Eds.), *Populist challenges to constitutional interpretation in Europe and beyond* (1st ed., 3–28). Routledge.

TASR (2020, December 9). Major judicial reform passed in parliament. *Newsnow TASR*. Retrieved June 25, 2021, from https://newsnow.tasr.sk/policy/major-judicial-reform-passed-in-parliament/

Tatlow, D. K. (2012, October 23). Behind China's high abortion rate: New sexual freedoms. *The New York Times*. Retrieved June 25, 2021, from https://cn.nytimes.com/china/20121023/c23abortion/dual/

Tomczak, M. (2020, November 30). Poland's Government creates constitutional crisis it will find hard to resolve. *Balkaninsight*. Retrieved June 26, 2021, from https://balkaninsight.com/2020/11/30/polands-government-creates-constitutional-crisis-it-will-find-hard-to-resolve/

Tong, Z. (2009). 宪法适用如何走出"司法化"的歧路 [How the constitutional application walks away from the "Judicialization"]. *Political Science and Law, 1*, 10–15

Trocsanyi, L., Sulyok, M. (2015). The birth and early life of the basic law of Hungary. In A. Z. Varga, A. Patyi, & B. Schanda (Eds.), *The basic (fundamental) law of Hungary: A commentary of the New Hungarian Constitution* (revised ed., pp. 1–34). Clarus Press.

Walker S. (2020, November 11). Hungarian government mounts new assault on LGBT rights. *The Guardian*. Retrieved June 24, 2021, from https://www.theguardian.com/world/2020/nov/11/hungarian-government-mounts-new-assault-on-lgbt-rights

Xu, C., Niu, W. (2019). *Constitutional law in China* (3rd ed.). Wolters Kluwer.

Zahradnicek-Haas, E. (2020, October 26). Polish women in Prague protested Poland's new abortion laws over the weekend. Expats.cz. Retrieved June 25, 2021, from https://www.expats.cz/czech-news/article/polish-women-in-prague-protest-poland-s-new-abortion-this-weekend

Zhang, C., Qin, Q., & Zhang, X. (2018). 推进合宪性审查, 加强宪法实施监督 [To advance the constitutionality review, and to strengthen the supervision of the implementation of constitution]. *China Law Review, 4*, 1–19.

Zhang, T., & Ginsburg, T. (2019). China's turn toward law. *Virginia Journal of International Law, 59*(2), 306–389.

Zhao, D. (2020). 合宪性审查制度能力研究: 以匈牙利为例 [*The Studies on institutional capacity of the constitutionality review: Take Hungary as an example*] (1st ed.). Shanghai Sanlian Press.

Chapter 7
Conclusion

> *Two roads diverged in a yellow wood. And sorry I could not travel both. And be one traveler, long I stood. And looked down one as far as I could. To where it bent in the undergrowth.*
> — *The Road Not Taken*, by Robert Frost (1915)

Abstract In this chapter, the author will address the following four parts. The first part is a comprehensive review of the whole research work. The second part mainly focuses on the different conditions in each state and how it led to a different road in China and the Visegrad States. The third part dealt with the contemporary constitutional development in China and the V4 countries, the author argued the rule by constitutionalism has been (re)established in the respective countries. The fourth one is how the constitutionalism has been developed in China and the Visegrad States after the transformation period, and the last one is a brief conclusion of this research work.

Finally, this research work is drawing to a close. This chapter contains the following four parts. The first is a comprehensive review of the entire work. The second focuses on the different conditions in each state and how they led to different roads in China and the Visegrad states. The third explores how constitutionalism developed in China and the Visegrad states after the transformation period. Finally, there is a brief conclusion.

7.1 Brief Review

After the Second Word War, numerous countries regained their independence, and countries in the Visegrad region were also "liberated" by the Allied military, especially the Soviet Union's Red Army. At the Yalta Conference, the three Great Powers agreed that Eastern Europe lay under the Soviet sphere of influence. Therefore, the communist party in each state established a communist regime, and communist constitutions were also adopted. In China, the Chinese won the Second Sino-Japan

War, and four years of civil war broke out the same year. In 1949, the CPC established the PRC. The constitutional document the Common Program was adopted the same year. Five years later, in 1954, the Constitution of the PRC was adopted by the NPC. The 1954 Constitution was more or less a hybrid of the Chinese Common Program and the 1936 Soviet Union Constitution. In the section of this monograph comparing the first communist constitutions of China and the Visegrad states, the author drew attention to the context and structure of the constitutions in each state. Their contexts were similar, since all were strongly influenced by the 1936 Soviet Union Constitution and the Soviet Union dominated the socialist family. Three parts of the context are compared in this part: the preamble to the Constitution, the fundamental rights and duties of the citizens and the supreme organ of state power.

The communist parties in the Visegrad states and China did not appear out of thin air. Therefore, the author explains in detail the birth of the communist parties in each state.

The communist ideology spread in the Visegrad region in the late nineteenth century. The unsuccessful land reforms in the Habsburg Empire or so-called Austro-Hungarian monarchy and the development of industrialization forced an increasing number of farmers to leave the countryside and live in the city as workers. A significant number of working-class people formed trade unions and other political groups. Under such conditions, the communist ideology was introduced from Western Europe to the Visegrad region and gradually won significant support among workers. In the Chinese case, the communist ideology was brought to China by Chinese students who studied abroad, mostly from France and Japan. Zhou Enlai, the most famous and popular prime minister of the PRC, and Deng Xiaoping, the reform and opening-up policy maker and protector, both studied in France. The earliest CPC leaders, Li Dazhao and Chen Duxiu, spent their university time in Japan, where these young intellectuals received the communist ideology; when they returned to China, the communist ideology was considered as one theory to save the old empire from colonization by the Great Powers. The courses of the spread of communist ideology in the Visegrad states and China differed. Namely, the working class in the Visegrad region had the chance to learn the communist ideology. However, in China, it was mainly promoted by young intellectuals, and its spread was from top to bottom. It also affected the course of communist development in China. In China's Communist Party regime, the most notable movements were promoted by the central government and the Party rather than the people.

The first pivotal moment in the development of the communist parties in each state occurred after the world's first communist regime was established in 1917. With the operation of the Communist International in Moscow,[1] an increasing number of people heard communist ideology and spread it around the world. Among these

---

[1] Communist International or Third International is a communist organization which established in 1919 in Moscow. The Communist Interntional (1919–1943). Retrieved June 24, 2021, from https://www.marxists.org/history/international/comintern/index.htm.

communist comrades, Bela Kun,[2] the Hungarian communist, was sent back to Hungary. He soon found an opportunity to establish a Soviet Republic in March 1919, although a provisional Soviet Constitution was drafted by the communist party. Nevertheless, this Soviet experiment barely lasted 100 days. China's Communist Party formed in 1921. In the 1930s, Mao Zedong conducted a Soviet experiment in a communist-controlled area in Jiangxi Province, and an Outline of Constitution of Soviet Republic of China was drafted. However, it never came into force.

Examining the development of the constitutions in China and the Visegrad states, a crucial point must be noted, that is, the declaration of the establishment of socialist states in the constitutions. This is examined in the reform period in this thesis. China's 1954 Constitution basically reflected the conditions in China at that time. However, this Constitution was soon abandoned by the leadership, a rule of man policy was employed by the governor and later the ten-year Cultural Revolution movement initiated by the leader of the Party. Under such circumstances, the 1975 Constitution announced that the socialist system was fully established in the PRC. However, looking back at this announcement now, it appears more like an affirmation of the Cultural Revolution. States in the Visegrad region also announced the establishment of socialist systems in their constitutional documents. Hungary declared the Hungarian People's Republic a socialist state in 1972. Czechoslovakia made a similar announcement much earlier, and the socialist system was fully established there in 1960. The Polish People's Republic adopted the 1976 amendment to the 1952 Constitution, in which it became a socialist state.

The next vital moment in the development of constitutions in China and the Visegrad states occurred in 1989. Revolutions broke out first in this region and later in other socialist states. After the Revolutions of 1989, although the socialist constitutions were not immediately invalid, several crucial constitutional amendments were adopted by the legislatures in the Visegrad states. The most dramatic change was that these countries abandoned the socialist system, and the constitutional provisions related to the socialist system were modified. Constitutionality review systems were (re)established in the Visegrad states. In China, the Tiananmen Incident occurred, however, the CPC did not lose its sovereignty, and several amendments were adopted by the NPC. The reforms focused mainly on the economy, while so-called socialism with Chinese characteristics was enshrined in the Constitution.

A new chapter has been added on the constitutional development in China and the Visegrad states after the transformation period. The most notable development is constitutionality review. China established its own constitutionality review in this period, developing it slowly but surely. The first new case was reported in the annual Report of the Filing and Reviewing Working of Commission of Legislative Affairs of the Standing Committee of the NPC in 2020. It mentioned a case on constitutionality review of regulations on teaching languages in some ethnic minority autonomous regions. The regulations were ruled unconstitutional because the current Chinese

---

[2] Bela Kun, the founding father of Hungarian Communist Party, he was sent to Hungary in the end of 1918, before the funding of Communist International. Bela Kun Archive (1886–1937). Retrieved June 24, 2021, from https://www.marxists.org/archive/kun-bela/index.htm.

Constitution reads, "The State promotes the nationwide use of Putonghua (common speech based on Beijing pronunciation)". In addition to the comparative analysis of the development of the constitutions in China and the Visegrad states, the new chapter conducts a comparative analysis of constitutionality review, makes conclusions about trends in constitutionality review in the different countries, and holds that self-restraint will be a strategy used by most constitutionality review organs. Additionally, in this part, the author analyzes the different reasons for the same result (different structures of constitutionality review in China and the Visegrad states, however, led to the position of self-restraint).

Finally, the gap between the law in books and in action should be noted. Given that this monograph mainly focuses on the law in the real-world context, each state's constitutional provisions may operate differently from what the law declares to the public. The Chinese case of disrespecting the law from the late 1950s to the late 1970s had a disastrous impact on the country's economy.

7.2 Reasons for the Different Roads

It is also worth inquiring why socialist states chose different roads to develop their constitutions. This part, after examining the development of constitutions in China and the Visegrad states, presents four possible reasons why China and the Visegrad states made such different choices.

7.2.1 Socioeconomic Conditions

Karl Marx made a famous speech arguing that sooner or later, economic changes will transform the superstructure (Marx, 1977). Therefore, it is important to study socioeconomic conditions in each state. In this part, the author analyzes economic development during the communist period in China and the Visegrad states.

When communist states were established in China and the Visegrad states, the economic conditions in the Visegrad states were much better than those in China.[3] Here is a brief introduction to the economies in the Visegrad states. After the First World War, Czechoslovakia and Poland were newly established countries in the region. Czechoslovakia inherited most of the industry of the former Austro-Hungarian monarchy, and Poland also gained a large territory and population in the

---

[3] Take the GPD per capita (current US $) in 1991 as an example, GDP per capita in mainland of China was 310.9 US$, in Poland the number was 2235.5 US$; in Slovakia part, the number was 2680 US$, in Czechia part, it was 2878.7 US$; and Hungary reached the highest number, 3349.8 US$. The statistics of the GDP per capita of the V4 is available from the World Bank. Retrieved June 24, 2021, from https://data.worldbank.org/indicator/NY.GDP.PCAP.CD?end=1991&locations=CZ-CN-PL-HU-SK&start=1986.

region. Spulber divides these countries, according to their levels of economic development, into three categories: Czechoslovakia was the only industrial country, and Hungary and Poland belonged to the second category as agricultural countries with relatively significant processing facilities (Spulber, 1966).

China's economic conditions were much worse than those of the Visegrad states. The development of industry in China at establishment of the PRC was still relatively low. At that moment, China was a primarily agricultural economy (Brandt, Ma, & Rawski, 2016), and although industrialization slowly increased, the two huge wars severely damaged its economy.

More proof can be found in the Maddison Project database. In 1950, the GDP per capita in Czechoslovakia was the highest, reaching 3501; Hungary and Poland were more or less in the same place, at approximately 2400; and the PRC was at only 448.[4] These states' economic positions did not change during the entire communist period. In 1988, the eve of the collapse of the socialist system in the Visegrad states, Czechoslovakia reached 8709, Hungary was in second place at 7031, and Poland was at 5789. However, the PRC was still much worse, at only 1830.[5] Therefore, during nearly 40 years of economic development, the economic conditions in the Visegrad states were much better than those in China.

Eagerness in the Visegrad states to join the market economy should also be considered. To integrate into Western Europe's market economy, not only was the democratic political system established in the Visegrad states, but the planned economy was abandoned and privatization and other economic policies were gradually implemented. In China, the 1993 constitutional amendment declared that the country would have a socialist market economy. This ensured the stability of the political system and the CPC's ruling position in China.

7.2.2 Culture

The Visegrad states undoubtedly belong to the continent of Europe. Before 1918, Czechoslovakia and Hungary and a large portion of Poland belonged to the Austro-Hungarian monarchy, which is considered a constitutional monarchy. In Hungary, noble-led liberalism was more successful in practice than the monarchy's Slavic provinces from the German perspective. However, the goal of building a bourgeois society developed at that time. "Free press, free association and better education"—such bourgeois slogans spread in the monarchy's territory. Meanwhile, in the Czech territory, liberalism was much more popular than in other Slavic lands, and the Tabor movement of 1868–70 was supported by over one million people (Okey, 2002).

---

[4] Maddison Project Database. Retrieved June 24, 2021, from http://www.ggdc.net/maddison/maddison-project/home.htm.

[5] Maddison Project Database. Retrieved June 24, 2021, from http://www.ggdc.net/maddison/maddison-project/home.htm.

In China, the influence of Confucianism should be noted. As mentioned in the last chapter, the legal system in ancient China was a hybrid of Legalism, Confucianism and Taoism. In particular, Confucianism required the masses to be loyal to the governor and the governor to take care of his subjects (Korolkov, 2017; Zhang, 2011). In the 1960s and 1970s, society was fully overtaken by political fanaticism, and several political movements, especially the Cultural Revolution, dramatically damaged civil society in China.

7.2.3 International Relationships with the Soviet Union

In addition to the internal reasons, the external reasons should be studied. The relationships between these socialist states and the Soviet Union merit particular attention.

The rise of communist regimes in the Visegrad region, as most constitutions in the Visegrad states stated, was due to liberation by the Soviet Union.

Before the communist party seized power in each state, local communists had already operated with the support of the Soviet Union; even in the Nazi-controlled period, communists participated in the anti-Nazi movement. At the end of the Second World War, the Red Army was sent to the Visegrad region and helped locals defeat the German army.

In Hungary, as noted earlier, the Soviet experiment occurred in 1919, led by Bela Kun, the founder of the Hungarian Communist Party. Although the experiment soon failed, Hungarian communists still operated locally with a low profile. After the Second World War, communists in Hungary used "salami tactics" (Granville, 2004)[6] and gradually came to power. In Czechoslovakia, the Communist Party played an important role in the coalition government and kept crucial government posts, such as minister of internal affairs. Finally, communists in Czechoslovakia launched a coup d'état in February 1948 and took control of the entire country. In Poland, Stalin asked local communists to "move gradually towards socialism by exploiting elements of the bourgeois democratic order such as the parliament and other institutions" (Karmer, 2009). After the establishment of communist regimes in the Visegrad region, local people tried to change these regimes and the constitutions. However, such efforts, like the Hungarian Revolution of 1956, Poznan protests the same year and Solidarity Movements in 1979 and 1980 in Poland, and the 1968 Prague Spring in Czechoslovakia, were in vain because of suppression by the Soviet Army or the military of the Warsaw Pact (Fowkes, 1993).

The Soviet army is also credited with establishing the PRC, and the Soviets helped China establish its own industry in the 1950s. However, the honeymoon between the two countries did not last long. The Sino-Soviet split finally occurred in 1960, and

---

[6] The so called "salami tactics" was a strategy which employed by the Hungarian Communist Party, communist member Matyas Rakosi and his comrades gradually disarmed the power of non-communist parties.

open disputes between China and the Soviet Union caused international tensions. In early 1960, China publicly criticized the ideology of the Soviet Union. The Soviets also reacted to China, such as by withdrawing Soviet experts from the country (Jersild, 2014; Li, 2012).

7.2.4 Relationships with(in) the European Union (EU)

In addition to the relationships with the former Soviet Union, the relations with(in) the EU must be examined here. Relationships with the EU influenced constitutional development in China and the Visegrad states in the new era, namely, after the transformation period. All of the Visegrad states joined the EU in 2004, and China is considered one of the EU's largest trading partners.[7] In this part, the author first examines how the EU influences constitutional development in the Visegrad states and then how the relationship between China and the EU makes its own contribution to constitutional development in China.

The Visegrad countries joined the EU in 2004, and prior to that, they all amended their constitutions to meet the EU membership criteria, including "stable institutions guaranteeing democracy, the rule of law, human rights and respect for and protection of minorities".[8] Such efforts started after the Revolutions of 1989. For instance, the Hungarian Constitutional Court abolished capital punishment, ruling it unconstitutional. In a concurring opinion, Justice Solyom P. stated that abolishing capital punishment was considered a general trend at the Council of Europe (Solyom & Brunner, 2000). Of course, this case did not directly suggest Hungary's intention to access the EU. However, it at least showed that Hungary was inclined to follow the legal criteria of Europe. In books edited by Anneli Albi and Samo Bardutzky, legal scholars from Hungary, the Czech Republic, Slovakia, and Poland explain how their respective countries dealt with the European Arrest Warrant and ESM Treaty within the EU and how to amend their constitutions (Albi & Bardutzky, 2019).

Recently, with the emergence of populism in the Visegrad states, the narrative of Euroskepticism has gained considerable support there (Csechi & Zgut, 2021).[9] EU authorities are usually described as a group of bureaucratic elitists in Brussels who try to intervene in internal affairs in various countries. The weak EU and the overwhelming populism have made constitutionalism in the Visegrad states turn in a different direction.

Because China is not an EU member state, its relationship with the EU did not directly affect its constitutional development. In general, the EU influences economic

---

[7] According to the EU Commission, China is the biggest source of imports and its second-biggest export market of the EU, the trade between China and EU reached over 1 billion Euro a day. Retrieved June 24, 2021, from https://ec.europa.eu/trade/policy/countries-and-regions/countries/china/.

[8] Conditions for membership, European Commission. Retrieved June 24, 2021, from https://ec.europa.eu/neighbourhood-enlargement/policy/conditions-membership_en.

[9] A notable study of the typical Eurosceptic populism at the region.

reforms, not constitutional changes in China (Yu, 2007).[10] However, this does not mean that the EU plays no role in China's rule of law. In fact, China-EU trade helps China follow EU regulations at a certain level. A notable case is the development of the intellectual property law (IP Law), with specialized IP courts created in major Chinese cities. With economic development, China has become the most prolific country in terms of filing for IP rights.[11] Additionally, China is the top trademark applicant at the EU Intellectual Property Office, with one IP law expert in the EU Chamber of Commerce in China noting, "Chinese companies had learned how to use IP as 'shields and swords' for their own interests" (Ho, 2021).

7.3 Rule by Constitutionalism in China and the Visegrad States After the Transformation Period

This monograph took considerable space to review the constitutional development prior to the Revolutions of 1989, and a new chapter was developed to explore how the contemporary constitutions developed after the transformation period. In this part, the author argues that China and the Visegrad states are using constitutionalism in an instrumental way. Given the different conditions in China and the Visegrad states (with the triumph of populism in the Visegrad countries and the special arrangement of state powers in China), rule by constitutionalism, rather than rule of constitutionalism, is implemented or advocated in these states. By employing constitutionalism, these countries have adopted well-written constitutions and established specific organs to protect them (by reviewing the constitutionality) with different stages of implementation (Blokker, 2019; Drinoczi & Bien-Kacala, 2019; Halmai, 2019; Zhai, 2020; Zhang, 2012).[12] In this part, the author analyzes how constitutionalism as an instrument is (re)established in China and the Visegrad states and defends Chinese constitutionalism by distinguishing thin and thick constitutionalism.

After the Revolutions of 1989, the Visegrad states embraced Western constitutionalism and replaced their socialist constitutions with democratic ones. To establish constitutionalism, they created key institutional organs (such as the constitutional

---

[10] Prof. Yu Xingzhong holds a different view, in his article, he argued that EU constitutional practice may improve Chinese Constitution with its theory and practice. Also, Prof. Yu believes China may learn from EU, on the constitutional experiment in Hong Kong.

[11] WIPO, World Intellectual Property Indicators 2020. Retrieved June 24, 2021, from https://www.wipo.int/edocs/pubdocs/en/wipo_pub_941_2020.pdf.

[12] The idea of to use the constitution as an instrument is a sufficient condition of constitutionalism is presented by Paul Blokker. However, Prof. Gabor Halmai holds a different view. Here, the author shall not involve in the debate of what is the authentic constitutionalism. In most cases, constitutionalism as a term is widely used in the Visegrad States and China. For instance, in Zhai Han's monograph, there is a chapter to discuss the "Modern Constitutionalism in China and the Fundamental Structure". Also, in Prof. Zhang Qianfan's book, a Chapter of "the future of China's constitutionalism" has been presented. For the Visegrad States' case, see Timea Drinoczi and Agnieszka Bien-Kacala's article.

court and ombudsman).[13] Initially after their establishment in each state, these organs played important roles in the transitional period. Hungary's Constitutional Court, for instance, issued a series of progressive rulings on different topics of fundamental rights (Solyom & Brunner, 2000).[14] With such progress, all the Visegrad states joined the EU. To enter the EU, they adopted constitutional amendments to meet EU criteria. The EU-friendly approach, nevertheless, faces challenges at home. Populism has emerged in each Visegrad state, and populist parties are in ruling positions. These parties use an anti-elitist mentality and protection of national interests as rhetoric (Halmai, 2019; Hlousek & Kaniok, 2020)[15] to establish a nonliberal constitutionalism that is trending in the Visegrad states (notably in Hungary and Poland) (Drinoczi & Bien-Kacala, 2019).

China, at the same time, developed a different constitutionalism thanks to its economic development. As this study noted, the constitutional amendments in China mostly focused on the economy.

Very significant changes were made in 2018 in the latest amendment. The first article states that the "leadership of the CPC is the defining feature of the socialism with Chinese characteristics". The current constitution did not clearly declare "the leadership of the CPC" until the adoption of the 2018 amendment. Doing so reflected the Four Self-Confidences (confident in our chosen path, confident in our guiding theories, confident in our political system, and confident in our culture) promoted by President Xi Jinping. Second, the new amendment required all state officials to take a public oath of allegiance to the Constitution when assuming office. After the adoption of the amendment, President Xi took this oath publicly after the NPC elected him President of the PRC for a second term.[16] Third, to respond to the criticism or suggestion that a constitutionality review system was lacking (Lin, 2015),[17] the Law Committee of the NPC was replaced by the Constitution and Law Committee, and the new organ is expected to perform the task of constitutionality review. The fourth revision has received great attention at home and abroad. Namely, the presidential term limits were removed. According to Hu Jinguang, a prominent constitutional

---

[13] Poland established the Constitutional Tribunal in 1985, other three countries established the Constitutional Courts in the beginning of 1990s. Also, the Ombudsman (may have different names in each State, e.g. the Commissioner for Fundamental Rights in Hungry, Public Defender of Rights in Czechia and Slovakia, and Commissioner for Human Rights in Poland) has been established in respective countries.

[14] In Solyom, the former Chief Justice's book, a series of selected Decisions have been presented.

[15] With the slowly economic development, the Visegrad States become impatient and lost their illusion as joined the EU, the economic conditions of the Visegrad States will be as good as their western neighbors. Therefore, two mentalities getting popular in the Visegrad States:1. Populism, to maintain its own history, culture, and national identity and against the elites in Brussels become a popular and handy tool to use. See the speech of Viktor Orban on the case of defying the Sargentini report, in his speech, Hungary was portrayed as an innocent member state who just want to protect its own needs. Viktor Orban, 'In the Debate on the So-called Sargentini Report' cited in Gabor Halmai's article. Euroscepticism as a strategy for elections is widely used in this region.

[16] A video of President Xi took an oath is available at the Xinhua net. Retrieved June 24, 2021, from http://www.xinhuanet.com/politics/2018lh/zb/zxxfxs/index.htm.

[17] Prof. Lin Yan expressed the needs of an operational constitutional review system.

law professor in China, this revision will help strengthen and perfect the office of the head of state (Hu, 2020).[18] The last significant revision that may greatly affect Chinese constitutionalism is the new constitutional organ the National Supervisory Commission. It exercises supervisory power independently in accordance with the provisions of law.

Such constitutional developments contribute to Chinese constitutionalism. However, China's theory and practice of constitutionalism do not fit the criteria of liberal constitutionalism. As Professor Dieter Grimm notes in his article, since "all essential characteristics of constitutions are missing", the "socialist Constitutions are the anti-type to these (constitutionalism)" (Grimm, 2012). To be fair, the Chinese Constitution, as a socialist constitution, does not meet all the essential characteristics of constitutions required by liberal constitutionalism.[19] Nevertheless, the failure to meet all the requirements of the liberal constitutionalism checklist does not mean there is no constitutionalism in China. Jothie Rajah's defense against the criticism of illiberalism in Singapore (Rajah, 2012) employs Peerenboom's idea of the thick and thin rule of law, in which the thin rule of law only requires law in formal or instrumental terms, whereas the thick rule of law may involve "a particular institutional, cultural and values complex" (Peerenboom, 2003). Here, the author argues that constitutionalism in China at least meets the criteria for thin constitutionalism, i.e., a formal constitution and a series of constitutional organs.

Constitutionalism has been (re)established in China and the Visegrad states in different ways. It cannot be said that there is rule of constitutionalism in these countries. As critics note, in the Visegrad states, especially Hungary and Poland, constitutionalism as a handy instrument is used by political leaders not only in the countries but also within the EU (Drinoczi & Bien-Kacala, 2021). In China, as Li Bin states, "China's position towards global constitutionalism is pragmatic rather than normatively inspired" (Li, 2018). Constitutionalism is being used in a pragmatic way in China.

Thus far, the strategy of rule by constitutionalism has functioned in China in an economic way, while in the Visegrad states (EU member states), it has attracted criticism at home and abroad. Will rule by constitutionalism be good enough for Chinese (economic and political) development? For how long can the Visegrad states maintain rule by constitutionalism within the EU framework? These questions must be followed in the next stage.

---

[18] In practice, the President of the PRC is also the General Secretary of the CPC. And there is no limitation for the term of the General Secretary of the CPC, according to the Constitution of the CPC.

[19] For instance, as Prof. Grimm argued in his chapter, the separation of powers. In the Chinese constitutional practice, all of the national organs are created by the people's congress, to which they are responsible and by which they are supervised.

7.4 Conclusion

As noted at the beginning of this chapter, there are two roads, and only one can be taken. After the Revolutions of 1989, the PRC continued along the socialist road and kept its socialist constitution; countries in the Visegrad region chose other roads and abandoned their socialist constitutions.

Why did China and the Visegrad states choose different roads? The author suggests four reasons. First, the socioeconomic conditions in each state differed. The statistics presented above show that the living standards in China and the Visegrad states differed dramatically; education and entertainment in the Visegrad states were much more advanced than in China, and it was easier to form a civil society in the Visegrad region. Second, culture in each state played a very important role, and the influence of Confucianism made Chinese citizens much more apt to accept a centralized government. Third, international relationships with the Soviet Union must be considered. Hungary, Czechoslovakia, and Poland joined the Warsaw Pact and formed the so-called Eastern Bloc. The Soviet Union must be considered the exclusive leader of the organization, and Soviet troops were stationed in these countries. For normal citizens, the fear of the Soviet Union was constant and indelible. Therefore, when the Revolutions of 1989 broke out, the Visegrad states immediately split with the Soviet Union. The Sino-Soviet relationship, in contrast, was more equal, and the establishment of a socialist state was more likely to be favored by Chinese people themselves. The final reason is the relationship with the EU, especially in contemporary constitutional development. All the Visegrad states accessed the EU in 2004, and therefore, each state's constitutional development in the new millennium was heavily influenced by the EU. For China, trade with the EU helped it establish a full legal system rather than directly affecting its constitutional development.

There is an old Chinese saying: "The history mirrors both thriving and calamity". Studying the development of the constitutions in China and the Visegrad states also reminds us of the importance of the rule of law and respect for fundamental rights, especially in the Chinese case. The disaster of the Great Leap Forward and the Cultural Revolution also demonstrate the importance of implementation of the constitution and full enforcement of laws. It is difficult to determine the best way to develop a constitution since each state has its own conditions.

However, some lessons may be learned from this research study by comparing the development of constitutions in China and the Visegrad states. First, in the modern era, a prosperous country cannot exist without a constitution. The establishment of a People's Republic in each state always went along with the constitution-making process. Czechoslovakia adopted a communist constitution in 1948, and Hungary, Poland and China did so in the late 1940s and first half of the 1950s. Second, the constitution must be respected and fully enforced. The lessons from the PRC during the Cultural Revolution show us the disastrous consequences of disrespecting the law. In the transformation period, to protect their constitutions, the Visegrad states established constitutionality review systems. These guarantee that the constitution is respected by the people and the government and that its provisions will be implemented. Finally, there are some common features in constitutions around the world. However, the early experiences of China and the Visegrad states in copying the Soviet Constitution demonstrated that there is no single model that every country can follow, and each state's constitution should reflect its own conditions.

References

Albi, A., & Bardutzky, S. (Eds.). (2019). *National constitutions in European and Global Governance: Democracy, rights, the rule of law* (1st ed.). Springer.
Blokker, P. (2019). Populism as a constitutional project. *International Journal of Constitutional Law, 17*(2), 536–553.
Brandt, L., Ma, D., & Rawski, T. (2016). *Industrialization in China* (Institute of Labor Economics Discussion papers, No. 10096). Retrieved June 24, 2021, from https://www.econstor.eu/bitstream/10419/145230/1/dp10096.pdf
Csechi, R., & Zgut, E. (2021). 'We won't let Brussels dictate us': Eurosceptic populism in Hungary and Poland. *European Politics and Society, 22*(1), 53–68.
Drinoczi, T., & Bien-Kacala, A. (2019). Illiberal constitutionalism: The case of Hungary and Poland. *German Law Journal, 20*(8), 1140–1166.
Drinoczi, T., & Bien-Kacala, A. (2021). *Illiberal constitutionalism in Poland and Hungary: The deterioration of democracy, misuse of human rights and abuse of the rule of law* (1st ed., online version). Routledge Taylor & Francis Group.
Fowkes, B. (1993). *The rise and fall of communism in Eastern Europe* (1st ed.). Macmillan Press Lltd.
Frost, R. (1915). *The road not taken*. Retrieved June 24, 2021, from https://www.poetryfoundation.org/poems/44272/the-road-not-taken.
Granville, J. C. (2004). *The first Domino: International decision making during the Hungarian Crisis of 1956* (1st ed.). Texas A&M University Press.
Grimm, D. (2012). Types of constitution in contemporary history from 18th century classic liberal to post-colonial and post authoritarian. In M. Rosenfeld & A. Sajo (Eds.), *The Oxford handbook of comparative constitutional law* (1st ed.). Oxford University Press.
Halmai, G. (2019). Populism, authoritarianism and constitutionalism. *German Law Journal, 20*(3), 296–313.
Hlousek, V., & Kaniok, P. (Eds.). (2020). *The European Parliamentary Election of 2019 in East-Central Europe: Second-Order Euroscepticism* (1st ed.). Palgrave Macmillan.
Ho, M. (2021, May 5). Intellectual property: China's evolution from 'norm taker' to 'norm setter'. *South China Morning Post*. Retrieved June 24, 2021, from https://www.scmp.com/news/china/politics/article/3131750/intellectual-property-chinas-evolution-norm-taker-norm-setter
Hu, J. (2020). 改革开放与1982年宪法 [The reform and opening-up and the constitution of 1982]. In D. Han (Ed.), 新中国宪法发展70年 *[70 Years constitutional development of the New China]* (1st ed., pp. 244–358). Guangdong People's Publishing House.
Jersild, A. (2014). *The Sino-Soviet Alliance: An international history* (1st ed.). The University of North Carolina Press.
Karmer, M. (2009). Stalin, Soviet policy, and the consolidation of a communist bloc in Eastern Europe, 1944–53. In V. Tismaneanu (Ed.) *Stalinism revisited: The establishment of communist regimes in East-Central Europe* (1st ed., pp. 51–101). CEU Press.
Korolkov, M. (2017). Legal process unearthed: A new source of legal history of early imperial China. *Journal of the American Oriental Society, 137*(2), 383–391.

References

Li, B. (2018). China's socialist rule of law and global constitutionalism. In T. Suami et al. (Eds.), *Global constitutionalism from European and East Asian perspectives* (1st ed., pp. 58–99). Cambridge University Press.

Li, M. (2012). *Mao's China and the Sino-Soviet Split: Ideological dilemma* (1st ed.). Routledge.

Lin, Y. (2015). Constitutional evolution through legislation: The quiet transformation of China's constitution. *International Journal of Constitutional Law, 13*(1), 61–89.

Marx, C. (1977). *A contribution to the critique of political economy*. Progress Publishers. The work has been completed in 1859. Retrieved June 24, 2021, from https://www.marxists.org/archive/marx/works/1859/critique-pol-economy/preface.htm

Okey, R. (2002). *The Habsburg Monarchy, 1765–1918: From enlightenment to eclipse (1st ed.)*. Palgrave Macmillan.

Peerenboom, R. (2003). *Varieties of rule of law: An introduction and provisional conclusion*. UCLA School of Law Research Paper Series. Retrieved June 24, 2021, from https://doi.org/10.2139/ssrn.445821

Rajah, J. (2012). *Authoritarian rule of law: Legislation, discourse and legitimacy in Singapore* (1st ed.). Cambridge University Press.

Solyom, L., Brunner, G. (2000). *Constitutional judiciary in a new democracy: The Hungarian constitutional court* (1st ed.). The University of Michigan Press.

Spulber, N. (1966). *The state and economic development in Eastern Europe* (1st ed.). Random House.

Yu, X. (2007). *The European constitution and its implications for China*. Cornell Law Faculty Publications. Paper 992. Retrieved June 24, 2021, from http://scholarship.law.cornell.edu/facpub/992

Zhai, H. (2020). *The constitutional identity of contemporary China* (1st ed.). Brill.

Zhang, Q. (2012). *The constitution of China: A contextual analysis* (1st ed.). Hart Publishing.

Zhang, Z. (2011). 中华法系道德文化精神及对未来大中国法的意义 [The spirit of ethical culture of Chinese legal system and its meaning for Greater China law in the future]. *Law Science, 5*, 45–50.